THE
Thirty-three Articles of Faith

As Published in the

MARTYR'S MIRROR
With Apocrypha Ref. Omitted

Second Edition 1953

Third Edition 1961

Published by the
Publication Board of the Church of God in Christ, Mennonite
Hesston, Kansas

Printed in U S A

PREFACE

In presenting this booklet to the reader, containing the thirty-three Articles of Faith, as published in the Martyrs Mirror, and named· "The Confession of Faith, According to the Holy Word of God," we feel that we are rendering a much needed and wished for service. (Apocrypha references were omitted upon the recommendation of the General Conference of 1950)

Old and young and all seekers of truth may read with pleasure and profit, to enrich their faith, the faith for which great sacrifices have been made, being believed, taught and practiced by the faithful at a very early age, and by the Mennonites as early as the sixteenth century.

We recommend this booklet for use in the studying of doctrine, and it should prove both interesting and helpful in establishing the Christian faith firmly in the great doctrines of the Bible

It may also be used in Bible schools and study groups, for the layman as well as for the ministry.

We are sending it forth, dedicated to the glory of God and a blessing to our fellowmen.

The Publication Board.

INDEX

Ascension	56
Avoidance	104
Baptism	76
Christ, Human and Divine	51
Church of God	63
Church Distinguished From Other People	66
Communion of Believers	63
Creation of All Things	14
Damnation	112
Death of Christ	56
Death of the Body	109
Discipline of the Christian Church	100
Electing and Sending Ministers and Deacons	72
Essential Knowledge of Jesus Christ	51
Eternal Life	116
Faith (Saving)	35
Fall and Punishment of Man	17
Feet Washing	87
God	5
Good Works	88
Government and Secular Powers	96
Grace of God	24
Heaven	116
Hell	112
Holy Ghost	9
Incarnation of Christ	44

Infant Baptism Not Recognized	76
Judgment	112
Kingdom of Heaven	116
Last Day	108
Law of Moses and Gospel of Christ	31
Life of Christ	56
Lord's Supper	83
Man a Free Moral Agent	24
Marriage	92
Non-Resistance	96
Office of Christ and Purpose of His Coming	60
Ordinances of the Church	72
Providence of God	28
Regeneration and New Creature	39
Rejection of Unbelievers	28
Restoration or Justification	20
Resurrection of Christ	56
Resurrection of the Dead	109
Second Coming of Christ	108
Separation of Offending Members	100
Son of God	7
Suffering of Jesus Christ	56
Swearing of Oaths	94
Triune Godhead	10
Works and Their Reward	88

CONFESSION OF FAITH, ACCORDING TO THE HOLY WORD OF GOD

Article I

Of the only God of heaven and earth. By the grace of God, according to the import of the holy Scriptures, we believe with the heart, and confess with the mouth, that there is one only, eternal, almighty, and true God; who is the Creator of heaven and earth, with all things visible and invisible, so that all things derive their origin and being from Him alone, and are all sustained, governed and upheld by His almighty Word. He is a just, perfect, holy, incomprehensible and indescribable, spiritual Being; consisting of or through Himself (Ex 3:14), and not needing the help or assistance of any thing, but is Himself the origin and fountain of every good thing. From His overflowing goodness every good and perfect gift proceeds and descends. And He is the living One, eternal, without beginning or end, an almighty, true God and Lord of Hosts, a commanding King over all, and above us all in heaven and earth, a terrible Judge, and an avenging, consuming fire; the true Light, just, righteous, and holy, full of grace and peace, and a God of love and of all comfort, longsuffering and of great mercy.

And this only good, and only wise, exalted God, who is all in all, dwells with His worshipful, glorious existence above in heaven, in a light which no man has seen, nor can see, and is present everywhere with His Spirit, and power, filling heaven and earth, so that heaven is His throne, and the earth His footstool. From His all-seeing eye nothing is hid, but He is an omniscient hearer and beholder of the hearts and secret intents and thoughts of all men; all things being naked and open unto His eyes (I Cor 4:5, Heb 4:13).

And since He is such an omniscient God, full of all grace and mercy, and a God of all comfort, with whom alone the fountain of wisdom and all good gifts are to be found; and since He will not give this His divine honor to another, therefore all men are in duty bound, to seek, by ardent prayer and with a desiring heart, all grace, peace, forgiveness of sins, and eternal life, in God alone and in none other.*

And to this only Potentate, the King of kings, and Lord of lords, before whose worshipful majesty the angels stand with trembling, whose Word is true, and whose command is powerful; who is a righteous Judge over all; finally every knee shall bow, and every tongue confess, that He alone is Lord, to the praise of His glory.

And this only, eternal, true God of Abraham, Isaac, and Jacob, consists in one true Father, and one true Son, and one true Holy Ghost And besides this only God there never has been another, nor ever will be

Concerning this only, eternal God read· "Hear, O Israel The Lord our God is one Lord" (Deut 6 4; Mark 12:29).

Through Isaiah He speaks. "For I am God, and there is none else; I am God, and there is none like me" (Is 46 9; 45 5; 44.6; 43:11; 41:4).

Through Paul he says. "That an idol is nothing in the world, and that there is none other God but one" (I Cor 2 4; 12·6; Eph 4·6).

And in this only God we must necessarily believe to salvation, as the beginning and foundation of the Christian faith. Read· "For he that cometh to God must believe that he is, and that he is a rewarder of them that diligently seek him" (Heb. 11:6).

---

*Since God knows everything, believers can call upon Him with a firm confidence, for He hears their cry and knows their wants

To believe in this God, is also called a principle of the Christian doctrine. (Read: Heb. 6.1; Jas. 2:19; John 17.8; 14 1; Gen. 15 6; Rom. 4.9.)

Article II

Of the eternal birth and Godhead of the only and eternal Son of God, we confess: That the Son of God was born and proceeded from all eternity, in an ineffable manner, from the true God, His Father; of the essence and substance of the almighty God, as a Light from the true Light, true God from the true God; being in the form of God, the likeness of the invisible God, the brightness of His glory, and the express image of His person; so that He was born and proceeded from God His Father as the brightness of the everlasting light, the immaculate reflection of the power of God, and the image of His goodness; being equal with His Father in essence, form, and attributes; as eternal, almighty, holy, and the like For it is an inevitable consequence that like produces like.

Thus, as the stone spoken of by the prophet Daniel, which was cut out of the mountain without hands, and itself became a great mountain, is of the same essence and substance with the mountain; so also the precious, elect corner stone, Jesus Christ, was born or proceeded from God the almighty Father (who is called a mountain and rock forever), and is of the same essence and substance with Him. Hence, Christ Jesus, the only begotten Son of God, is to be believed in, confessed, served, honored, and worshipped by all believers, as the true God with His Father. But as this is also a matter of faith, and not of reason or comprehension, all this must be viewed, believed, judged, and spoken of, not humanly, nor carnally, but divinely and spiritually.

Concerning this high, eternal birth, issue, and Godhead of the Son of God, read "Thou art my Son; this day have begotten thee" (Ps 2 7) "For unto which of the angels said he at any time Thou art my Son, this day have I begotten thee? And again, I will be to him a Father, and he shall be to me a Son. And again When he bringeth in the first begotten into the world" (Heb. 1:5, 6).

"So also Christ glorified not himself to be made a high priest, but he that said unto him, Thou art my Son, today have I begotten thee" (Heb 5 5)

"And we declare unto you glad tidings, how that the promise which was made unto the fathers, God hath fulfilled unto us their children, in that He raised up Jesus again; as it is also written in the second Psalm, Thou art my Son, this day have I begotten thee" (Acts 13 32, 33) Observe, that this passage of Paul has reference not only to the raising up of Christ from the dead, but chiefly to His eternal birth from God His Father.

The prophet Micah, speaking of Bethlehem, says: "Out of thee shall he come forth that is to be ruler in Israel, whose goings forth have been from of old, from everlasting" (Micah 5 2; John 16:28, 30)

Again Paul says "Who is the image of the invisible God, the first-born (mark, *the first-born)* of every creature" (Col 1 15; Rev 3 14).

Also John "No man hath seen God at any time; the only begotten Son (mark, *the only begotten Son)* which is in the bosom of the Father, he hath declared him" (John 1·18 and 14)

Read also Prov. 8 23; Dan. 2.34, 45; Rom 8 29. Concerning the Godhead of Christ, read Ps. 45 6; Heb 1 8, John 1·1 and 20·28; Rom 9 5; I John 5 20.

Article III

Of the Holy Ghost we believe and confess That there is a true, real Holy Ghost, also comprehended in the only, eternal, divine essence; who proceeds from the Father and the Son and is the power of the Most High, by whom the Father and the Son operate, and through whom heaven and earth, and all the heavenly host were made Hence, the divine attributes are ascribed to Him; as eternal, almighty, holy, omniscient; who searches the deep things of the Godhead, knows what is in God, and goes through and searches all spirits, however subtle they may be He is therefore confessed as the true God with the Father and the Son. And He is the subtle breath of the power of God, who with His divine inspiration illuminates and enkindles the heart of man, and confirms and leads him into all truth. He is given by God unto all who obey Him. All that are led by this Spirit, are the Sons of God He that has not this Spirit, does not belong to God. He is called the real and earnest of the inheritance of all true children of God He who blasphemes this Spirit, must never expect forgiveness Christ also commands to baptize believers in the name of the Holy Ghost.

Concerning this only Spirit of God, read "In the beginning God created the heaven and the earth And the earth was without form and void; and darkness was upon the face of the deep. And the Spirit of God moved upon the face of the waters" (Gen 1 1, 2)

Through Paul we are taught "There are diversities of gifts, but the same Spirit" (I Cor. 12 4). "But all these worketh that one and the selfsame Spirit, dividing to every man severally as he will For by one Spirit are we all baptized into one body, whether we be Jews or Gentiles, whether we be bond or free; and have been all made to drink into one Spirit" (I Cor 12:11, 13. Read also: 2

Sam. 23 2, Eph 4 4; Matt 10 20; Luke 12 12, Matt. 3 16; John 1 32; Matt 28 19; Mark 16 16)

Article IV

How Father, Son, and Holy Ghost are to be distinguished in certain attributes. Of this we confess That in the only eternal Divine Being there are not three mere names; but that each name has its true signification and attributes; so that there is a true, real Father, of whom all things are; and a true, real Son, by whom are all things; and a true, real Holy Ghost, through whom the Father and Son operate. The Father is the true Father, who begat the Son before all time, and from whom the Son proceeded and came, and by whom He (the Father) created and made all things; and through whom the Son was sent to be the Savior of the world The Son was born of, proceeded and came from the Father, by whom the Father created all things and who was sent by the Father, and came into the world, and through the effectual power of the Most High was conceived by Mary, and born as man He suffered, was crucified, died, rose from the dead, ascended to heaven, and sitteth at the right hand of His Almighty Father in heaven The Holy Ghost is He that proceeds from the Father and the Son, and is sent by them; through whom the Father and the Son operate and work He speaks not of Himself, but whatsoever He has heard from the Father; He takes of the things of Christ, to show them to His own.

Hence there are, in the same divine essence, in heaven, three true witnesses· the Father, the Word, and the Holy Ghost; of whom the glory of the only begotten Son of God appeared really and distinctively, in the form of a servant, on earth, and was also seen by John the Baptist, at the Jordan. And the Holy Spirit was also distinctively seen by the same John to descend, in the form of a dove, from God out of heaven, upon Christ and abide upon Him   And the Father who is an invisible Spirit, and cannot be seen by mortal eye, let His voice be heard from heaven: "This is my beloved Son, in whom I am well pleased."

These three true witnesses are distinctively spoken of as follows   "If I bear witness of myself, my witness is not true   There is another that beareth witness of me" (John 5 31, 32).

"I am not alone, but I and the Father that sent me   It is also written in your law that the testimony of two men is true   I am one that bear witness of myself, and the Father that sent me, beareth witness of me" (John 8·16-18, 29, 54); I John 5 20; John 16·32 and 15 24)

Again, Paul says "There is one God, and one Mediator between God and men, the man Christ Jesus" (I Tim 2 5)

"Whosoever transgresseth, and abideth not in the doctrine of Christ, hath not God. He that abideth in the doctrine of Christ, he hath both the Father and the Son" (2 John 1 9)

Of the Holy Ghost, Christ says· "I will pray the Father, and he shall give you another Comforter, that he may abide with you forever; even the Spirit of truth; whom the world cannot receive" (John 14 11, 17, Matt 12 32).

"But if I depart I will send him unto you   For he shall not speak of himself; but whatsoever he shall hear, that shall he speak   He shall glorify me; for he shall receive of mine, and shall shew it unto you" (John 16·7, 13, 14).

How John, the man of God, saw the Holy Ghost in the form of a dove, read· "And the Holy Ghost descended in a bodily shape like a dove upon him, and a voice came from heaven, which said, Thou art my beloved Son; in thee I am well pleased" (Luke 3·22)

"And John bare record, saying, I saw the Spirit descending from heaven like a dove, and it abode upon him and I knew him not: but he that sent me to baptize with water, the same said unto me, Upon whom thou shalt see the Spirit descending and remaining on him, the same is he which baptizeth with the Holy Ghost And I saw, and bare record that this is the Son of God" (John 1 32-34) Read also Mark 1·10

"And Jesus, when he was baptized, went up straightway out of the water; and, lo, the heavens were opened unto him, and John saw the Spirit of God descending like a dove, and lighting upon him" (Matt 3 16)

Mark, how awfully they sin against the Most High, who, contrary to all these express words of the Holy Ghost, still dare say and maintain that John did not see the Holy Ghost, but only a natural or created dove

Hear also how the voice of the Father was heard from heaven· "And lo a voice from heaven saying This is my beloved Son, in whom I am well pleased" (Matt 3·17)

"For he received from the Father honor and glory, when there came such a voice to him from the excellent glory" (2 Pet 1 17. Read also Psalm 110·1; John 1:1; 1 Cor 12:5; 1 John 5:7).

"For there are three that bear record in heaven, the Father, the Word, and the Holy Ghost" (1 John 5 7, 1 Cor. 12.4; Rev. 3:14)

Article V

That these three true witnesses are but one only true God. Hereupon we confessed: That this must certainly follow, from the fact, that the Son proceeded or came forth from the eternal essence and substance of the Father; and that the Holy Ghost truly proceeds from the Father and the Son in the only, eternal Divine Being.*

Moreover, this is abundantly testified and confirmed by the divine works and attributes, which are ascribed in the holy Scriptures jointly to the Father, the Son, and the Holy Ghost, of which no angels in heaven, much less, any other creatures are capable, but which belong and are peculiar to the only God alone; as, the creating, governing, and upholding of heaven and earth with all things visible and invisible; the gracious Gospel sent from heaven; the sending out of the apostles to preach the same among all nations; the raising of man from the dead, and the giving of eternal life; and all divine worship, honor and reverence. Hence they are perfectly one, not only in will, words, and works, but also in essence, and in the eternal and indescribable godhead. Thus also in the divine works, so that whatsoever the Father does, the Son does likewise; and as the Father raises up the dead, even so the Son quickens whom he will; and all this they do in the power and with the co-operation of the Holy Ghost; and hence they can with reason and truth be called the *one God of heaven and earth*. Besides him, there has been no other God, neither shall another be found in all eternity. Hence in the term *one God*, Father, Son and Holy Ghost are comprehended.

On this subject read the prophet Jeremiah. "The gods that have not made the heavens and the earth, even thy shall perish from the earth, and from under these heavens. He hath made the earth by his power, he hath established the world by his wisdom" (Jer. 10:11, 12; Is. 44:24; Ps. 96:5).

"By the word of the Lord were the heavens made; and all the host of them by the breath of his mouth" (Ps. 33:6; Heb. 3:4; Acts 4:24).

---

*These things are very difficult to understand, and above human reason, hence they are not to be comprehended by reason, but must reverently be embraced in faith.

"All things were made by him (Christ); and without him was not anything made that was made" (John 1 3 and 5 19)

Concerning this perfect unity read "My Father, which gave them me (says Christ) is greater than all; and no man is able to pluck them out of my Father's hand I and my Father are one" (John 10 29, 30)

Christ said to Philip "He that hath seen me hath seen the Father Believest thou not that I am in the Father, and the Father in me?" (John 14 9, 10; 12 45; 17 21)

How the Holy Ghost is also called God, read what Peter said to Ananias "Why hath Satan filled thine heart to lie to the Holy Ghost?" And a little further on "Thou hast not lied unto men, but unto God" (Acts 5 3, 4)

"Them that have preached the Gospel unto you with the Holy Ghost sent down from heaven" (I Pet 1 12)

"The grace of the Lord Jesus Christ, and the love of God, and the communion of the Holy Ghost, be with you all Amen" (2 Cor 13 14).

"For there are three that bear record in heaven, the Father, the Word, and the Holy Ghost; and these three are one" (1 John 5 7; Deut 6·4; Mark 12 29; 1 Cor 8 6; Gal 3 20)

Article VI

Of the creation of all things visible and invisible, and of the creation of man we confess That the only, almighty, and wonderworking God, who is the origin of all good, and for whose sake all things are created, and have their being, created, among other invisible things, also a multitude of many thousand angels, whom He has put as ministering and immortal spirits in His worshipful glory, to minister unto their Creator, and to offer Him praise, honor, and thanks; and who are sent forth by God, as messengers, to minister in manifold ways for men who shall be heirs of salvation; and with which angels of God, Christ Jesus shall appear in the clouds of heaven, to hold judgment over all men And He shall glorify all that believe and please God, and make them like the glorious, immortal angels, and crown them with all holy angels in everlasting glory

But as some of these angels became unfaithful and apostate to God, their Creator, they were, through their own voluntary sin or pride, rejected by the holy and righteous God, who is of purer eyes than to behold evil, and were cast down from the glorious estate of heaven to hell, bound with chains of darkness and reserved until the great day of judgment, to be sentenced with all unbelievers to eternal damnation.

These impure spirits or devils are called the prince of darkness and spirit of wickedness, who rules in the air and works in the children of disobedience; with whom all unbelievers, who are governed and seduced by Satan, are in fellowship. And as all believers are in the society or brotherhood of the holy angels, and shall enjoy eternal salvation with them; so, on the other hand, shall all unbelievers have to endure everlasting damnation with all impure or apostate angels, with whom unbelievers are in fellowship

Likewise, God Almighty, in the beginning, from nothing, in a most wonderful manner, and above all human reason and comprehension, created heaven, the earth, and the sea, with all their glorious adornment, He the Blessed, only saying "Let heaven and earth be made; and His Word was a perfect work." He also adorned the heavens with many glorious lights; two great lights, one to rule and illume the day, and the other to rule the night; together with many glorious stars, which He ordained to the honor of their Creator, and the service of men.

Thus also, the Lord Almighty endowed the earth with many glorious fountains and running rivers, and adorned it with manifold trees and animals, and with all that lives and moves thereon And He created the sea with great whales and various kinds of fish, for the wants of man, together with all that lives and moves therein And He established the earth out of the water and in the water, by His almighty and everlasting Word. They shall be preserved until the last great day of judgment

After God, the Lord, in five days had most wisely and excellently created heaven, and earth, and the sea, togther with all visible things, He, on the sixth day, formed man from the earth, and breathed into him the breath of life; and from his rib made Eve, a woman, and gave her to him as a helpmeet Moreover, He loved them above all other creatures, and clothed them like Himself with divine virtues, which are righteousness and true holiness; endowing them with wisdom, speech, and reason, that they might know, fear, and love their Creator, and serve Him in voluntary obedience He placed them as lords over all creatures, endowing them with immortality that they might be and live before Him, and rule and reign over all creatures which God the Lord created

Concerning this wonderful creation, read: "Thou art worthy, O Lord, to receive glory and honor and power· for thou hast created all things, and for thy pleasure they are and were created" (Rev 4 11).

"For by him were all things created, that are in heaven, and that are in earth, visible and invisible, whether they be thrones, or dominions, or principalities, or powers all things were created by him, and in him" (Col 1 16; Ps. 33 6)

Regarding the angels, read "He maketh his angels spirits, and his ministers a flame of fire Are they not all ministering spirits, sent forth to minister for them who shall be heirs of salvation?" (Heb. 1.7, 14; Ps 104·4).

Concerning the apostasy of the angels, read "For if God spared not the angels that sinned, but cast them down to hell, and delivered them unto chains and darkness, to be reserved unto judgment" (2 Pet. 2 4; Jude 6; Luke 10 18; Is. 14 8; Rev. 12·4).

Regarding the creation of the visible things, read: "In the beginning God created the heaven and the earth" (Gen 1.1; John 1:3; Ps. 33 6).

"Through faith we understand that the worlds were framed by the word of God, so that things which are seen were not made of things which do appear" (Heb 11 3; Acts 17·24; Ps 146 6; 148·5).

Concerning the creation of man, read "Let us make man in our image, after our likeness" (Gen 1 26)

"And the Lord formed man of the dust of the ground, and breathed into his nostrils the breath of life; and man became a living soul" (Gen 2 7; Acts 17 25; I Cor 15 45)

How man was created, read "This only have I found, that God hath made man upright" (Eccl. 7 29; Gen. 1· 26; 5 1)

"And that ye put on the new man, which after God is created in righteousness and true holiness" (Eph 4 24)

"And God saw everything that he had made, and, behold, it was very good" (Gen 1 31; Deut 32 4)

Article VII

Of the fall and punishment of man we confess The first man, Adam, and Eve, having been thus gloriously created after the likeness of their Creator, unto eternal life, did not continue long in this estate; but as they were created with a free will, to choose what they would, so that they could fear, serve and obey their Creator, or, disobey and forsake Him; and as their Creator had given them a command, not to eat of the tree of the knowledge of good and evil, for in the day that they should eat thereof, they should surely die; they, notwithstanding this, in their vain desire to be equal to their Creator in wisdom and knowledge, were led and drawn away from God, and deceived by Satan; and thus they disobediently and voluntarily transgressed the command of their Creator The woman, last created, was first deceived and turned her ears away from God to Satan, and, also seducing her husband, they, through this sin, fell under the wrath and disfavor of God, and, with all their posterity, became subject that very day to temporal and eternal death, and were thus divested of the divine virtue, which is righteousness and true holiness, and became sinful and mortal.

On this account, God, the holy and righteous Judge, in whose sight wickedness can not endure, but who is of purer eyes than to behold evil, or to look on iniquity; and who threatens from heaven with His wrath and disfavor all disobedience and ingratitude of men; was so incensed by the sin thus committed by Adam and Eve, that thereby they not only fell into eternal condemnation, together with all their posterity, but God the Lord moreover imposed upon Adam and Eve divers temporal, bodily punishments, which also continually extend themselves into all their generations Who are so corrupted in Adam, that they are all from their youth, by nature, inclined to sin and evil, and are therefore deprived of the beautiful pleasure-garden, or paradise, but must eat their bread, all their life, in sorrow and in the sweat of their face, from the uncultivated earth, which because of this first sin was so cursed and marred, that it brings forth of itself weeds, thorns, and thistles; and cover the shame of their bodies made naked by sin. The woman, as the chief transgressor, has to subject her will and power to the man, and was constrained to bring forth her children in pain and anguish This punishment continues upon all men, until they finally return to the dust and ashes whence they came

Concerning how Adam, together with the whole human race, through sin, fell into temporal and eternal death, and in consequence of this, became sinful, read: "Wherefore, as by one man sin entered into the world, and death by sin; and so death passed upon all men" "Nevertheless death reigned from Adam to Moses, even over them that had not sinned," etc "And not as it was by one that sinned . . . for the judgment was by one to condemnation," etc "For if by one man's offense death reigned," etc "Therefore, as by the offense of one judgment came upon all men to condemnation," etc "For as by one man's disobedience many were made sinners," etc (Rom 5·12, 14-19).

"For since by man came death, by man came also the resurrection of the dead For as in Adam all die, even so in Christ shall all be made alive" (I Cor 15 21, 22)

"Behold, I was shapen in iniquity, and in sin did my mother conceive me" (Ps 51 5)

"Who can bring a clean thing out of an unclean?" (Job 14·4).

Read further, how God announced unto Adam his punishment on account of sin, which punishment God extends unto all his posterity· "Because thou hast hearkened unto the voice of thy wife, and hast eaten of the tree, of which I commanded thee, saying, Thou shalt not eat of it cursed is the ground for thy sake, in sorrow shalt thou eat of it all the days of thy life, thorns also and thistles shall it bring forth to thee; and thou shalt eat the herb of the field in the sweat of thy face shalt thou eat bread, till thou return unto the ground; for out of it wast thou taken for dust thou art and unto dust shalt thou return" (Gen. 3 17-19, 23, 24). Concerning the punishment of the woman, read: Gen. 3:16; I Cor. 14 34; I Tim. 2·12

Article VIII

Of the restoration or justification of man We confess that Adam and Eve having thus fallen under the wrath and the disfavor of God, and into death and eternal condemnation, together with all their posterity, so that no remedy or deliverance was to be found in heaven or earth, among any created beings, who could help, and redeem them, and reconcile them to God, the Creator of all things, who is the Almighty God (against whose majesty they had sinned, and who alone could heal them), who is rich and abounding in all grace and mercy, had compassion upon Adam and his posterity, and, hence, promised them His only begotten Son as a comforting Redeemer and Saviour, whom He would put as enmity between Satan and the woman and their seed, to the comfort and help of fallen mankind, in order thus to bruise the head of Satan, and to deprive him of his power; and, in this manner, to deliver Adam and his posterity from the prison of sin, the power of the devil, and eternal perdition, and to reconcile them to God.

And even as God the Lord, through this promise, clothed Adam and his seed internally, according to the soul, with His grace and mercy, He, in token of this, also covered the outward shame and nakedness of the body, making coats of skins, and clothing them therewith

And even as Adam, through this his first, one sin, brought not only himself but with him also his whole posterity, without exception of persons, and without their own actual evil works, into eternal death and condemnation; so also, God Almighty, through this promise of the only Savior Christ Jesus, redeemed, delivered, and justified from condemnation, and placed into the state of grace and reconciliation, all men, without exception of persons, without any of their good works, only from pure grace and mercy Seeing that Adam's race was not born of him when he stood under disfavor and condemnation before God; but as all men proceed from Adam as being in a state of grace, peace, and reconciliation with God, he could bring forth none but such as stand with him in the same reconciliation.

Thus none of Adam's race are created or born to condemnation, but all are born and brought forth into the world in the same state of grace and reconciliation with God Hence, we hold it to militate not only against the holy Scriptures, but also utterly against the nature of God, which is just, righteous, holy, and merciful, that God should punish with eternal death and damnation, simply on account of Adam's sin, so great a number of Adam's race who die in their infancy in a state of innocence, before they have followed Adam in sin; seeing the good God, through Christ and for Christ's sake, so graciously forgave Adam, (who had himself committed the sin) and placed him in a state of grace

But men having attained the knowledge of good and evil, and, through the lust of the flesh, and their own desire, having been drawn away from the path of virtue and innocence, so that they follow Adam in sin, hence it comes that they separate themselves from their Creator, and, consequently, do not perish, nor are condemned on account of Adam's transgression, but because of their own unbelief and evil works

But the righteous God, who does indeed forgive sin, yet ofttimes does not suffer it to go entirely unpunished, permitted the temporal, bodily punishment to remain upon Adam and Eve, and their posterity, by which they ought to learn to know, fear, and serve their Creator, and to shun sin; such as this, that from their infancy they are by nature inclined to sin and evil, against which they have a continual warfare, are barred out from the beautiful paradise, must cover their nakedness; the women must subject their power and will to their husbands, and must bring forth their children in pain and anguish; and all must eat all the days of their life, with sorrow, of the corrupted earth, until they return to dust of the earth, whence they have come.

But all believers receive in this life the restoration or justification of Christ only through faith, in hope, and afterwards in the resurrection of the dead they shall receive it truly and actually, and shall enjoy it forever

Concerning these glorious and comforting promises of salvation, read; "And I will put enmity between thee and the woman, and between thy seed, and her seed; it shall bruise thy head" (Gen. 3:15; Eph. 2:14, 15).

As to how this promise was renewed in the seed and race of Adam, read "The Lord thy God will raise up unto thee a prophet from the midst of thee, of thy brethren, like unto me; unto him ye shall hearken" (Deut. 18:15; Acts 7 37) To Abraham (Gen 12 3; 22:18; Acts 10 43)

Concerning the fact that this promise of justification does not extend only to a particular class of persons, but to all men without distinction, read· "Therefore as by the offense of one, judgment came upon all men to condemnation; even so by righteousness of one the free gift came upon all men unto justification of life. For as by one man's disobedience many were made sinners, so by the obedience of one shall many be made righteous" (Rom 5:18, 19).

"For since by man came death, by man came also the resurrection of the dead For as in Adam all die, even so in Christ shall all be made alive" (1 Cor. 15 21, 22).

"That was the true Light, which lighteth every man that cometh into the world" (John 1:9, 29).

"And he is the propitiation for our sins and not for ours only, but also for the sins of the whole world" (1 John 2 2).

"For it pleased the Father that in him should all fullness dwell, and, having made peace through the blood of his cross by him to reconcile all things unto himself; by him, I say, whether they be things in earth, or things in heaven" (Col 1 19, 20).

"For the grace of God that bringeth salvation hath appeared to all men" (Tit 2 11) Read also Rom 3 24, 11 32; 1 Tim 4 10; 2 Cor 5 19, 1 John 4 10, Isa 53 6, 1 Pet 2 24

As to how the kingdom of heaven is promised by Christ to infants, without respect of persons, read "Then were there brought unto him little children, that he should put his hands on them, and pray and the disciples rebuked them But Jesus said, Suffer little children, and forbid them not, to come unto me; for of such is the kingdom of heaven" (Matt. 19 13, 14; 18 3; Mark 10 13, Luke 18·15)

"The soul that sinneth, it shall die The son shall not bear the iniquity of the father, neither, neither shall the father bear the iniquity of the son the righteousness of the righteous shall be upon him" (Ezek 18 20, 4) "The fathers shall not be put to death for the children, neither shall the children be put to death for the fathers every man shall be put to death for his own sin" (Deut 24 16; Jer 31 29).

"Because he hath appointed a day in the which he will judge the world in righteousness" (Acts 17 31; Ps 7 11, 2 Tim 4 8)

"But he that believeth not shall be damned' (Mark 16 16) "Tribulation and anguish, upon every soul of man that doeth evil" (Rom. 2.9).

Article IX

Of the free will or power of man before and after the fall, and of the saving grace of God Of this we confess That God Almighty in the beginning created the man Adam and his wife in His image and likeness, endowing them, above all creatures, with virtues, knowledge, speech, reason, and a free will or power; so that they could know, love, fear, and obediently serve their Creator; or could voluntarily and disobediently forsake their God; as appeared in the first transgression, when Adam and his wife, through the subtlety of the devil, who appeared in the form of a deceitful serpent, departed from the commandment of God; hence they did not sin through the foreordination or the will of God; but as they had been created with a free will, and to do as they would, they sinned through their own voluntary desire, and transgressed the command of God contrary to His will

The man Adam and his wife having thus through their own sin fallen under the wrath and disfavor of God, whereby they became sinful and mortal, were again received into favor by God their Creator; so that they were not utterly divested of their former wisdom, speech, and knowledge, above all other creatures, nor of their previous free will or power, as may be seen from their voluntarily accepting God's gracious promises unto life, and obeying the voice of the Lord; and as also clearly appears from the fact that God the Lord very strictly appointed an angel with a flaming sword to keep the tree of life from Adam; lest through his free will or power he should eat of the tree of life and live forever; which would have been in Adam's power And this free will or power has been transmitted to all their descendants, who proceed from them as branches from their stem; so that even as men are endowed of God with knowledge, reason and voluntary power, by which they can perform manifold works, and seek and desire from God the health of their diseased and infirm bodies, and are not without action, as the irrational creatures, blocks and stones, so likewise, man through the grace of God, and the moving of the Spirit, by which men live, and are moved, may open the door of the heart to the salutary grace of God—which through the Gospel is offered to all men, and through which death and life is set before man—and seek the health of his wounded soul; or he may voluntarily resist, reject and neglect this offered grace and moving of the Spirit Thus also, as men have eyes and ears, to see and to hear, yet not of themselves, but only from God the Giver, so they also, through the grace of God, have a free will or power to do the good and to leave the evil.

But men, considered in themselves, seeing they are without the grace of God, are of themselves incapable of thinking anything that is good, much less are they able to do it But it is almighty God, who through His Spirit of grace works in man both to will and to do, moves, draws, and chooses them, and accepts them as His children, so that men are only recipients of God's saving grace Hence all Christians are in duty bound to ascribe the beginning, middle and end of their faith, with all the good fruits thereof, not to themselves, but only to the unmerited grace of God in Christ Jesus

We confess moreover That this saving grace of God is not limited to a few particular men, but even as the Almighty God lets His sun rise and shine on the evil and on the good, so He has extended His grace to all of Adam's race, as it is also evident that God, in His goodness, did not leave Himself without witness among the heathen, doing them good, and so moving their hearts, that their thoughts and consciences accused and excused them, so that they could do by nature, without the hearing of the law of Moses, the things contained in the law This appears in still greater clearness in the coming of Christ, that Almighty God has proclaimed the saving grace through the Gospel to the whole world, for a witness unto all nations, by which all excuse is taken from men, and as an evidence, that God is not willing that any should perish, but that all should repent and be saved According to the import of the holy and everlasting Gospel, a righteous, eternal, and irrevocable judgment shall be pronounced, in the last day, through Christ Jesus, the blessed, over all nations Hence all men who now in this time of grace believe and accept the Gospel, attain unto life; but all who do not believe the Gospel, but voluntarily reject it, will receive death as their portion

On the other hand, we reject the belief of those who say that Almighty God has indeed caused the Word of reconciliation to be preached to all, or many, but does nevertheless withhold His grace from many of them, so that the greater part of mankind cannot accept the Word of reconciliation and be saved, but will, through the purpose of eternal counsel and will of God, inevitably have to perish forever, and be damned

God the Lord said to Cain "If thou doest not well, sin lieth at the door. and unto thee shall be his desire, and thou shalt rule over him" (Gen 4 7).

Concerning man's free will, read· "Let him do what he will, he sinneth not; let them marry Nevertheless he that standeth steadfast in his heart, having no necessity, but hath power over his own will" (I Cor 7 36-38)

"And whosoever offereth a sacrifice of peace offerings unto the Lord to accomplish his vow, or a free will offering" (Lev 22 21, 23).

And Paul also says· "For to their power, I bear record, yea, and beyond their opower they were willing of themselves. Now therefore perform the doing of it;

that as there was a readiness to will, so there may be a performance also" (2 Cor. 8:3, 11; Phil. 14; Mark 14:7; 1 Cor. 7 36).

Man can do nothing good of himself, by his own power; but through the grace of God, he, in his imperfectness, is able to keep God's commandments For it is God which worketh in you both to will and to do his good pleasure" (Phil 2:13)

"Thou dwellest in the midst of a rebellious house, which have eyes to see, and see not; they have ears to hear, and hear not" (Ezek. 12:2)

"For to will is present with me; but how to perform that which is good I find not" (Rom. 7:18-21).

Read here all the Scriptures which unanimously testify that God does not desire the death of the sinner, but that he be converted, and live (Ezek 18:32; 33 11; Is. 55:7)

And that God has extended His saving grace not only to the elect, but to all of Adam's race; and that He also died for those that perish Concerning this, read: "For the grace of God that bringeth salvation hath appeared to all men" (Tit 2:11)

"Look unto me, and be ye saved, all the ends of the earth" (Is 45:22).

"Therefore, as by the offense of one judgment came upon all men to condemnation; even so by the righteousness of one the free gift came upon all men unto justification of life" (Rom 5 18)

"Who in times past suffered all nations to walk in their own ways Nevertheless he left not himself without witness," etc. (Acts 14 16, 17; Rom 1 19; 2:15)

"But there were false prophets also among the people, even as there shall be false teachers among you, who privily shall bring in damnable heresies, even denying the Lord that bought them, and bring upon themselves swift destruction" (2 Pet 2 1).

"And that he died for all, that they which live should not henceforth live unto themselves, but unto him which died for them, and rose again" (2 Cor 5:15)
"For God so loved the world, that he gave his only begotten Son," etc (John 3:16)
"Behold the Lamb of God, which taketh away the sin of the world!" (John 1:29)
"For this is good and acceptable in the sight of God our Saviour; who will have all men to be saved, and come unto the knowledge of truth" (1 Tim 2 3, 4)
"He is longsuffering to usward, not willing that any should perish, but that all should come to repentance" (2 Pet 3 9, Rom. 2:4; Jas 4 6; Acts 13 46 Read also: Matt 23:36. 37; Luke 13:34)

As to how God the righteous Judge will pronounce the final judgment upon those who disobey* the Gospel, read "When the Lord Jesus shall be revealed from heaven with his mighty angels in flaming fire, taking vengeance on them that know not God, and that obey not the Gospel of our Lord Jesus Christ" (2 Thess 1.7, 8; Mark 16:16).

Article X

Of the providence of God, the election of believers, and the rejection of unbelievers Of this we confess: As we believe and confess that God is omnipotent; and that with Him nothing is impossible; so likewise is He also prescient and omnisicient, so that nothing is hid from Him in heaven and in earth, neither that which is to take place until the end of all things, nor that which has taken place from all eternity. And through this exceeding high prescience (foreknowledge), knowledge and wisdom of God, which are unfathomable, He very well saw and knew from the beginning in eternity

---
*The original says OBEY, which evidently is an error.—Trans.

until the consummation of the world, who would be the truly believing recipients of His grace and mercy; and, again, who should be found unbelieving despisers and rejecters of said grace And, consequently, He from the beginning and from eternity knew, foresaw, elected and ordained all true believers to inherit eternal salvation through Christ Jesus; and on the other hand rejected all unbelieving despisers of said grace to eternal damnation Hence the perdition of men is of themselves, and their salvation only through the Lord their God, without whom they can do nothing that is good

But in no wise is it true that the gracious, merciful, and righteous God (who conforms to His holy nature) has from eternity foreseen, ordained or predestinated, and created, at a convenient time, by far the greater number of the human race unto eternal damnation; or that, they having fallen through the sin of the first man, Adam, He let them remain without help in eternal death and condemnation, into which they had come without their knowledge and own actual evil works, without having in this case seen and known the just cause of their rejection. Far be it from us, to believe this from the only good and righteous God!

But, on the other hand, all true followers of Christ believe and confess· That the righteous God, in the beginning created man good and upright, and gave him an existence, and He hates none of those things which He has created And when through the subtlety of the devil they had fallen into eternal death, the blessed God, whose mercy is over all flesh, and who is not willing that any should perish, out of pure love and mercy, redeemed, bought, and delivered, through the atonement of our Lord and Savior, Jesus Christ, the whole human race, without exception of persons, from eternal condemnation; so that, in consideration of the death of Christ, none shall perish on account of Adam's sin;

but God the righteous Judge will judge the world in righteousness, giving assurance unto all men, and rendering to every man according to his own works and deeds. The believers, who by patient continuance in well-doing seek for eternal life, attain glory and honor and immortality, but the unbelieving and disobedient, tribulation and anguish, and the everlasting wrath of God.

Concerning the foreknowledge or prescience of God, read "And hath determined the times before appointed, and the bounds of their habitations" (Acts 17 26; Deut 32 8)

"My substance was not hid from thee, when I was made in secret, and curiously wrought in the lowest parts of the earth. Thine eyes did see my substance, yet being unperfect; and in thy book all my members were written, which in continuance were fashioned, when as yet there was none of them" (Ps 139 15, 16)

Here it is to be observed with attention, how God, through His presence, from the beginning elected the believers in Christ, and rejected the unbelievers. Read "Hearken, my beloved brethren, hath not God chosen the poor of this world rich in faith?" etc (Jas 2·5).

"But God hath chosen the foolish things of the world to confound the wise, and God hath chosen the weak things of the world to confound the things of the world, and things which are despised, hath God chosen," etc (1 Cor 1 27, 28)

"I have even from the beginning declared it to thee; before it came to pass I shewed it thee for I knew that thou wouldest deal very treacherously, and wast called a transgressor from the womb" (Is 48 5, 8; Mal 1 2; Rom. 9 13, Eph 3 11; 2 Tim 1·9)

"And who, as I, shall call, and shall declare it, and set it in order for me, since I appointed the ancient people?" (Is. 44:7).

"We know that all things work together for good to them that love God, to them who are the called according to His purpose For whom he did foreknow, he also did predestinate to be conformed to the image of his Son, that he might be the firstborn among many brethren Moreover, whom he did predestinate, them he also called and whom he called, them he also justified" (Rom 8 28-30)

"Before I formed thee in the belly I knew thee, and before thou camest forth out of the womb I sanctified thee," etc (Jer 1·5)

"According as he hath chosen us in him before the foundation of the world," etc (Eph 1 4; 2 Tim 1 9; John 15 16; Acts 13·48)

Article XI

Of the written Word of God, the law of Moses, and the Gospel of Christ We confess That the old law which was given by Moses and received by the disposition of angels, was a perfect doctrine and rule for the descendants of Abraham, Isaac, and Jacob, with whom God had made and established this His covenant According to the doctrine and tenor of this law, this people had to conduct and regulate themselves, without transgressing any part of it, or taking away from, or adding to it, or following their own opinion in regard to it, on pain of being exterminated, and falling under a great curse On the other hand those who hear, believe and fulfill this law, are promised life, and many glorious blessings This blessing and cure extended mostly to temporal and bodily things.

This law of God—the five books of Moses—embracing also all kings, priests and prophets, who prophesied and spoke, through the Spirit of God, among this people, Israel (agreeing with the law of Moses), which is the entire Old Testament, has through the grace of God been made known to us in the Bible This law is also spiritual, the bringing in of a better hope, and the schoolmaster to Christ. By its various figures and shadows, as the Levitical Priesthood, ceremonies and sacrifices, the land of Canaan, kings, the city of Jerusalem, and the temple it pointed and led to Christ Jesus, because the old law was an intolerable yoke of bondage, which brought condemnation upon all who did not continue in and perform all that is written in the book of the law And since men, through the weakness of the flesh, could not perfectly keep all this, they could not obtain the eternal blissful life through the law, but would have had to remain under the wrath and anger of God But Christ Jesus came, who is the end and the fulfilling of the old law, and the beginner and author of the new law, of perfect liberty, and the real, true light, to which all the dark shadows pointed, He came sent from God, with full power in heaven and on earth and is the One who has abolished death, and brought life and immortality to light through the Gospel

He has made a new covenant with the house of Israel, and the house of Judah, and has invited thereto all the Gentiles and nations of the earth, who in time past were strangers and enemies, but not now, through grace, are all invited, and for whom the way unto life has been opened and well beaten; so that by obedience through grace, they may now become fellow-citizens with the saints, and of the household of God And this is the Word of reconciliation, by which Almighty God, through His Spirit, works faith, regeneration, and all the good fruits resulting therefrom in men; in which Word of the New Testament are proclaimed to us full grace and peace, forgiveness of sins, and eternal life, together with all things that pertain unto life and godliness, yea, all the counsel of God. According to this proclamation all believing children of the New Testament must necessarily regulate and conduct themselves in all matters relating to the faith; in accordance with which, finally an eternal judgment will be held And it is so much worthier, and better established than the Old Testament, as it was given through a higher and worthier ambassador, and was sealed with a more precious blood; and it shall not cease, but continue till the end of the world And as a man's covenant, if it be confirmed, may not be changed, or anything taken from or added to it, so this New and Everlasting Covenant, which is confirmed with the precious death and blood of our Lord Jesus Christ, may still much less be diminished, or anything added thereto, nor may it be bent and distorted according to one's own individual opinions; but all Christians are in duty bound to bow their whole heart, mind and soul under the obedience of Christ and the mind of the Holy Spirit expressed in the holy Scriptures, and to regulate and measure their whole faith and conversation according to the import thereof

The Old Testament is to be expounded by and reconciled with this New Testament and must be distinctively taught among the people of God· Moses with his stern, threatening, punishing law over all impenitent sinners as still under the law; but Christ with His new, glad tidings of the holy Gospel over all believing, penitent sinners as not under the law, but under grace.

To this new law of Jesus Christ all decrees, councils and ordinances made contrary to it by men in the world, must give place; but all Christians must necessarily, as far as the faith is concerned, regulate and conduct themselves only in accordance with this blessed Gospel of Christ And as the outward man lives outwardly by the nourishment of bread; so the inward man of the soul lives by every Word proceeding from the mouth of the Lord. Therefore the Word of God must be purely and sincerely preached, heard, received and kept, by all believers

Of the law of Moses. how it was written with the finger of God on tables of stone, and given by the disposition of angels, concerning this read Ex. 20·2, Deut 5 6; John 1 17; Acts 7.53; Ex. 31 18; 32 16.

Of the severity of the law, and how we must neither take away from nor add to it; in regard to this, read· "Cursed be he that confirmeth not all the words of this law to do them and all the people shall say, Amen" (Deut 27 26; Gal 3 10)

"What thing soever I command you, observe to do it thou shalt not add thereto, nor diminish from it" (Deut 12 32, 8; 29 19; Prov 30 6; Deut 4 2)

Of the imperfectness of the law, read "For the law having a shadow of good things to come, and not the very image of the things," etc (Heb 10·1, Col 2 17)

"For the priesthood being changed, there is made of necessity a change also of the law For there is verily a disannulling of the commandment going before, for the weakness and unprofitableness thereof For the law made nothing perfect, but the bringing in of a better hope did" (Heb 7 12, 18, 19; Gal. 2.16, Acts 13 39; Rom 8 3)

How Christ is the end and fulfilling of the law; with regard to this read "For Christ is the end of the law for righteousness to every one that believeth" (Rom 10 4, Matt 5 17; Rom 7 4; Gal 1 19)

Of the power and dignity of the holy Gospel, read "For I am not ashamed of the Gospel of Christ for it is the power of God unto salvation to every one that believeth," etc (Rom 1 16; John 1 17; Luke 16 16; Mark 1 15; 1 Pet 1 12).

"Who hath abolished death, and hath brought life and immortality to light through the Gospel" (2 Tim. 1 10; 1 Pet. 1:25).

Of the usefulness and power of the holy Gospel, read "And that from a child thou hast known the holy Scriptures, which are able to make thee wise unto salvation through faith which is in Christ Jesus All Scripture is given by inspiration of God, and is profitable for doctrine for reproof, for correction, for instruction in righteousness that the man of God may be perfect, thoroughly furnished unto all good works" (2 Tim 3 15-17; 2 Peter. 3:15).

"Search the Scriptures; for in them ye think ye have eternal life " "He that believeth on me, as the Scripture hath said," etc (John 5·39; 7 38; James 1 21; Matt 4 4; Deut 8 3; Revelation 22·18, Deut 4 2; 12 32; Prov 30 6).

"For whatsoever things were written aforetime were written for our learning, that we through patience and comfort of the Scriptures might have hope" (Rom. 15 4)

How Christ Jesus will pronounce the last judgment upon the obedience of the Gospel, read· "The word that I have spoken, the same shall judge him in the last day" (John 12.48)

"When the Lord Jesus shall be revealed from heaven with his mighty angels, in flaming fire, taking vengeance on them that know not God, and that obey not the Gospel of our Lord Jesus Christ who shall be punished with everlasting destruction from the presence of the Lord," etc. (2 Thess. 1:7-9; Matt. 24·14; Heb. 4·12; Rev 20:12).

Article XII

Of saving faith. We confess. That saving faith is not a vain or hidden thing unborn in man; nor does it consist in us having a historical knowledge derived from the holy Scriptures, and that we have much to say about it, without having the real substance or signification thereof But the real and true faith, which avails before God, is a sure knowledge of the heart in a sure confidence, which we receive from God, not through our own power, will or ability, but through the hearing of the Word of God; and which, through the illumination of the Holy Spirit, is imprinted on, and written in, the heart, and works so effectually in us, that we are drawn away by it from all visible and perishable things, to the invisible and living God; acquiring thereby a new spiritual taste for that which is heavenly, and not for that which is earthly For saving faith, accompanied with hope and love, is of such a nature that it conforms to things not seen Hence, all true believers gladly and obediently submit themselves to all the commandments of God, contained in the holy Scriptures, and, when necessary, testify to and confess them with the mouth before kings, princes, lords, and all men, not allowing themselves to be drawn away therefrom by any means whatever, though, on account thereof, money, property, body and life be sacrificed unto spoiling, water, and fire For the power of God, which preserves them in the faith, strengthens them, so that they esteem all the sufferings of this time brief and light, not avenging themselves, but praying for their persecutors, gladly suffering for the name of the Lord what is imposed upon them, because of the faith, hope, and love which they have to their Creator and His heavenly riches

Where this true faith is received in the heart, there the fruits of the Holy Spirit, as witnesses of the same, must follow and flow out On the contrary, unbelief, with its unfruitful works of darkness must flee, as darkness before the clear sunlight . By this faith, which is the beginning of the Christian doctrine, we become children of God, overcome the world, are armed against all the subtle wiles of the devil, become sanctified, justified, saved, and partakers of all the benefits of God shown in Christ Jesus; and without this faith it is impossible to please God.

In this true faith we cannot stand still, but, with humble fasting, praying and supplicating in the Spirit, we must plead for help, assistance, and new strength in all divine virtues, unto the end, in order that God may strengthen and preserve us in the same Where this is neglected men may fall from the faith; the good Spirit may be taken away, and their names blotted out of the Book of Life, and written again in the earth To this true faith, which is a noble gift of God, all men, who have attained to understanding and knowledge, so that they can hear and understand the Word of God, without distinction of persons, are called through the divine Word, and invited to come; but all infants, and those whom God permits to remain in their infancy, are herefrom excepted and excluded They are under the grace and pleasure of God through the atonement of Jesus Christ, by which He, through His blood, cleansed and redeemed the whole human race from the fall of Adam, without requiring of them any other means than faith, hope, love, and the observance of certain commandments of God It is therefore a great error that some ascribe faith to new born infants; or (that they say) that without this they cannot be saved It is a sure sign that said persons do not know the true faith, and do not believe the Words of Jesus Christ, who has promised the kingdom of heaven to infants without this.

For, as true faith consists in hearing, believing and accepting the good things which God offers us through His Word; and, again as unbelief consists in despising and rejecting those things; and since infants have neither knowledge, ability, inclination, nor emotion concerning any of these things, as all intelligent persons see and know; therefore it must truly follow that neither faith nor unbelief may be attributed to infants; but they are simple and ignorant, and in this state perfectly pleasing to God, He having set them as examples for us, that we should imitate them in their simplicity

How the true faith is a gift of God, and is wrought in the hearts of men through the hearing of God's Word, read "For by grace are ye saved through faith; and that not of yourselves it is the gift of God" (Eph 2 8; Rom 12 3; Col. 2·12; Phil. 1 29; Jude 3)

"So then faith cometh by hearing, and hearing by the word of God" (Rom 10:17; Heb 6 2).

With regard to how we must believe in God through His Word, read. "Neither pray I for these alone, but for them also which shall believe on me through their word" (John 17 20; Eph. 1 9; John 7 38; 14 1; Heb 11.6; 1 Pet 1·21; 2 Tim. 3·15).

Concerning how true faith is not vain, but manifests its effectual power and nature, read: "By whom we have received grace and apostleship, for obedience to the faith among all nations," etc (Rom. 1 5; 16 25; Acts 6.7).

When ye received the word of God which ye heard of us, ye received it not as the word of men, but, as it is in truth, the word of God, which effectually worketh also in you that believe" (I Thess 2:13).

"In Jesus Christ neither circumcision availeth anything, nor uncircumcision; but faith which worketh by love" (Gal 5·6)

He that does not evince from his faith the seven virtues required, "is blind, and cannot see afar off," etc (2 Pet. 1 9; Jas. 2·26).

"But the just shall live by faith" (Heb. 10 38; Rom. 1.17; Gal. 3 11).

By faith we become righteous and partakers of the benefits of God (Acts 26.18; Rom. 10 10; Gen. 15 6; Rom. 4:3; Gal. 3·6; Mark 16:16).

We must pray to God to be strengthened and kept in the faith (Luke 17.5; 1 Pet 1 5)

When the grace of God is neglected through unbelief and evil works, one may fall away from the faith, and be blotted out of the Book of life Now the Spirit speaketh expressly, that in the latter times some shall depart from the faith (1 Tim 4 1; 2 Peter 2 1; 1 Tim 6.10).

"Which for a while believe, and in time of temptation fall away" (Luke 8.13)

"The Lord said unto Moses, Whosoever hath sinned against me, him will I blot out of my book" (Ex 32.33; Rev 3.5; Ps 69 29; Isa 1 2; 30 1; Jer 18 7)

How infants are simple and ignorant, and that therefore neither faith nor unbelief may be imputed to them; but that they are well-pleasing to God through His grace, without any other means, read "Moreover, your little ones, which ye said should be a prey, and your children, which in that day had no knowledge between good and evil, they shall go in thither, and unto them will I give it, and they shall possess it" (Deut. 1.39; Matt 19 14)

"When I was a child, I spake as a child, I understood as a child, I thought as a child· but when I became a man, I put away childish things" (1 Cor. 13 11; Heb 5 13)

"Brethren, be not children in understanding· howbeit in malice be ye children" (1 Cor 14 20; Eph 4 14; Matt. 18.2; 19.13; Mark 10.13; Luke 18.15).

Article XIII

Of regeneration and the new creature, we confess· Inasmuch as our first parents, Adam and Eve, through their transgression, separated themselves from God, and fell into temporal and eternal death, with all their posterity, and, consequently, lost the image of God, which is righteousness and true holiness; became depraved in their nature, and inclined to sin and wickedness from their youth; so that of all men none can attain unto faith and a godly conversation through the power of their first birth, which has sprung and proceeded from the sinful seed; because that which is born of the flesh is flesh, and hence, carnally minded, and the natural man does not receive the things of the Spirit of God; therefore, all men, having come of the earth, shall return to dust and earth, and, in part, are also like to the corrupted earth, which of itself does not bring forth good grain, but must thereto be prepared anew, and sown with good seed Thus also, all men, when they have passed their youth, and have come to understand and discern good and evil, we perceive, that their carnal hearts and earthly life, being conceived in sin, are inclined to sin, which conceives by its own lust, which awakens sin in them, and allures and moves them to actual sin; and thus they fall from grace,—to which they had been redeemed through the atonement of Christ —which plunges them into death of sin

Hence, God the Lord requires and demands through His Word, of all men of understanding. a true reformation and renewing from these their own actual sins; that is, that through the hearing of the Word of God they receive the faith, become regenerated from above, of God, be created anew in the inner mind of the heart, according to the image of God, and circumcised, being translated from the carnal into the spiritual, from unbelief into faith, from that which is earthly-minded and like Adam into that which is heavenly-minded and like Jesus Christ; that they crucify and mortify their earthly members, and feel, prove and taste that which is heavenly, and not that which is earthly To this, God promises life, peace, and all heavenly riches; and it is the sanctification in the spirit of the mind, and the appropriation of all the benefits of Christ (which have been lost through our own actual sin) and has the promise of eternal salvation.

And wherever this renewing and conversion of the mind and heart is not found (among all those who know sin have served it), there Christ and the life do not exist; and without this renewing neither circumcision nor uncircumcision, baptism nor Supper, nor any ceremonies, however glorious they may appear, avail anything

And as man in the beginning is brought forth with pain and anguish from the flesh, so the second, spiritual generation is also called a birth; and it takes place with godly sorrow over sin, and with the crucifying and mortifying of the earthly members

And as men by the fall of Adam were not altogether deprived and divested of all godly virtues and qualities, so as to become like Satan in evil, but through the grace of God have retained many good principles, so the innate sinful nature, affection for, and proneness to sin are not utterly removed by regeneration, but remain until death in the regenerated; so that the flesh lusts against the Spirit, and the lust or indwelling sin wars against the law of the new mind, so that the regenerated enter upon a continuous warfare, and must constantly crucify and mortify the lusts of the flesh, tame and bring into subjection their bodies, and abstain from fleshly lusts, which war against the soul; and thus fighting, they must keep the victory unto death

On the other hand, the assertion of those who ascribe regeneration to new-born infants, and say that without this they cannot be saved, is rejected as a grave error. Some of these found regeneration upon infant baptism, maintaining that as soon as thy have their children baptized they are also, through this ceremony of baptism, regenerated Others build the regeneration of infants on the justification or general redemption of Christ, by which the human race has been reconciled from the fall of Adam and put in a state of grace; saying that children are regenerated as soon as they are conceived by the mother; thus putting regeneration, against all right and probability, before the first birth which is of the flesh Some can not tell whether infants become partakers of regeneration before, in, or after baptism; from which it is judged that the aforesaid persons treat of regeneration without the holy Scriptures and all true reason, as the blind man of colors; since Almighty God, nowhere in His holy Word speaks of the regeneration of infants And though children are conceived in sin, or born from sinful seed, yet they have never known, served, or practiced sin, from which they might be regenerated, converted, and renewed in their mind and heart; but they have without this been born, and placed by God in so holy and God-pleasing a state, through the atonement of Christ, that no adult person can, through regeneration and the putting off of the sinful body of the flesh, and the renewing of the mind, become more sinless, holy and God-pleasing; seeing the innate sinfulness, lust or inclination to sin remains in the most pious, regenerated adult persons until death (not less then in children, in their infancy), against which they carry on a constant warfare; and besides this, Almighty God, by His Word, requires of all men that have served sin, no higher or greater reparation than that they be converted by regeneration, and become like unto children in sin and malice With what reason, then can regeneration be applied to children, who have never committed sin, from which they could be regenerated; seeing infancy has already the innocence which is acceptable to God, and has been set as an example before men, after which all the regenerated must labor and strive until death

Of this heavenly birth from God, and how it is effected through the Spirit and the Word of God, read "Seeing you have purified your souls in obeying the truth through the Spirit unto unfeigned love of the brethren, see that you love one another with a pure heart fervently being born again, not of corruptible seed, but of incorruptible, by the Word of God, which liveth and abideth forever" (1 Pet 1 22, 23; 2 2, James 1 18; 1 Cor 4 15, Gal 4 19; Philemon 10)

"Not by works of righteousness which we have done, but according to his mercy he saved us, by the washing of regeneration and renewing of the Holy Ghost," etc. (Tit 3 5)

That regeneration is not a vain or hidden thing, but demands a new life and the following of Christ, and that eternal salvation is promised thereupon, read "Verily, I say unto you, that ye which have followed me, in the regeneration, when the Son of man shall sit in the throne of his glory, ye also shall sit upon twelve thrones, judging the twelve tribes of Israel (Matt 19.28)

"For in Christ Jesus neither circumcision availeth anything, nor uncircumcision but a new creature And as many as walk according to this rule peace be on them, and mercy, and upon the Israel of God" (Gal 6 15, 16).

"But as many as received him, to them gave he power to become the sons of God, even to them that believe on his name which were born, not of blood, nor of the will of the flesh, nor of the will of man, but of God" (John 1 12, 13)

To all who have served sin, and have not been regenerated, the kingdom of God is denied Concerning this, read "Verily, verily, I say unto thee, except a man be born again, he cannot see the kingdom of God"

"Except a man be born of water and of the Spirit, he cannot enter into the kingdom of God That which is born of the flesh, is flesh; and that which is born of the Spirit is spirit Marvel not that I said unto thee, Ye must be born again The wind bloweth where it listeth, and thou hearest the sound thereof but canst not tell whence it cometh, and whither it goeth· so is every one that is born of the Spirit" (John 3 3, 5-8)

That the regenerated do not become perfect in this life, but must fight unto death against the flesh, the world, and sin, read "Not as though I had already attained, either were already perfect but I follow after," etc (Phil 3 12, 1 30; Col 1·29; Rev. 2·10)

"I keep under my body, and bring it into subjection lest that by any means, when I have preached to others, I myself should be a castaway" (1 Cor 9 27).

"For the flesh lusteth against the Spirit, and the Spirit against the flesh; and these are contrary the one to the other; so that ye cannot do the things that ye would But if ye be led by the spirit," etc (Gal 5 17, 18; 1 Pet 2 11; Rom 7 18, 23; Jas 3·2)

Article XIV

Of the incarnation of the eternal and only begotten Son of God We confess That the exalted and true God faithfully kept and fulfilled His exceeding great and precious promises, which He had made in the beginning concerning His Son, who had been foreordained to this end before the foundation of the world, but in these last times was manifest for our sakes.

This glorious and cheering promise was originally given to fallen Adam and Eve, and was afterwards renewed in their seed, as in Abraham, Isaac, and Jacob, Moses and David Of Him did all the prophets prophesy, and on Him did all the pious fathers hope, with a firm confidence (as though they had seen Him), that Shiloh would come from Judah, and that this beautiful star would arise out of Jacob. This truly and really took place as follows When everything was in tranquility, when the royal sceptre had departed from Judah, and the seed of Jacob was under tribute to the heathen; then the gracious God remembered His holy covenant, and sent His true, real Word or Son out of heaven, from His royal throne; having to this end foreordained and elected the righteous Joseph, of the house and generation of David, whose espoused wife was Mary, whom God had blessed and chosen for this purpose above all other women

To this Joseph and Mary the Holy Ghost points from generation to generation, as well as to the town of Bethlehem, out of which this Light long before promised was to arise and come forth; in order that all the pious who waited and hoped for this salvation, might have a certain consolation and knowledge from which tribe, city and place they were to expect this Savior of the world.

Thus Mary received the message through the angel of God, and believed it, being overshadowed by the power of the Highest, and conceived of the Holy Ghost the true, real Word, which was in the beginning with God and by which all things were created The same, through the effectual power of the Almighty God, became flesh or man in her, and was born of her, the Son of the Most High God, whom she had before conceived of the Holy Ghost

Thus the eternal and only begotten Son of the living God became a visible man subject to suffering He was wrapped in swaddling clothes, laid in a manger, and was brought up at Nazareth under the care of His (imputed) father and His mother He hungered, thirsted was wearied with walking, sighed and wept, and increased in wisdom and stature, and in favor with God and man; so that the eternal, only begotten Son of the living God, in the time of His incarnation, did not continue like His heavenly Father in an invisible, impassive, immortal, and spiritual form, but for our sakes, humbled Himself into a visible, passive, mortal and servile form, became like unto us men in all things, except sin; in order thereby to heal us from the poisonous bite of the serpent, and from everlasting torment.

Hence, all true witnesses of Jesus Christ are bound, by virtue of the holy Scriptures, to believe and confess: That this same Word, which was in the beginning with God, and was God, by which all things were made, proceeded from God His Father, came into the world, and, through the power of God, became Himself man or flesh, so that the glory of the only begotten Son of the Father, full of grace and truth was touched and seen

Thus He who before was like unto His Father in brightness and glory—not given or usurped Godlikeness, but one peculiar thing to Him by nature—left His brightness and glory, and humbled Himself, and became in form like unto us men; He who before was greater than the angels, and in an invisible, immortal form, like unto God His Father, was now made lower than the angels, and became like unto His brethren in a visible and mortal form He who could have had joy with His Father, and was surrounded by eternal riches, became poor for our sakes, and suffered on the cross, despising the shame He who in the presence of the apostles ascended heavenward, was the same who before had descended from God out of heaven into the lower parts of the earth; and the same ascended above all heavens. This is the mystery of godliness, which is great, but on account of their carnal and flickering reason, is believed by but few that God the Son was thus manifest in the flesh and that He appeared, as a true Redeemer and Savior, and eternal Light, to them who sat in darkness and in the shadow of death.

And as the food which the Israelites ate in the wilderness, is called bread from heaven or heavenly bread, because the substance of the bread was no fruit of this earth, but had come from heaven, though the same, was in the world prepared in the form of bread, so also Christ Himself calls His flesh the true bread which came down from heaven; and says that the Son of man should ascend up where He was before, because His flesh or body became flesh, not of Mary or of any created substance, but only of the Word of life which had come down from heaven

He it was who spake with Moses on the mount and in the wilderness; and Him the fathers tempted in the wilderness, and resisted His Spirit This is the same who was from the beginning Him the apostles touched with their hands, and beheld with their eyes, herein the life was manifested, that they saw and proclaimed to men, that which was with the Father, and was manifested unto them, and was even the same Word which spake with them

And though it is true that the eternal Son of the living God forsook His divine glory, and, for a brief time, was made lower than the angels, and appeared in the visible form of a servant; yet He did not thereby lose His eternal Sonship and Godhead with His Father; but when God the Father brought this His first and only begotten Son into the world, He prepared Him a body, not of any created substance, but only of the Word of life, which became flesh, and which by all the angels of God is honored and worshiped as the true God

Likewise, Christ glorified Himself before His apostles, on Mount Tabor, that His face shone as the bright sun, and He was confessed by His Father from heaven as His beloved Son. Thus have also the highly enlightened apostles of Christ, and all true believers, confessed, pronounced, honored and worshiped this visible and palpable Christ Jesus as the true God, and Son of God Hence all true believers, according to these testimonies of holy Scripture, and the examples of all the saints of God, must necessarily, unto salvation, follow, believe, and confess, that the whole crucified Christ Jesus, visible and invisible, mortal and immortal, is the true God, and the Son of God, God and man in one undivided person To Him be praise forever and ever Amen

Of these promises concerning the Savior, read, how, God the Lord, in the beginning promised fallen Adam and Eve, to put Him as enmity between Satan and the woman, and between their seed "And I will put enmity between thee and the woman, and between thy seed and her seed; it shall bruise thy head, and thou shalt bruise his heel" (Gen 3·15; Col. 1 19; 3·15; Eph 2·15)

"The Lord thy God will raise up unto thee a prophet from the midst of thee, of thy brethren, like unto me; unto him ye shall hearken" (Deut 18 15; Acts 7 37; Read also Acts 3·25; Gal 3·8; Gen. 49 10; Num 24 17; Matt 2 2; Jer. 23 5; 33.15; Is. 9 6; 11·1; Acts 10·43)

And that this Savior of the world originally did not spring from the fathers, Mary, or any creature, but was sent and came from God, and was conceived and brought forth by Mary, read· "Behold, a virgin shall be with child, and shall bring forth a son" (Matt 1 23; Is 7 14; Luke 2 21; Gal. 4 4) "When as his mother Mary was espoused to Joseph, before they came together, she was found with child of the Holy Ghost " And further "Joseph, thou son of David, fear not to take unto thee Mary thy wife for that which is conceived in her is of the Holy Ghost" (Matt. 1:18, 20)

The angel of God said unto Mary: "Behold, thou shalt call his name Jesus. He shall be great, and shall be called the Son of the Highest; and the Lord God shall give unto him the throne of his father David. and he shall reign over the house of Jacob forever, and of his kingdom there shall be no end Then said Mary unto the angel, How shall this be, seeing I know not a man? And the angel answered and said unto her, The Holy Ghost shall come upon thee, and the power of the Highest shall overshadow thee therefore also that holy thing which shall be born of thee shall be called the Son of God" (Luke 1·30-35)

Read in this connection St John, who also gives thorough information regarding this matter "In the beginning was the Word, and the Word was with God, and the Word was God The same was in the beginning with God And the Word was made flesh, and dwelt among us (and we beheld his glory, the glory as of the only begotten of the Father) full of grace and truth" (John 1 1, 2, 14; Zach. 2·10).

And further· "That which was from the beginning, which we have heard, which we have seen with our eyes, which we have looked upon, and our hands have handled, of the Word of life; (for the life was manifested, and we have seen it, and bear witness, and shew unto you that eternal life, which was with the Father, and was manifested unto us,)" (1 John 1 1, 2; John 8 25; Micah 5 2; 2 Peter 1 16; John 20 28)

Of the humbling of the eternal and only Son of God (Mark especially the word *made*, for nowhere do we find anything about *assuming* man) read· "Who, being in the form of God, thought it not robbery to be equal wtih God but *made* himself of no reputation, and took upon him the form of a servant, and was *made* in the likeness of men and being found in fashion as a man," etc (Phil 2 6-8)

"Thou madest him a little lower than the angels " "But we see Jesus, who was made a little lower than the angels for the suffering of death, crowned with glory and honor" (Heb. 2.7, 9; Ps. 8·5).

"For ye know the grace of our Lord Jesus Christ, that, though he was rich, yet for your sakes he became poor, that ye through his poverty might be rich" (2 Cor 8 9, Eccl 9 15)

"Looking unto Jesus the author and finisher of our faith, who for the joy that was set before him endured the cross, despising the shame," etc (Heb 12 2)

"I am the living bread which came down from heaven if any man eat of this bread, he shall live forever and the bread that I will give is my flesh, which I will give for the life of the world" (John 6 51 Read also verses 58 and 63)

How the saints of God confessed and worshiped this humiliated Jesus also in the days of His flesh, as the true God, and the Son of God, read "Whom do men say that I, the Son of man, am?" And after a few more words "Simon Peter answered and said, Thou art the Christ, the Son of the living God" (Matt. 13.16) Understand, the true Son who was born and came forth from the essence of the Father; and not a Son become so in time, or assumed, as believers, who because of the faith, are also called sons and daughters" (2 John 1 3; John 1 49, 10 36; 11 27; Acts 8 37; Matt 27 54)

Jesus said to the blind man "Dost thou believe on the Son of God? He answered and said, Who is he, Lord, that I might believe on him? and Jesus said unto him, Thou hast both seen him, and it is he that talketh with thee And he said, Lord, I believe And he worshiped him" (John 9 35-38)

"Thomas answered and said unto him, My Lord and my God Jesus saith unto him, Thomas, because thou hast seen me thou hast believed," etc. (John 20 28, 29)

"In his Son Jesus Christ. This is the true God, and eternal life Little children, keep yourselves from idols. Amen" (1 John 5:20, 21; Rom 9.5).

Article XV

Of the knowledge of Jesus Christ, God and man in one person, and the necessity of believing it Of this we confess· That it is necessary for all Christians to believe that the knowledge of the only Son of the Father, is, as one of the principle articles of our faith, in the highest degree essential unto salvation It is therefore not sufficient to know Christ only after the flesh, or His humanity; as, that He was born of Mary, and became like unto us in all things, except sin, but we must also (which is the most important) know Him after the Spirit, and His eternal Godhead; that is, that He before all time, in eternity, in an unspeakable manner, was born of or proceeded from the true God His Father, and that He is the true, real Word and Wisdom, which proceeded from the mouth of the Most High, and which for this reason, was equal with His Father in brightness, glory, power, might and eternal Godhead, before the foundation of the world And that this only Son of God, for our justification became a visible man, that by His present, visible humanity—which is not of this tabernacle or sinful substance, but in essence far different from sinners—He might give us a holy, unblamable example in doctrine and conversation, in order thus to incite all men to follow Him

And that according to His divine power and might He was able to deliver us from the captivity of sin, hell, the devil, and death, and save us forever; seeing no other means or name in heaven or on earth is given unto men for salvation To this end, Christ was made unto us, of God, wisdom, and righteousness, and sanctification, and redemption Hence neither Moses with His threatening and punishing law of commandments, nor Aaron with the entire Levitical priesthood, and all their sacrifices and offerings, which were made only for remembrance of sins, and consequently, passed by polluted mankind without affording them any help (for no corruptible man could redeem his brother, and reconcile him with God; as all human, sinful substance was not able to redeem the soul from eternal death); but this was fulfilled and accomplished by the slain Lamb, which was foreordained and was manifest in these last times. He restored that which He had not taken away. He, the innocent one, took the guilt of us all upon Him, and only He was found worthy in heaven and earth, to open the book with its seven seals. And by His coming into this world (which can never be sufficiently praised), He opened the entrance to the kingdom of God, which was closed by sin, not by the blood of bulls and goats, or of any corruptible man, nor by corruptible silver or gold; but Christ paid and accomplished this by His own dear and precious blood, thereby obtaining an eternal redemption.

And as the sun in the heavens is endowed by God with a glorious splendor, so that it is the eye of the world, which illuminates the darkness, and spreads its beautiful light over all visible things, and receives nothing from any of them; so also Christ Jesus, the true Sun of righteousness, and what is still more, the Creator and Ruler of the sun, and of all things, did not take to His assistance any created substance, by which to accomplish the work of our salvation; but came with His most praiseworthy light from God out of heaven, and shone into this dark world, where He was received, and arose, as the beautiful day-star, in the hearts of many men; and was thus a Giver, but not a recipient. Hence, the praise and honor for this redemption must be ascribed to the only God of heaven and earth, and not to any created man; otherwise we would rob the Creator of His proper honor, and ascribe the same to sinful, created flesh like unto ourselves; thereby making flesh our arm, Redeemer, God and Savior; and thus departing with our hearts from God our Salvation, we should fall into damnable idolatry, seeking life from the dead, where it cannot be found

Herein we are to know the love and goodness, and also the severity of God, and how greatly the Almighty God hates sin;—His severity and justice, from the fact, that through the one sin of the first man, the whole human race became corrupted; and that this could be paid and atoned for by no other means than through the death and blood of God's own, only begotten Son God's goodness and everlasting love are known from this, that He, the Blessed, so graciously looked upon and recognized, the weakness and nothingness of man, and, hence, as He often sent angels, as faithful messengers, in human form to men, upon the earth, knowing that this sinful, mortal, earthly flesh and blood is not able to behold the immortal, eternal, holy splendor and glory of the eternal Creator of all things; therefore the eternal, invisible, and immortal Son of God, through His unfathomable love, had Himself to become a visible, mortal man, for a little while lower than the angels, and to appear in the form of a servant, like unto His brethren, so that the glory of the eternal and only begotten Son of God was felt and seen in human form, that He might be a true example for us to follow His footsteps. Herein we may especially know the love of Christ, which passes knowledge that the holy, heavenly, only begotten, blessed Son of God, Jesus Christ, became man, died and rose for us, when we were yet ungodly and His enemies

And though Christ suffered for us in the flesh, and was crucified and died; yet it was not possible that He should be held by death, or that His holy flesh should see corruption But He had Himself the keys of death and hell, and to take it again; and He it is that liveth, and was dead, and behold, He is alive forevermore

Hence all true believers must believe that the true knowledge of Jesus Christ, both of His true divinity, and pure, immaculate humanity, is necessary to salvation, And to this, life and eternal salvation are promised by the Holy Ghost; and that Christ would build His church upon this foundation, and that the gates of hell should not prevail against her. On the other hand that all unbelievers, who confess not that Jesus Christ is come in the flesh, (that is, that the Son of God became man, and thus coming, appeared in the flesh), are not of God, but of the spirit of Antichrist, who began already in the days of the apostles, and is to exalt himself still more in the last times

Of the necessity of this knowledge of Jesus Christ, read "And this is life eternal, that they might know thee the only true God, and Jesus Christ, whom thou hast sent" (John 17:3; Hosea 13 4)

"If ye had known me, ye should have known my Father also," etc (John 14 7)

"Though we have known Christ after the flesh, yet now henceforth know we him no more" (2 Cor 5 16)

"And that every tongue should confess that Jesus Christ is Lord, to the glory of God the Father" (Phil. 2 11; Rom 14 11; Col 2 2; Phil 3 8).

And Jesus said to Peter, after the latter had confessed and pronounced the man Jesus, to be Christ, the Son of the living God "Blessed art thou, Simon Bar-jona for flesh and blood hath not revealed it unto thee, but my Father which is in heaven. And I say also unto thee, That thou art Peter, and upon this rock I will build my church; and the gates of hell shall not prevail against it" (Matt 16 17, 18).

And after the apostle Thomas had confessed the visible and the palpable man Jesus as his Lord and God, Christ did not reprehend him for it, but accepted it as the belief of the truth, saying: "Thomas, because thou hast seen me, thou hast believed blessed are they that have not seen, and yet have believed" (John 20 29, 17 20; 1 Pet 1.8).

Read in this connection the various Scripture passages, how the apostles through the Holy Ghost, labored with all their might, to impress on men, not that the eternal Son of God dwelt concealed in the man Jesus; but on the contrary, that the visible man Jesus was the Christ, that is, the Anointed, and the Savior of the world, sent down from heaven; and to this, the promise of life is given Read "And many other signs truly did Jesus in the presence of his disciples, which are not written in this book· but these are written, that ye might believe that Jesus is the Christ, the Son of God; and that believing ye might have life through his name" (John 20 30, 31).

"Whosoever shall confess that Jesus is the Son of God, God dwelleth in him, and he in God" (1 John 4 15; 1 John 5 5; 2 John 1 3; John 6·47)

"Whosoever believeth that Jesus is the Christ is born of God" (1 John 5·1, 5, 10; Acts 18 5, 28)

"Who is a liar but he that denieth that Jesus is the Christ? he is antichrist, that denieth the Father and the Son" (1 John 2·22).

Hereby know ye the Spirit of God every spirit that confesseth that Jesus Christ is come in the flesh (that is, that the eternal Word became flesh, and being thus flesh, came into his own) is of God and every spirit that confesseth not that Jesus Christ is come in the flesh is not of God. and this is that spirit of antichrist, whereof ye have heard that it should come; and even now already is it in the world" (1 John 4 2, 3; 2 John 1:7).

Read further, how we have been redeemed and bought by no other means, than only by the death of the Son of God

"For God so loved the world, that he gave his only begotten Son," etc (John 3.16; Rom. 5 8)

"For if, when we were enemies, we were reconciled to God by the death of his Son," etc (Rom 5 10; Heb 5 9)

"If God be for us, who can be against us? He that spared not his own Son, but delivered him up for us all," etc (Rom 8 31, 32; 1 John 3·16)

"Ye know that ye were not redeemed with corruptible things, as silver and gold, from your vain conversation received by tradition from your fathers; but with the precious blood of Christ, as of a Lamb without blemish and without spot" (1 Pet 1·18, 19)

"In this was manifested the love of God toward us, because that God sent his only begotten Son into the world, that we might live through him" (1 John 4 9)

Article XVI

Of the life, suffering, death, burial, resurrection, and ascension of Jesus Christ and of His again receiving His glory with His Father. Of this we confess. That the Lord Jesus, in the time of His humiliation in the flesh, being about thirty-three years, did not only with words, but also by works and deeds, set us a holy, godly example, to be looked to as the Captain of the faith, by all believers, and followed in the regeneration; for in His youth He was subject to His father and mother. And when His time was fulfilled, He entered in full obedience toward His heavenly Father, on the office and ministry imposed upon Him, proclaimed unto them His Father's good pleasure, made the deaf to hear, the dumb to speak, the blind to see, cleansed the lepers, cast out devils, raised the dead from their graves, forgave men their sins and promised eternal life to those who believe in Him

These things Christ did not do in the same manner and form as His apostles and others, who performed miracles through a power and gift only received, which had been conferred upon and given them by Christ But such was not the case with Christ; for He Himself had all power in heaven and earth; so that He said to the two blind men "Believe ye that I am able to do this?" And further "That ye may know that the Son of man hath power on earth to forgive sins" And still further: "I will raise them up at the last day; and I give unto them eternal life"

Thus the Lord Jesus completely fulfilled and accomplished the works of His Father, and shone as a clear heavenly light into this dark world, convincing the same of her evil works, and pointing them out to her; by which He incurred the hatred of the blinded scribes and Pharisees, who did not know the light of truth, and who, from hatred and envy, censured Him for all these divine deeds, attributing them to the devil, and thus they delivered this innocent One into the hands of the unbelieving heathen, Pontius Pilate They also examined this dumb Lamb with many severe threats, mocked Him, spat in His face, smote Him with their fists, scourged Him, wounded His head with a crown of thorns, and finally stripped Him and stretched Him naked on the cross, nailed His hands and feet thereon, and thus suspended Him, as the Prince and Captain of all malefactors, between two murderers In His bitter thirst they gave Him vinegar to drink, mixed with gall; they pierced His side with a spear, so that blood and water flowed out therefrom Thus He gave up the ghost with a loud voice, commending it into the hands of His Father And when He had died, heaven and earth were convulsed by this precious death and resurrection; so that the sun lost his brightness, and darkness came over all the earth; the earth quaked; the vail of the temple was rent in twain from the top to the bottom; and many bodies of the saints arose from their graves, and went into the holy city, and appeared unto many

And as in the time of His flesh, suffering and death, He showed that He had become man, so He also showed herein that this very man was also true God with His Father; and that He had the keys of the power of death and hell, that He could again raise up the broken temple of His body in three days, and had the power to lay down His life, and to take it up again; so that it was impossible that He should be held by death, or that His holy flesh should see corruption, but rose triumphantly from the dead, on the third day, by the glory of the Father, revealed Himself to His apostles and others, and miraculously appeared unto them, as they were assembled with doors closed, ate and drank with them, and for forty days spake with them of many things pertaining to the kingdom of God Then, in the presence of the apostles, He was taken up to heaven by a cloud, and sat down on the right hand of His Almighty Father in heaven

Thus the only begotten Son of God suffered, was crucified and put to death according to the flesh; but thereby was again glorified and made alive according to the spirit, and again fully received His previous divine glory, and His equality with the Father He will now die no more, neither will death have any more dominion over Him; but He shall live and rule as a reigning King of kings, and Lord of lords over mount Zion and the house of Jacob, forever and ever

Of the unblamable life and conversation of Christ, and how He was subject to His father and mother, read Luke 2 51; John 8 46; Acts 1 1

And after His time was fulfilled, how He entered on the ministry imposed upon Him, and performed many glorious deeds in His Father's name, read: Mark 1:15;

Matt. 8:16; 9.35; 11:5; 12.15; John 10; Acts 10:38; Is 53:7; 1 Pet 2:24

And how He, as a light in the world, testified of their dark and evil works, and thus fell into the hands of sinners, read: "The world cannot hate you; but me it hateth, because I testify of it, that the works thereof are evil" (John 7:7; 1:5, 3:19; Matt. 27:18)

How Christ in the time of His humiliation in the flesh was obedient to His heavenly Father, read: "He humbled Himself and became obedient unto death, even the death of the cross" (Phil. 2:8).

"Though he were a Son, yet learned he obedience by the things which he suffered" (Heb. 5:8).

Of the suffering, death, and burial of Christ, read Ps 22:16; 60:9, 21; Is 53:7; 63:3; Acts 8:32, Matt 27; Mark 15; Luke 23; John 19; Acts 3:15; 1 Cor 15:4, 20; Matt 27:57; Is 53:9.

Of the resurrection of Christ, read: Matt 28:7; Mark 16:6; Luke 24:7; 1 Cor 15:4, 20; Acts 3:26; 10:40

How Christ again received the divine glory and likeness which He had forsaken; and how He ascended unto heaven, read: "And Jesus came and spake unto them, saying, All power is given unto me in heaven and in earth" (Matt. 28:18, Ps 8:6).

"Ought not Christ to have suffered these things, and to enter into his glory?" (Luke 24.26).

"Thou madest him a little lower than the angels; thou crownedst him with glory and honor, and didst set him over the works of thy hands: thou hast put all things in subjection under his feet" (Heb. 2:7-9; John 17:5).

"The God of our fathers raised up Jesus, whom ye slew and hanged on a tree Him hath God exalted with his right hand to be a Prince and a Savior," etc (Acts 5:30, 31; Phil 2:9; Acts 2:33, 36).

"And when he had spoken these things, while they beheld, he was taken up; and a cloud received him out of their sight And while they looked steadfastly toward heaven as he went up," etc (Acts 1 9, 10; Mark 16 19; Luke 24.51).

Article XVII

Of the office of Christ, and the specific reason of His coming into the world We confess That Christ is the true promised Prophet, High Priest, and King, whom Moses and all the prophets foretold and proclaimed, and to whom the former priests and kings pointed as figures and shadows And the specific reason of His coming into the world was to destroy the works of the devil, to seek that which was lost, to deliver the whole human race from the captivity of sin, and the power of the devil, and to reconcile them with God His Father, and thus to save sinners

According to His prophetical office He went out from God, and came into the world to proclaim unto men, through the Gospel, the full counsel and will of God, which had been hid from the beginning of the world, and thus to preach deliverance to the captives, the Gospel to the poor, and the acceptable year of the Lord, according to which as the last declaration and will of God, all the children of the New Covenant are required to live and walk, according to a perfect rule of faith, which shall obtain until the end of the world.

According to His office as High Priest He fulfilled and changed the Levitical priesthood; and by His one offering made on the cross, He opened the closed entrance to the Holy of holies; and through this His one offering, which is of eternal value, He fulfilled and finished the sacrifice of the law, and obtained an eternal redemption And thus reconciling mankind with the Father, He sat down on the right hand of the Majesty in heaven, and is become the believers' only Advocate, Mediator, High Priest, and Intercessor with God His Father, and ever lives to make intercession for them

And according to His office as King He came with full power from His almighty Father from heaven, to reestablish, as a mighty King of Kings, and commander of the people, judgment and righteousness on earth; and He was the end and fulfillment of all the kings of Israel But as His kingdom was not of this world, and He was a spiritual, heavenly King, He avoided all earthly kingdoms of this world, and desired and had only a spiritual, heavenly kingdom. Among His subjects He reformed, improved and fulfilled the commandments, laws, and customs, given by Moses As a commanding king He dissuaded and prohibited His followers from all revenge, whether with words or by deed, (and taught them) that they should beat their swords into ploughshares, and their spears into scythes and sickles, and should learn war no more; but that, on the contrary, they, according to the example of Christ, their Captain, should love their enemies, and pray for those who injure and persecute them—very far indeed from allowing them to wage war against their enemies with carnal weapons But Christ armed His people only with the armor of God, and the sword of the Spirit, which is the Word of God, with which to fight against flesh and blood, the world, sin, and the manifold wiles of the devil, and thus finally to receive, through grace, from this eternal King, the crown of everlasting life, as their recompense and exceeding great reward

How Christ is the prophet promised by God, whom we must hear and follow as the perfect teacher of the will of God, read "The Lord thy God will raise up unto thee a prophet from the midst of thee, of thy brethren, like unto me; unto him ye shall hearken" (Deut 18 15; Acts 7 37; 3·22; Matt. 17:5).

"We have also a more sure word of prophecy; whereunto ye do well that ye take heed, as unto a light that shineth in a dark place" (2 Pet 1 19)

"God, who at sundry times and in divers manners spake in time past unto the fathers by the prophets, hath in these last days spoken unto us by his Son," etc (Heb 1 1, 2)

Of His prophecies, read: Matt 24 throughout; Luke 17 20, 19 41-44.

Of His priestly office, read "And having a high priest over the house of God; let us draw near with a true heart in full assurance of faith," etc (Hebrews 10 21, 22).

"For the priesthood being changed, there is made of necessity a change also of the law" (Heb 7 12; 8 6; 10.12).

"But Christ being come a high priest of good things to come," etc (Heb 9:11)

Of His preaching, read Matt 9 35, Mark 1 14; Matt. 5 2; 11 1; Luke 4 15)

Of His office of King, read "Rejoice greatly, O daughter of Zion; shout, O daughter of Jerusalem, behold, thy King cometh unto thee," etc (Zech 9 9; Matt 21:5).

"Behold, the days come, that I will raise unto David a righteous Branch, and a King shall reign and prosper, and shall execute judgment and justice in the earth" (Jer 23 5; 33 15; Is. 32.1).

"Rabbi, thou art the Son of God; thou art the King of Israel" (John 1 49; Acts 10 36, II Cor. 4 5; Phil 2 11)

Of His spiritual kingdom and dominion, read "And the Lord God shall gave unto him the throne of his father David and he shall reign over the house of Jacob forever; and of his kingdom there shall be no end" (Luke 1 32, 33).

"For he is Lord of lords, and King of kings and they that are with him are called, and chosen, and faithful" (Rev 17 14)

"But ye are a chosen generation, a royal priesthood," etc (1 Pet 2 9; Ex 19 6; Rev. 5 10, John 18 36, 37; Ps 22 28)

Of His government, read "Behold, I have given him for a witness to the people, a leader and commander to the people" (Is 55 4)

"There is one lawgiver, who is able to save and to destroy," etc. (Jas 4·12; 1 Cor 9 21, Matt 12 8, 28 20; Jas 1 25)

Article XVIII

Of the church of God and the communion of believers Concerning this we believe and confess Whereas men by reason of the natural birth of the flesh, follow sin and wickedness when they attain to their understanding, and thereby depart from God their Creator, therefore the high and holy God, before whom the sinners and ungodly cannot stand from the beginning of the world, called and chose, from all the unbelieving nations of the world, an own special people, and separated them from all other nations These are they who turn their ears to the calling voice of God, and thereby have separated themselves from the world with all its sinful lusts, and all false worship, and have again united themselves to Christ, bowing, as obedient members and sheep of Jesus Christ, under His head and commanding voice, and shunning everything strange which militates against this These are they who are renewed in the inward man, and are circumcised, changed, and converted, and live after the Spirit

This church of God was first commenced on earth, with Adam and Eve in Paradise, and afterwards, with

Enoch, Noah, and all those who with them honored and called upon the high name of God; which was the first period of time, that is, before the law.

After this God the Lord established His covenant or church with Abraham and his seed, giving them circumcision as a sign of the covenant, together with many laws, ceremonies, statutes, and customs; which continued till the coming of Christ, and was the second period, or the time of the law of Moses

Finally God sent His Son, who, as a potentate in heaven and earth, established a new and perfect covenant with the house of Israel, calling to the same all the Gentiles and nations of the earth, all those who amend their sinful life, and obediently yield their bodies under this covenant With all these Christ has established His church and congregation; this is the third and last period, which shall thus continue, without change in faith, walk, and laws, until the reappearing of Christ from heaven

And though the people of God in these three periods, had different and special laws and ceremonies, according to which they had to live and walk; yet this was the will of God, and they were nevertheless only one people of God, and were moved and led by one Spirit.

This church and congregation of believers has not always been visible to the eyes of all men, but has frequently vanished from the sight of the sinful and bloodthirsty world, the latter not being worthy of them This can be seen in the case of Noah with his families in the ark, who concealed themselves from the whole world; in the people of Israel in the Red Sea, and here and there during the forty years in the wilderness; in the pious in Judah from the bloody sword of Manasseh; and in all the godfearing in Israel from the awful threats of Jezebel Thus also the bride of the Lamb, the church of Jesus Christ, had to hide herself in the wilderness, forty-two months, or three times and a half time,* from the abominable beast of Antichrist, which with his tyrannical sword and burning, exalted itself above everything which is called and worshipped as God Afterwards, through the grace of God, she again came to the light, and was built upon the first, ancient apostolical foundation

And as Solomon's temple was destroyed, and the second building continued until the first coming of Christ in the flesh, so we hold that the church of Jesus Christ, rebuilt upon the foundation of the apostles and prophets, shall also continue openly in the light until the second coming of Christ from heaven.

This church of God, that is, all believers, are, as members of one body, joined together by faith and the bond of love: they are like-minded one toward another according to Christ Jesus; they live according to the same rule of the divine Word, and are bound together by the same love, thus having fellowship with one another. Those whom God has blessed with spiritual gifts, minister with them to the souls of their neighbors out of love. And those whom God has provided with temporal possessions, minister with them to the temporal needs of their neighbors; thus showing that they have their temporal and spiritual goods in common, and suffer no want in spiritual and temporal gifts This church of God has existed on the earth from the beginning of the world, either in greater or in smaller numbers, secretly or openly, and shall thus continue unto the end of the world, and Christ will be with her, with His Spirit, always.

Of the Christian church, that is, of all believing regenerated persons, gathered and purified by the Holy Spirit, read "The Lord thy God hath chosen thee to

---

*Understand, taking each time for a great year, there are as many years as there are days in three years and a half which is about 1260 years (Num 14 34, Ezek 4 5)

be a special people unto himself, above all people that are upon the face of the earth" (Deut 7 6, 14 2, 26 18; 1 Pet. 2·9)

How the church of God, which is built upon Christ, must be subject, as members to their head, read "And upon this rock (Christ) I will build my church, and the gates of hell shall not prevail against it" (Matt 16 18; 28 20).

"Husbands, love your wives, even as Christ also loved the church, and gave himself for it; that he might sanctify and cleanse it with the washing of water by the word, that he might present it to himself a glorious church, not having spot, or wrinkle, or any such thing; but that it should be holy and without blemish" (Eph 5 25-27, 29, 32, 1 22).

"That thou mayest know how thou oughtest to behave thyself in the house of God, which is the church of the living God, the pillar and ground of the truth" (1 Tim 3 15; Eph 2 20; 4 16; Heb 12 23).

Of the fellowship of believers, read "But if we walk in the light, as he is in the light, we have fellowship one with another, and the blood of Jesus Christ his Son, cleanseth us from all sin" (1 John 1 7)

They continued steadfastly in the apostles' doctrine and fellowship" (Acts 2 42, 4 34; 1 Cor. 12 12; Gal 3 28; John 17 21).

Article XIX

Of the signs of the church of God, by which it may be distinguished from all other peoples, we confess the following In the first place, all true Christians are known by the only saving faith, which works by love It is wrought, through the grace of God, in the heart of man by hearing of the Word of God, and hence, is not founded and built upon human decrees, but upon the Word of God alone; and it works so effectually that by it we are drawn and impelled from all visible things and sinful lusts of this world to the invisible God and His heavenly riches

Secondly All true children of God are known by the second or new birth, from above, of God; which is wrought by the Spirit of God internally in the heart, through the putting off of the sinful lusts of the flesh; so that, as man, through his first birth of the flesh, brings forth his human nature and mind; so, through regeneration, he becomes a partaker of the divine nature, by which he is also to bring forth godly and spiritual fruits, and the mind of Christ Jesus

Thirdly. The church, or the believers, are known by the good works which they evince as fruits of gratitude from their faith; which may not be done according to human instructions, in a self-selected holiness, but in which we follow Christ and His apostles, as they prescribed and walked And with these divine virtues all true believers must be clothed, that, as a light on the candlestick, and a city on the hill, they may excel and shine among all men, and may be known thereby, as a good tree is known and distinguished by its good fruits.

Fourthly The church of God is known by the glorious appellations by which she is described and honored by the Holy Spirit, as a city and temple of the living God, in which God will dwell and walk; the bride of the Lamb, the daughter of Zion; a chaste virgin, joined to Christ by faith; so that, even as with all cities which are subject to the command of their lord and king, and it may thereby properly be known, under whose power and dominion they belong, so also the church of God is known by this that she recognizes and obeys Christ Jesus as her only Head and King, in all matters of faith, and observes His commandments. And as a pure virgin and bride forsakes father, mother, and all strange company and subjects herself to the will and obedience of her only bridegroom, so all true children of God must separate themselves from all false worship, flee from the stranger's voice and unite themselves to Christ, to hear and obediently follow His voice, which is proclaimed by the ministers sent by Him

Fifthly The people of God are known by their faithful ministers, who, according to the doctrine of Paul, are unblamable in doctrine and life, and feed the sheep of Christ, not for the milk and wool, but with a willing mind, with knowledge and understanding; speaking not their own words, but only the words of their Lord, and executing His work; rightly dividing and dispensing the Word of God, and bringing forth fruits with it; in order that through this good message of the ways of the Lord men might, according to the counsel and will of God, be converted from their evil ways, and won to God

Sixthly, and lastly All true disciples of Jesus Christ are known by the unfeigned godly love, which our Saviour Himself has put as a sign, by which His disciples should be specially known; which is comprehended in these things That we love the Lord God our Creator with all our heart and strength, above all other things, which consists principally in the keeping of His commandments And besides· That we love our brethren or neighbors as ourselves, not only in word or tongue, but in deed and in truth; so that those to whom God has given spiritual gifts, minister therewith, from love, to the souls of their neighbors; and those whom God has blessed with temporal possessions, minister therewith unto the temporal needs of their neighbors, in order that thus among this true Israel of God, there may be found no poor, nor any lack in spiritual or temporal things Finally, we must show charity to all men, though they be our open enemies, who persecute and kill us, whom we may by no means resist with carnal weapons; but, as Christ did not open His mouth in revenge upon His enemies, but, as an humble and dumb lamb, prayed for them, so we must also follow this infallible example And as all soldiers forsake their former vocation, and wear the livery of their lord and king, as a sign to distinguish them from all strange servants, and that they are bound to their captain even unto death; so, also, must all true servants of Jesus Christ be armed with the aforesaid marks, that thereby they may be known and distinguished from all other people

Where, therefore, men believe with the heart, in the Father the Son and the Holy Ghost, and in the incarnation, justification or redemption, suffering, death, resurrection, and ascension of Jesus Christ, and the resurection of the dead and the eternal judgment; and where, besides, the ordinances of the Lord, as baptism, Supper, separation, and the like, are rightly observed, according to Scripture, and Christ is followed therein, in the clean fear of the Lord, and in the regeneration— there is the city and church of the living God, the pillar and firm ground of the truth, the tabernacle of God with men, in which God will dwell and walk with His Spirit Such a body (church) has Christ for its Head, Preserver, and Savior But where said marks do not exist, and where the ordinances of men are the rule of action, there is no church of God, but a vain boasting of the same

How the true faith is to be known, read "So then faith cometh by hearing, and hearing by the word of God" (Rom 10 17).

"He that believeth on me, as the scripture hath said, out of his belly shall flow rivers of living water" (John 7·38).

"That your faith should not stand in the wisdom of men, but in the power of God" (1 Cor. 2 5).

"For in Jesus Christ neither circumcision availeth

anything, nor uncircumcision; but faith which worketh by love" (Gal 5 6; Heb 11 1; Hab 2 4; Heb. 10 38; Rom 1:17).

How the children of God are to be known by regeneration or the new birth, read "Being born again, not of corruptible seed, but of incorruptible, by the word of God, which liveth and abideth forever" (1 Pet. 1·23).

"Jesus said unto them, Verily I say unto you, That ye which have followed me, in the regeneration when the Son of man shall sit in the throne of his glory, ye also shall sit upon twelve thrones, judging the twelve tribes of Israel" (Matt. 19:28)

"For in Christ Jesus neither circumcision availeth anything, nor uncircumcision, but a new creature" (Gal. 6·15, John 3 8; 2 Cor. 5:17).

How the true members of Christ are to be known from their godly conversation, read "Every tree that bringeth not forth good fruit is hewn down, and cast into the fire Wherefore by their fruits ye shall know them Not every one that saith unto me, Lord, Lord, shall enter into the kingdom of heaven; but he that doeth the will of my Father which is in heaven" (Matt 7 19-21; 5:16; 12:50; John 15:14).

"Do all things without murmurings and disputings: that ye may be blameless and harmless, the sons of God, without rebuke, in the midst of a crooked and perverse nation, among whom ye shine as lights in the world; holding forth the word of life" (Phil. 2:14-16).

"Little children, let not man deceive you· he that doeth righteousness is righteous, even as he is righteous He that committeth sin is of the devil" (1 John 3 7, 8).

How the people of God are to be known from this that they have separated themselves from all other people, and put themselves under Christ their Head, hearing only His voice, and observing His commandments, read: "Wherefore, my dearly beloved, flee from idolatry. Ye cannot drink the cup of the Lord, and the cup of devils ye cannot be partakers of the Lord's table, and of the table of devils" (1 Cor 10 14, 21).

"Be ye not unequally yoked together with unbelievers for what fellowship hath righteousness with unrighteousness? and what communion hath light with darkness? Wherefore come out from among them, and be ye separate, saith the Lord, and touch not the unclean thing (2 Cor. 6.14, 17; Rev. 18.4; Is. 52:11, Jer. 15 19, 51 6).

"As I said unto you, My sheep hear my voice, and I know them, and they follow me. And a stranger will they not follow, but will flee from him; for they know not the voice of strangers" (John 10:26, 27, 5).

"Teaching them to observe all things whatsoever I have commanded you" (Matt. 28.20, 2 Thess 2:15; John 8 31; 14 21; 15:10; Matt. 11·28, 29; 1 John 3:7).

How the false prophets are to be known and distinguished from the true servants of Jesus Christ, read: "Beware of false prophets, which come to you in sheep's clothing, but inwardly they are ravening wolves. Ye shall know them by their fruits" (Matt. 7:15, 16; Deut. 13·1)

"He that speaketh of himself seeketh his own glory; but he that seeketh his glory that sent him, the same is true, and no unrighteousness is in him" (John 7 18).

"For he whom God hath sent speaketh the words of God" (John 3 34; 8 31, 1 Pet. 4·11)

"But if they had stood in my counsel, and had caused my people to hear my words, then they should have turned them from their evil way, and from the evil of their doings" (Jer. 23·22, 31; Is. 55.11; Matt. 23 throughout; Col 1.6; read also Tit. 1 6; 1 Tim. 3 throughout). .

How Christians are to be known by their love, read "An new commandment I give unto you, That ye love one another; as I have loved you, that ye also love one another By this shall all men know that ye are my disciples, if if ye have love one to another" (John 13 34, 35, 1 John 3:23).

"In this the children of God are manifest, and the children of the devil; whosoever doeth not righteousness is not of God neither he that loveth not his brother" (1 John 3:10; 15 12; Matt 22 39; Eph 5 2; 1 Pet 1 22; 2 Pet. 1:7).

Article XX

Of the ordinance of the church of God, and the sending and electing of ministers Of this we confessed· That, as a house, city, or country cannot subsist unless it have laws and ordinances by which to be governed and upheld, and as no human body can subsist without the members performing the service appointed by God for the needs of the body; so also, God the Lord has appointed in His church divers ordinances, laws and commandments, by which it is to be built up, edified, and improved.

And, as the necessities of the body require, as its chief and most indispensable members, eyes, mouth, hands and feet, to see, speak, and labor for the body, that it may thereby be fed and sustained; so Christ the Lord ordained as necessary in His church, first, by His own, present commanding voice, His apostles, whom He sent out to preach the Gospel among all nations, and teach them to observe His commandments, which He caused to be confirmed by signs and miracles

This the apostles, through the Holy Spirit again enjoined upon their followers; namely, that they should elect in the church, pastors, teachers, helpers and rulers, who as fit shining stars, by their good walk and sound doctrine, should shine to edification in the spiritual firmament, and, as messengers of peace, proclaim the good new tidings everywhere, that thereby men may be turned from their evil ways, added to the church, and thus the body of Christ be perfected and edified

And since it is a known fact that a lack of faithful ministers, and the erring of the sheep because of the lack of good doctrine, arise principally from the unworthiness of the people; therefore the people of God, needing this, should not turn to such as have been educated in universities, according to the wisdom of man, that they may talk and dispute, and seek to sell their purchased gift for temporal gain; and who according to the custom of the world do not truly follow Christ in the humility of regeneration But the true members of Christ, must, according to the counsel of God, with humble fasting and praying, turn to the Father of the harvest, who is the true Sender, that by His divine wisdom He will raise up men, whom He may set as faithful and wise stewards over His household, that they may give them proper meat in due season, and may enkindle them in their hearts with His Spirit, and urge them into His harvest, that they may feed the flock of Christ, not for the milk and wool, but of a ready mind, with knowledge and understanding, and lead them on the right way to the kingdom of God; and thus execute the ministry imposed upon them by God, with the strength which God gives

Hence, believers who are in need, in this respect, shall, after having sought the face of God with ardent prayer turn their eyes to a pious brother, who keeps his own body, and brings it into subjection, and in whom the fruits of the Holy Spirit are perceived and seen Having been chosen thereto by the voice of the Church, he shall be examined in the faith by the elder and pastors of the church, whether he, according to the Word of God, agrees with the church in every article, that he may teach others the way of truth, which he himself knows. And having been found to be sound, he may stand forth in the name of the Lord, to proclaim the will of God unto the people. And when it has thus been found that God has committed the preaching of the Gospel to him so that he rightly divides the Word of God, and brings forth fruits with it, the church, if she require it, and he, after examination, has been found, according to the Word of God, to be of the same faith with the church, may, by the voice of the church, choose him as an elder and teacher in the full ministry, and cause him to be confirmed by the imposition of the hands of the elders, and ordain him to labor and work in the vineyard of the Lord, and to administer and execute Christian baptism, and the Lord's Supper, with all that pertains thereto.

In like manner, the church shall, by the voice of the church, elect deacons over the poor, and, after they have been examined in the faith, and found to be sound, cause them to be confirmed by the imposition of the hands of the elders, as helpers and governors, that willing givers may give their contributions to them, that they may thereby supply the wants of the poor members of Christ who according to their ability diligently labor and work with their hands, and still are not able to support themselves, that there may be found no poor among the people of God, nor any want in temporal things, and that the good gifts of the donor may be hidden from men, but become manifest before God, according to the doctrine of Christ.

And if any of said ministers depart in faith or conversation from the adopted way of truth, the church which elected him when he was pious and sound, shall punish or remove him, according as his deeds deserve (Matt. 18:8; 1 Tim. 1:20).

Of the ordinances of the church of Christ, read "Joying and beholding your order, and the steadfastness of your faith in Christ" (Col 2 5, 1 Cor 11 33, 14 40, 2 Cor 8 19)

How men are to pray to God, who is the true Sender, for faithful laborers, read "The harvest truly is plenteous, but the laborers are few; pray ye therefore the Lord of the harvest, that he will send forth laborers into his harvest" (Matt 9 37, 38; Luke 10 2, Matt 23 34; Luke 11 49, John 13 20, Matt 10 40; Luke 10 16; Matt 25 14, Luke 19 12, John 20 21)

How necessary these ministers are, and how they shall teach the Word of God, and be qualified, read "Let the Lord, the God of the spirits of all flesh, set a man over the congregation, which may go out before them, and which may go in before them and which may lead them out, and which may bring them in; that the congregation of the Lord be not as sheep which have no shepherd" (Num 27 16, 17).

"I will give you pastors according to mine heart, which shall feed you with knowledge and understanding" (Jer 3 15).

"For him whom God hath sent, speaketh the word of God," etc (John 3.34; 7·18).

"If any man speak, let him speak as the oracles of God, if any man minister, let him do it as of the ability which God giveth; that God in all things may be glorified through Jesus Christ," etc (1 Pet 4 11)

"For the prophecy came not in old time by the will of man; but holy men of God spake as they were moved by the Holy Ghost" (2 Pet 1 21)

"For this cause left I thee in Crete, that thou shouldest set in order the things that are wanting, and ordain elders in every city, as I had appointed thee· if any be blameless." etc. (Tit 1 5, 6).

Of their qualifications, and how they are to minister

after their examination, read: 1 Tim. 3 throughout; 1 Cor 12 28; Rom 12 7; Eph 4:11.

Concerning the mode in which they are to be chosen, read "We have sent with him the brother, whose praise is in the Gospel throughout all the churches; and not that only, but who was\ also chosen of the churches to travel with us, with this grace, which is administered by us to the glory of the same Lord and declaration of your ready mind" (2 Cor 8 18, 19; Acts 1·23).

"As they ministered to the Lord, and fasted, the Holy Ghost said, Separate me Barnabas and Saul for the work whereunto I have called them. And when they had fasted and prayed and laid their hands on them, they sent them away" (Acts 13 2, 3; 20 28)

"The things that thou hast heard of me among many witnesses, the same commit thou to faithful men, who shall be able to teach others also" (2 Tim. 2 2)

"Feed the flock of God which is among you, taking the oversight thereof, not by constraint, but willingly; not for filthy lucre, but of a ready mind; neither as being lords over God's heritage, but being ensamples to the flock" (1 Pet. 5 2, 3).

Of the election and confirmation of deacons, read· "It is not reason that we should leave the word of God, and serve tables Wherefore brethren, look ye out among you seven men of honest report, full of the Holy Ghost and wisdom, whom we may appoint over this business" "Whom they set before the apostles and when they had prayed, they laid their hands on them" (Acts 6 2, 3, 6, 1 Tim 3 8-10).

Article XXI

Of Christian baptism we confess· That the same is a divine, evangelical transaction, practice and ordinance, which was first commenced by the man of God, John the Baptist, by the counsel and will of God, and was received by the worthy Son of God, Christ Jesus, who humbled Himself as a true example, and to whom the aforesaid John led and pointed with his doctrine and baptism, as being the true Baptizer with the Holy Ghost and with fire He proceeded and came from God with full power in heaven and earth, and sent out His apostles, commanding them to preach the Gospel to all nations, and to baptize all true hearers and believers of it, in the name of the Father, the Son, and the Holy Ghost, and to teach them before and after baptism, to observe all things which He had commanded them

This the apostles of Christ, as obedient ministers of God, practiced according to this manner, beginning at Jerusalem, and preaching the Gospel in every country And all who heard, believed and gladly received this heavenly doctrine were made disciples and followers, and were baptized with water, in the name of the triune God, and thus entered into covenant with Christ, to observe whatsoever He had commanded them

And inasmuch as the doctrines and commandments of Christ are not instituted for a certain time, but are commanded to be kept until the appearing of Jesus Christ from heaven; and as He will continue with His Spirit to the end of the world with His followers, therefore all believers and followers of Christ are bound in no wise, to alter or reject according to human opinions, these doctrines and commandments which God has commanded, but to practice and observe them constantly according to the form and institution of Christ and the practice of His highly enlightened apostles; to preach the Gospel to the people, and all who believe the same, manifest repentance from sin the amendment of life, and submit to the will of God, shall, by an unblamable minister ordained to this purpose, be baptized once with water, in the name of the Father, and the Son, and the Holy Ghost.

This outward baptism with water does not properly constitute the entrance of the kingdom of God, nor does the visible element of the water contain any power or holiness, neither is it able to give grace and salvation; but, as the waters of Jordan and Siloam did not, properly speaking, heal leprosy and blindness, but only the power of God, to which they were herein subject and obedient, so also the water in baptism has no power to forgive sins, and to cleanse the filthiness of our flesh, but is simply a token and proof of the grace and blood of Christ in the washing away of sin, which man, through faith and regeneration, by grace, has received, in the heart, before baptism, in putting off the body of the sins of flesh, which is proclaimed in baptism; and without this internal visible, water baptism is as useless and vain as the seal on an empty letter.

Since, then, Christian baptism is of such a nature that it was ordained and commanded by Christ only upon faith, repentance, and reformation, and was practiced and taught by His high apostles in this, and in no other wise; therefore we herewith reject, with good reason, the baptism of unintelligent, speechless infants, which we regard as a human institution, etc.* which ought justly to be rooted out and rejected. The principal originators of the same found this their infant baptism upon the fall of Adam, saying** that thereby all men are born and placed into the world in an unsaved or condemned state, and that by the power of water baptism are translated and changed from this unsaved and condemned state into a saved and God-pleasing condition; thus binding not only the salvation and condemnation of infants, but also the saving grace, death, and atonement of Christ to the willingness or unwillingness of

---

*Invented in the kingdom of Antichrist, says the writer

**This is an expression of the belief of the papists, who attach forgiveness of sins and salvation to the external water baptism

man, and the weak element of water; so that when an infant is baptized it is instantly saved, and when this is neglected, it dies condemned

Who that fears God can in no wise accept with a good conscience this human infant baptism, instead of the ordinance of God, since in the whole New Testament not the least is commanded or written concerning it, either by Christ or by His apostles

The pedobaptists themselves plainly confess, that in the sending forth of the apostles into the whole world by Christ, to teach and baptize, infant baptism is not commanded, nor comprehended in these passages, neither is there any advocate of the same able to point out in the Word of God the author and first foundation of infant baptism (though every divine ordinance has its beginning where it was first commanded by God)—how then shall this fabric of infant baptism, of which no foundation can be found, stand in the sight of God?

Infant baptism is in fact nothing less than a contemning and trampling under foot of the true baptism of Christ, militating in many respects against it, since Christ has attached to baptism the doctrine of the Gospel, faith and repentance, as a seal and token of the same

And, as infant baptism does not accord with, but militates against the baptism of Christ, even so does it not agree with the circumcision of the Jews, which was not commanded to children but to adults, namely, that on the eighth day, every male child among them should be circumcised, on pain of being cut off But it is not so with the baptism of Christ, concerning which no command is given to the parents, much less to any one else, to baptize their children, or to have them baptized But baptism is an ordinance of Christ, similar in part to the Supper, to another, but which Christian ordinance each must desire and receive by his own faith, for which reason it does in no wise apply to new born infants

And as unqualified as infants are to observe the Supper (in which every reasonable person will agree with us), even so unfit are they also to receive Christian baptism And, as infant baptism, for want of testimony from the divine Scriptures, is demonstrated only by arguments and uncertain conclusions, so also, by such and similar conclusions, the Supper may be approriated to infants, as was formerly done in the Roman church And as we may by no means, on such human conclusion, admit infants to the Supper, just as little may we on these conclusions admit them to baptism; but in all this all of us who do not wish to be seduced and deceived must necessarily adhere to the doctrine of Christ and His apostles But, as the Jews adhered unchangingly to the circumcision on the eighth day, without following in any wise their own opinion, even so should all Christians still much more, adhere unalterably to the doctrine of Christ, and administer baptism only upon faith and repentance, as Christ has ordained

But all Christians are commanded and in duty bound to walk before their children with a good example, and to bring them up in the fear of the Lord, by good teachings and instructions, without using on them baptism, the Supper, or any other ceremonies; since it is known that it is impossible for any one to unite another to the Lord, without his will and knowledge

But as soon as men grow up and arrive at the years of discretion, it is found, that through their innate sinful nature they live after the flesh, and thereby fall from grace, to which they had been bought by the blood of Christ Their souls then need the hearing of the Word of God, whence proceed faith and regeneration, and, as a consequence thereof, Christian baptism; which by Christ has been appended to faith and regeneration, and may never be separated therefrom; and which is represented as a grave in which men are to bury their own actual sins which they have put off, and are thus to rise with Christ to newness of life, and walk after the Spirit

And as no bath to wash off the filth of the body can be used on an unborn child, but the child must first be born; so Christian baptism, which is compared to the washing of newborn infants, can, according to the will of God, be given to none but those who are regenerated by faith, dead to sin, desire the same rise from the death of sin, and walk in newness of life, observing whatsoever Christ has commanded them

Hence no one can be recognized as a brother or sister in the church of Christ, with whom any Christian ordinance may be practiced, unless they have previously, according to the Word of God, received upon faith the Christian baptism here spoken of, which is the first ordinance and the reception into the Christian communion, by whch we submit and obligate ourselves to actually observe all the commandments and ordinances of God And as there is but one faith and one God, so there is only one Christian baptism, which, having been once received upon true faith, according to the institution of Christ, may not be repeated or renewed

Of the baptism of John, and how he as a messenger and forerunner sent before Chirst, preached the baptism of repentance, and pointed to Christ, read "John did baptize in the wilderness, and preach the baptism of repentance for the remission of sins" (Mark 1 4, Matt. 3 6,11)

"I indeed baptize you with water; but one mightier than I cometh, the latchet of whose shoes I am not worthy to unloose he shall baptize you with the Holy Ghost and with fire" (Luke 3 16; John 1 31)

How Christ Jesus commands His disciples to preach the Gospel, and to baptize only hearers and believers of it, and not unintelligent, ignorant children, read "All power is given unto me in heaven and in earth Go ye therefore, and teach all nations, baptizing them in the name of the Father, and of the Son, and of the Holy Ghost teaching them to observe all things whatsoever I have commanded you and lo, I am with you alway, even unto the end of the world" (Matt 28 18-20).

"He that believeth and is baptized shall be saved; but he that believeth not shall be damned" (Mark 16 16)

How the apostles, pursuant to this high injunction, preached the Gospel, and baptized only the hearers, believers, and self-desiring recipients, read "When they heard this, they were pricked in their heart, and said unto Peter and to the rest of the apostles, Men and brethren, what shall we do? Then Peter said unto them, Repent, and be baptized every one of you in the name of Jesus Christ for the remission of sins." "Then they that gladly received his word were baptized" (Acts 2 37, 38, 41)

"And the eunuch said, See, here is water; what doth hinder me to be baptized? And Philip said, If thou believest with all thine heart, thou mayest. And he answered and said, I believe that Jesus Christ is the Son of God And he commanded the chariot to stand still and they went down both into the water, both Philip and the eunuch, and he baptized him" (Acts 8 36-38)

How the apostles, according to this foundation, taught and baptized several households, after they had heard the Word of God, had believed, had been filled with the Holy Ghost, ordained to the ministry of the saints, and regarded as believers, read Acts 10 37; 16 15, 32, 1 Cor 16:15; Acts 18.8.

How the apostles in their epistles described Christian baptism as a burying of sins into the death of Christ, a rising and walking in newness of life, putting on of Christ, a washing of regeneration, a being baptized by one Spirit into one body, and the answer of a conscience toward God, read. Rom. 6·3; Col. 2:12; Gal. 3 27; Tit. 3 5; 1 Cor 12 13; 1 Pet. 3 21).

Article XXII

Of the Lord's Supper or the breaking of bread, we believe and confess As baptism is an ordinance and institution of the Lord, by which believers are united with each other by one Spirit in fellowship with Chrst; so the Supper is a worthy ordinance and institution of Christ, by which believers who have been baptized according to the ordinance of Christ, are taught and admonished, to live and walk in Christ even as they have received Him by faith in baptism, and to be bound by brotherly love to their neighbors, with whom they are to live and walk in the unity of the Spirit, according to the same rule of the divine Word, and that they are to remember hereby, with heartfelt contemplation, the bitter suffering and death of the Lord.

And in order to put men in remembrance of this, it pleased the Lord Jesus for this purpose to use bread and wine, things well known among men, and thereby to implant into the hearts of believers heavenly and hidden things; thereby teaching them to remember, that, as bread from many broken grains is made into one bread and the wine being pressed from many grapes and made one beverage thereby being necessary, useful and adapted as food and drink for the body of man, even so Christ, from ardent love, suffered Himself to be broken on the cross His blood to be shed, and trod the winepress of suffering alone, to minister by His flesh and blood, as necessary meat and drink, to the souls of men, by which we are taught, that like as bread is of many grains broken and prepared as bread, and wine is of many grapes pressed and made a beverage, so also, many believers, from various places, are by one faith become one bread or church, and bound together in fellowship, in order that thereby all those who worthily receive, and eat and drink with the mouth this bread and wine, may hereby through faith in the Spirit, receive, and become partakers of Christ and all His heavenly riches, and thus be strengthened in the faith, fed in the soul, and be bound together by fervent love, with God and their neighbors, as members of one body

But believers must in no wise place any confidence in these visible memorials, as though they in themselves were more sacred and worthy than other like, common meat and drink, or had power to give unto men grace and forgiveness of sins By so doing one should depart with the heart from his Creator, and seek grace from the creature, where it is not to be found But believers must receive these signs as nothing more than bread and wine, confide with a firm heart only in that which is thereby taught and signified and look upon and regard these signs as figures, as the Holy Ghost is wont, in the Holy Scriptures, to call the signs, that which is signified by them And as in this institution of the Supper by Christ the cup is called the New Testament in His blood, which cup is really not the New Testament itself, but is figuratively so called, because the blood of Christ, which He shed for the sin of the world, is proclaimed and recommended to us through the New Testament; which signifies, that as a testator by a testament bequeathes to his heirs his property, which they are to receive and enjoy after his death; so has Christ in His last Supper—since He could not remain with them—bequeathed His last will in the New Testament, together with all its heavenly riches, to His friends and followers; in order that all those who in this testament are specified and recorded as children of God and heirs of Christ, shall enjoy His glorious riches; whereupon they receive in the Supper, with the mouth, only natural bread and wine; but through faith there is received, according to the Spirit, Christ's flesh and blood, which He gave as an atonement for the human race, of which the natural bread and wine, and the Supper are figures, signs, and representations.

Hence, believers are to use this worthy institution of Christ among each other, and thereby through an ordained blameless minister, proclaim with great reverence the bitter suffering and death of the Lord

And after God has been thanked with an humble heart, for his boundless grace and mercy, and been called upon by fervent prayers, the bread shall be broken by the minister, the wine poured out, and be received by all believers baptized according to the ordinance of Christ, and each shall, examining himself, use and avail himself of the same, with heartfelt contemplation of the broken body and shed blood of the Lord Jesus This shall constantly be observed by believers in this manner, when time and place permit, until the appearing of Jesus Christ from heaven.

Of this institution and ordinance of Christ, read "And as they were eating, Jesus took bread, and blessed it, and brake it, and gave it to the disciples, and said, Take, eat; this is my body And he took the cup, and gave thanks, and gave it to them, saying, Drink ye all of it; for this is my blood of the New Testament, which is shed for many for the remission of sins But I say unto you, I will not drink henceforth of this fruit of the vine, until that day when I drink it new with you in my Father's kingdom" (Matt 26 26-29; Mark 14 22; Luke 22·19)

How the apostles in accordance with this also practiced and observed it in the same form and manner, with bread and wine, read· "I have received of the Lord that which also I delivered unto you That the Lord Jesus, the same night in which he was betrayed, took bread; and when he had given thanks, he brake it, and said, Take, eat; this is my body, which is broken for you this do in remembrance of me After the same manner also he took the cup, when he had supped, saying, This cup is the new testament in my blood: this do ye, as oft as ye drink it, in remembrance of me. For as often as ye eat of this bread and drink of this cup, ye do shew the Lord's death till he come. Wherefore whosoever shall eat this bread, and drink this cup of the Lord, unworthily, shall be guilty of the body and blood of the Lord But let a man examine himself, and so let him eat of that bread, and drink of that cup For he that eateth and drinketh unworthily, eateth and drinketh damnation to himself, not discerning the Lord's body" (1 Cor 11 23-29; Acts 2·42; 20 7, 11).

How the bread and wine in the Supper are not the real body and blood of Christ, but signs of His communion with the believer, read "The cup of blessing which we bless, is it not the communion of the blood of Christ? The bread which we break, is it not the communion of the body of Christ? For we being many are one bread, and one body for we are all partakers of that one bread Behold Israel after the flesh are not they which eat of the sacrifices partakers of the altar?" (1 Cor. 10 16-18)

Mark, the Israelites did not eat the altar, but only the sacrifice, and thereby were partakers of the altar. Thus, also, Christians do not eat and drink with the mouth the real body and blood of Christ, but only bread and wine, as figures; but according to the soul, they, by faith, receive Christ Jesus, with all His benefits, and are thus partakers of the true altar Christ Jesus.

Read in regard to this: "I am the bread of life: he that cometh to me shall never hunger, and he that believeth on me shall never thirst It is the Spirit that quickeneth, the flesh profiteth nothing the words that I speak unto you, they are spirit, and they are life" (John 6 35, 63).

Article XXIII

Of the feet-washing of believers we confess After our Leader Christ Jesus had celebrated the Supper with His apostles, He, before His suffering, used another ordinance with them, and commanded that they should observe it with each other. He rose from supper, girded Himself with a linen towel, poured water into a basin, washed the disciples' feet, and wiped them with the towel, saying to them "Ye call me Master and Lord and ye say well; for so I am If I then your Lord and Master, have washed your feet; ye also ought to wash one another's feet For I have given you an example, that ye should do as I have done to you" And He also added "If ye know these things, happy are ye if ye do them"

And we find that the apostles observed this ordinance of Christ in this manner, and that they counted it, in the ministry of the saints, among the good works, and required it of the believers Hence, the believers, as successors and followers of Christ and His apostles, ought also, when time and place permit, practice and observe this ordinance of Christ When their fellow believers, out of love, visit them, they shall, with heartfelt humanity, receive them with the kiss of love and peace into their houses, and as a ministration to their neighbors, according to the humiliation of Christ, wash their feet, sincerely considering how the most worshipful Son of God humbled Himself, not only washing the feet of His apostles, but much more washing and purifying with His precious death and blood, all our souls and consciences from the stain of eternal condemnation On this the pious ought herein to meditate with an humble heart

How Christ practiced this ordinance with His apostles, and commanded it to be observed, read, John 13:4-17.

And also, how the apostles required it of believers as one of the good works· "Let not a widow be taken into the number under three-score years old, having been the wife of one man, well reported of for good works; if she have brought up children, if she have lodged strangers, if she have washed the saints' feet," (1 Tim 5 9, 10).

How the pious fathers practiced this ordinance with the guests whom they received, read Genesis 18 4; 19·2 And also Luke 7 38; John 11:2; Acts 16 33.

Article XXIV

Of good works Of good works we believe and confess That for every true Christian it is not enough, in every respect according to the Scriptures, to confess the faith aright with the mouth, and to regard Christ Jesus as our only Head, Redeemer, and Savior, but that above this we must necessarily manifest from our faith, as a fruit of gratitude, virtuous works Thus also, it is not enough that we put off all the accursed works of the flesh, and seek to bury them by baptism into the death of Christ; but we must also rise from the death of sin, and live and walk after the Spirit in a new life adorned with good works; and thus we are not only to put off the old man with his evil deeds, but it is also our duty to put on the new man with his good deeds, in righteousness and true holiness, and to let our light so shine before men, that they may see our good works, and glorify our Father in heaven; in order that thus all believers, as a tree by its good fruits, may be known, and distinguished by their good works from all unfruitful and unbelieving men

These good works must not be performed through an outward appearance of holiness to please mortal men; nor must we follow herein the hypocrites and self-righteous Pharisees, and others, whose works mainly consist in (things of) their own choice, and self-invented commandments, which, according to the Scriptures, is only a vain and unavailing worship; but we must work out from our faith such divine virtues as are taught, and required of us in the holy Scriptures, and in which we have the example of Christ and His apostles, whose footsteps we are so highly commanded to follow; and all this we must do from the heart, to the honor of Him who created us; thus learning from Christ to be meek and lowly in heart, and thereby to put off all pride, which later is the beginning of all destruction, and proceeds from man's sinful heart, and manifests itself outwardly in the adorning of and display in dress (in the style of), living, and in words and works; and on the contrary, to adorn ourselves inwardly with an humbled spirit, which does not think much of itself, but in lowliness esteems his neighbor better than himself; and outwardly in our conversation after our lowly Head and Example, Christ Jesus.

Thus we must also put off avarice, which is called the root of all evil, whence proceed many sinful desires and unrighteous works, and, on the other hand, put on the love and mercy of our heavenly Father, and manifest it towards our neighbors and all men by works of mercy; seeing the practice of love and mercy is the chief sacrifice with which we can please our Creator in this present time.

Likewise we must put off all unclean lusts and desires, fornication, and all uncleanness, each preserving, on the contrary, his body chaste, holy, and pure, and abstaining also from all drunkenness, revelings and banquetings; in excessive eating and drinking, and on the contrary, live soberly, temperately, righteously, and godly in this world, with humble fasting and constant praying to God Almighty, and not to make provision for the flesh, to fulfill the lusts thereof.

We also must not walk in the way of sinners, nor hold fellowship with light-minded persons, where foolish talking and lies are bandied about; but we must associate with the pious, whose conversation treats of godliness, and who speak with tongues truly circumcised; and gladly attend the assembly of the believers, where we hear the praise of the Lord proclaimed; and furthermore, observe according to all our ability the commandments and ordinances of the Lord, and thus by patient continuance in well doing seek for eternal life, remembering that Almighty God has promised eternal life to that faith which in this manner works by love; just as He has pronounced the sentence of eternal death upon unbelief with its evil works; and that all boasted faith without good works (as the body without the spirit), in itself is dead But all the pious who thus evince divine virtue from their faith, and seek to excel in good works, must not suppose that they are able to merit salvation by their good works, or that God does owe them anything for them; but all true Christians are to consider themselves unprofitable servants, who of themselves can do nothing good; but that Almighty God, by His grace works in them both to will and to do that which is good and that they are encompassed with a body of sin, which lusts against the Spirit, against which they have a continual warfare until the last enemy, which is death, shall be vanquished For this reason all the pious fall far too short in good works; are very imperfect and frail; and hence, are in duty bound to pray daily, with an humble heart, to Almighty God for forgiveness and remission of sins, and to give heartfelt praise, honor and thanks to Him for His saving grace which He has manifested towards us And thus we hope to be saved only through the unmerited grace and mercy of our Lord and Saviour Jesus Christ, and not through our good works (Tit. 3:8; Luke 18·10).

Of the deadly works of darkness, which separate men from God and which we must put off and lay aside by faith, read "Seing that ye have put off the old man with his deeds; and have put on the new man," etc. (Col 3 9, 10)

Read further concerning the twenty-three sins which are worthy of eternal death (Rom 1·29-31)

Of the ten works of unrighteousness which shall not inherit the kingdom of God, read 1 Cor 6 9, 10

Of the seventeen works of the flesh to which the kingdom of God is denied, read Gal 5·19-21; Matt 7 23

Of the good and virtuous works which the believers are to manifest from their faith as fruits of gratitude, read "Let your light so shine before men, that they may see your good works," etc (Matt 5 16; 1 Pet 2 12, Phil 2 15)

"To them who by patient continuance in well doing seek for glory and honor and immortality, eternal life" (Rom 2 7; John 8 39; James 2·22; Gal 5 6).

"But (which becometh women professing godliness) with good works" (1 Tim 2 10).

"That they do good, that they be rich in good works," etc (1 Tim 6 18).

Of the nine beatitudes, read Matt 5 1-11

Of the seven works of mercy, read: Matt. 25 35, 36.

Of the nine fruits of the Spirit, Gal 5 22, 23

Of the seven cardinal virtues which we are to evince from our faith, and that where this does not follow, we are blind, read 2 Pet 1 5-7, "For as the body without the spirit is dead, so faith without works is dead also" (James 2 26) "And the sea gave up the dead which were in it; and death and hell delivered up the dead which were in them; and they were judged every man according to their works" (Rev. 20·13; 2 Cor 5:10).

How we are saved not through any works which we have done, but only through the grace of God, read "But we believe that through the grace of the Lord Jesus Christ we shall be saved" (Acts 15·11)

"Not by works of righteousness which we have done, but according to his mercy he saved us" (Tit 3.5; Eph. 2.5; 2 Tim 1 9; Luke 17·10; Acts 4 12; 15 11).

Article XXV

Of marriage Of marriage we confess That the same is honorable and an ordinance of God, who in the beginning instituted this state with the two human beings first created in the image of God, blessed it, and joined them together And since this divine ordinance, through the hardness of the heart and evil wantoness of man had fallen into great disorder, so that men through the lusts of the flesh, married whomsoever they would, and took unto them many wives, and then, for divers reasons, dismissed them by a bill of divorcement, and married others; therefore Christ, as a perfect Lawgiver, rejected and abolished the writing of divorcement and permission of Moses, together with all abuses thereof, referring all that heard and believed Him to the original ordinance of His heavenly Father, instituted with Adam and Eve in Paradise; and thus re-establishing marriage between one man and one woman, and so inseparably and firmly binding the bond of matrimony, that they might not, on any account, separate and marry another, except in case of adultery* or death

Hence, every believer who desires to enter into matrimony, must follow this doctrine of Christ and the above example, and unite himself in marriage only with one person, who has been, by a like faith with him, born from above, of God, and renewed, and created after the

---
*Fornication—Matt 5 32, 19 9, King James Version

image of God. And such persons, after their parents and the church have given their consent, shall, in the presence of the church, with fervent prayer to God, be joined together by a minister. This we believe to be marrying in the Lord, of which God is Himself the Author and Joiner (2 Pet. 1:1; John 3:3; 1 John 5:4).

But all unregenerated persons, who are not yet sanctified by faith in Christ, and do thus marry, we also regard as being in honorable matrimony, but not in the Lord (Heb. 13:4; 1 Cor. 7:12).

And, as Christ accepts none as His bride and a member of His body, but those alone who are united with Him by faith, so also, believers cannot sever their bodies which are sanctified and surrendered to God, as members of Christ and temples of the Holy Ghost from Christ, and unite them in marriage with the unregenerate, and thus be unequally yoked together with unbelievers, who are not known to the church, by faith and Christian baptism, as brethren or sisters in fellowship, seeing that baptism is the first Christian ordinance in the church, after which all other ordinances of God follow (Eph. 5:30; Gal. 3:26).

Thus marriage is advised by the Holy Ghost, to avoid fornication and all uncleanness; but if any one does not need this, and can without it, keep himself pure and undefiled, in a virginal state, in order to serve the Lord the better and without hindrance, it is commended still more highly. Hence, marriage is free for all, but no commandment.

How God the Lord in the beginning instituted marriage, read: "And the Lord God said, It is not good that the man should be alone; I will make him a help meet for him." "And the rib, which the Lord God had taken from man, made he a woman, and brought her unto the man." "Therefore shall a man leave his father and his mother, and shall cleave unto his wife. and they shall be one flesh" (Gen 2 18, 22, 24)

How Christ rejected all abuses of marriage, and renewed the ordinance of His Father, read· "Have ye not read, that he which made them at the beginning made them male and female and said, For this cause shall a man leave father and mother, and shall cleave to his wife and they twain shall be one flesh? Wherefore they are no more twain, but one flesh What therefore God hath joined together, let no man put asunder" (Matt 19 4-6, 8, 1 Cor 7:10)

"Marriage is honorable in all, and the bed undefiled: but whoremongers and adulterers God will judge" (Heb 13 4; 1 Cor. 7 2).

"The wife is bound by the law as long as her husband liveth; but if her husband be dead, she is at liberty to be married to whom she will; only in the Lord" (1 Cor 7 39; Gen 1 27; 24 4; Ex 34 16; Num 36 6; Deut 7 3)

Concerning the transgressors of this, and their punishment, read. Gen. 6 3; Num 25.1; Neh. 13.26, 27; 1 Kings 11:1.

Article XXVI

Of the swearing of oaths, we confess· That the people of the Old Testament were permitted to swear in various ways by the name of the Lord; either by lifting up their hand toward heaven, or by putting it on the thigh of someone, which was done in various ways, and into which practice, through the artifice of man, many abuses were introduced, so that they would swear by heaven ‑and · earth, ‑by Jerusalem, by‑ their ‑head, the temple, the gold of the temple, the altar, and the sacrifice, on account of which the Lord Christ, who had come from God, and been sent to execute judgment and righteousness, being the only lawgiver, utterly abolished and prohibited all the aforesaid swearing, whether permitted or feigned and, in place thereof, referred all His hearers and followers only to yea and nay, which is so in truth

And we also find that the high apostles of Christ, as obedient sheep of their only Shepherd, followed the doctrine of Christ in this respect Hence all believers are in duty bound obediently to follow this doctrine of Christ and the course of His apostles, putting away all lying, and dealing only in truth, and thus testifying in all true matters, whether before authority, or however the case may be, only with yea that which is yea, and with nay that which is nay, without adding anything more; and to keep these few words, little in sound, but great and strong in signification, as inviolable as an oath, thus showing themselves to be obedient followers of Christ and His apostles.

Of the rejection and abolishment of the ancient custom of swearing, and how Christ commanded yea and nay in place of it, read "Again, ye have heard that it hath been said by them of old time, Thou shalt not forswear thyself, but shalt perform unto the Lord thine oaths but I say unto you, Swear not at all; neither by heaven; for it is God's throne· nor by the earth; for it is his footstool neither by Jerusalem; for it is the city of the great King Neither shalt thou swear by thy head, because thou canst not make one hair white or black But let your communication be, Yea, yea; Nay, nay for whatsoever is more than these cometh of evil" (Matt 5 33-37; 23·21).

"But above all things, my brethren, swear not, neither by heaven, neither by the earth, neither by any other oath but let your yea be yea; and your nay, nay; lest ye fall into condemnation" (James 5 12)

"When I therefore was thus minded, did I use lightness? or the things that I purpose, do I purpose according to the flesh, that with me there should be yea, yea, and nay, nay? For all the promises of God in him are yea, and in him Amen" (2 Cor. 1:17, 20).

Article XXVII

Of the office of magistracy, and secular power, we confess: That the office of magistracy is an ordinance and institution of God who Himself willed and ordained that such a power should be over every country in order that thereby countries and cities might, through good policy and laws, for the punishment of the evil and the protection of the pious, be governed and maintained in quiet and peace, in a good civic life; without which power of authority the world, lying as it is in wickedness, could not subsist. Hence, all believers are in duty bound, not only for wrath, but also for conscience sake, to submit themselves to this power, and as good subjects, to obey it with fear and reverence; willingly and without murmuring to render unto their human ordinances and laws everything that is due to them, whether it be tribute custom or excise; and to pray with an humble heart for their life and welfare, and thus to seek with a faithful heart the prosperity of the country and city in which they reside; and though they, for the Word of God, may have to suffer persecution, the spoiling of their property, and death, from the authorities, they may not speak evil of them, nor resist them in any wise with weapons and defense, but commit vengeance to God alone, and expect consolation with God after this life (Rom 12:2; Ecc. 17:14).

But if the authorities, through Christian equity, grant liberty to practice the faith in every respect, we are under so much the greater obligation of submissive obedience to them; but so far as the authorities abuse the office imposed on them, which extends only to the temporal, bodily government of men in temporal things, and encroach on the office of Christ, who alone has power over the spirits and souls of men, seeking, through their human laws, to press and compel men to act contrary to the Word of God, we may not follow them, but must obey God rather than men, seeing Christ has been set by God His Father above all authority and power, the head in His church; and to this Father of Spirits we are directed, that in all things pertaining to the faith we should obey Him.

And as the kingdom of Christ is not of this world, but spiritual, He has dissuaded and prohibited all His servants and followers from all secular government and highness and has instituted in His church various ordinances, as pastors, teachers, helps and governments, by which the saints may be joined together, to edify the body of Christ; but the secular office* He left to the secular government, under which the followers of Christ as strangers and pilgrims, who have here no kingdom, power or continuing city, must sojourn, and fight only with spiritual weapons, which is the Word of God; seeing neither Christ nor His apostles prescribed to believers any laws or rules according to which they should govern the world; neither did they refer them to the laws of the Jews, much less to those of the Roman emperors, or heathen laws, according to which they might regulate themselves herein; but they prescribed to believers only good doctrines, how they should conduct themselves in all Christian propriety as obedient subjects, under the government of the authorities; referring them to His own example, who shunned all the greatness of this world, and showed Himself only as a poor servant. Thus must also all His followers avoid

---

*But not the office of authority, then says the writer

the office of magistracy in all its departments, and not administer it, following also in this the example of Christ and His apostles, in whose church said offices were not administered, as is well known to every intelligent person

But as all Christians are not permitted, but very strictly prohibited by God, to speak evil of, judge or condemn any one that is without their communion, we would with this still much less speak evil or injuriously of the magistracy, but trust in the only good God, who keeps all the alms of man as a signet, and his good deeds as the apple of the eye, and has promised a true reward to him who will give only a cup of cold water in the name of a disciple; that He, the Blessed, will also be gracious to, and not leave unrewarded the good deeds of all authorities, particularly those who administer their office aright according to the ordinances of God, which consists chiefly in protecting good, innocent defenseless people, and in punishing the evil Hence, all Christians are in duty bound to regard the authorities as God's ministers, and to pray for them, with a fervent heart, that it may please God to be gracious to them and give them eternal salvation

How government is of God, and for what purpose it is instituted, read "For there is no power but of God the powers that be are ordained of God Whosoever therefore resisteth the power, resisteth the ordinance of God and they that resist shall receive to themselves damnation For rulers are not a terror to good works, but to the evil. Wilt thou then not be afraid of the power? do that which is good, and thou shalt have praise of the same for he is the minister of God to thee for good But if thou do that which is evil, be afraid; for he beareth not the sword in vain; for he is the minister of God, a revenger to execute wrath upon him that doeth evil" (Rom. 13 1-4).

"Jesus answered Pilate Thou couldst have no power at all against me, except it were given thee from above" (John 19 11; Dan 2 21; 4 25; 5 21; Jer 27 5)

How Christ taught His followers not to accept magisterial office, read "But Jesus called them to him, and said unto them, Ye know that they which are accounted to rule over the Gentiles exercise lordship over them; and their great ones exercise authority upon them But so shall it not be among you but whosoever will be great among you, shall be your minister and whosoever of you will be the chiefest, shall be servant of all. For even the Son of man came not to be ministered unto, but to minister, and to give his life a ransom for many" (Mark 10 42-45; Matt 20 25; Luke 22 5)

Mark the words *But so shall it not be among you* This can not be applied to the apostles only, who were equal servants, the one being no greater than the other, and they soon separating from each other to preach the Gospel to all nations, could not, on this account, show to each other alone the duty of servants here required; hence the word, *among you,* must necessarily be understood of the whole church, seeing Christ spoke to His twelve apostles many others of His principal doctrines and commandments, which relate to all believers, as His blessed lips say in the Gospel: "And what I say unto you I say unto all" (Mark 13:37).

"Jesus answered, My kingdom is not of this world. if my kingdom were of this world, then would my servants fight, that I should not be delivered to the Jews but now is my kingdom not from hence" (John 18:36; 6 15; Matt 5 39; 2 Cor. 10:4; Eph. 6.13; Is 2:4; Micah 4 3; Zech 9 10; Ps. 76:3).

Read, further, not according to what law the believers are to govern the unbelievers, but only how the church of Christ shall be obedient to government "Let every soul be subject unto the high powers." "Wherefore ye must needs be subject, not only for wrath, but also for conscience' sake." "Render therefore to all their dues; tribute to whom tribute is due custom to whom custom, fear to whom fear" (Rom 13 1, 5, 7).

"Render therefore unto Caesar the things which are Caesar's and unto God the things that are God's (Matt 22 21; Mark 12 17).

"Submit yourselves to every ordinance of man for the Lord's sake whether it be to the king, as supreme; or unto governors, as unto them that are sent by him for the punishment of evil doers, and for the praise of them that do well" (1 Pet 2:13, 14).

"Put them in mind to be subject to principalities and powers, to obey magistrates, to be ready to every good work, to speak evil of no man, to be no brawlers, but gentle, showing all meekness unto all men" (Tit 3 1, 2; 1 Tim 2 2; Jer 29 7)

Article XXVIII

Of the discipline of the Christian Church and separation of offending members. Of this we confess That, as a house or city cannot be maintained without doors, gates and wall by which evil men may be expelled, excluded and debarred, and the good and pious be taken in and protected; so Christ, for the preservation of His church, gave her the key of heaven, which is His Word, that by and according to the same, she should judge and reprove according to truth, for their reformation, all those in her communion that are found to offend in doctrine and conversation, that is, to act contrary to any commandment or ordinance which God has given to His church; and thus to separate the disobedient from her communion, that the church may not be leavened and stained by their false doctrine and impure walk, and become a partaker of other men's sins; and that the pious thereby may be brought to fear and restrain themselves from the commission of similar offenses

And, as God through Moses commanded this punishment of transgressors to be inflicted according to the magnitude of the offense, so that those who through ignorance, weakness and otherwise, offended by minor sins against any of the commandments of the Lord, were reconciled to God by various offerings and the intercessions of the priests, but the open, great transgressors of the law could not be reconciled by such offerings, but had to die without mercy under two or three witnesses; so Christ in the New Testament also taught to inflict Christian punishment according to the magnitude of the offense; not in man's destruction, as in the punishment of Israel, which was death, by which the transgressor was cut off from repentance, and reformation; but Christ having come to save men's souls, instituted this punishment for the reformation of sinners and ordained that if any one see his brother commit a transgression which is obviously a sin, but not so great as to have brought forth death in him, he shall out of Christian love for his soul, speak to him privately, with the Word of God, and reprove him of his sin and admonish him If he receive this Christian admonition, he has gained his brother, and shall, out of fervent charity, conceal and cover his sin (1 Pet 4·8). But if he heareth him not, he shall take one or two more with him, so that in the mouth of these witnesses every word may be established But if he shall neglect to hear them then the matter must be brought before the church; and if he neglect to hear the church, all the members of which are judges, he shall be excluded from the brotherhood.

But if any one fall into open works of the flesh, from which the church perceives that through these sins he has separated himself from his God, and incurred the divine wrath, such an one the church shall, without any of the aforesaid admonitions and words as in the case of the offending sinner, on account of his sins, exclude from the brotherhood, and point him to repentance and reformation, by which he may again find grace with God, even as he has become separated from God through the evil works of the flesh Thus the church shall knowingly keep none in her communion who are separated from God through their sins; nor separate any from her communion save those who have previously through their sins become separated from God; nor again receive any, and promise life and peace to them, except those who through faith and true repentance have first been received into grace with God

This true repentance possesses the following properties· 1 That we have a sincere sorrow before Almighty God for all the sins we have committed; 2 that we confess our sins from the heart, before God and men; 3 that we desist from and do not continue any longer in sin, and according to our ability, seek to make amends for the evil we have done, by doing good This repentance and reformation again opens the entrance to the kingdom of God, which before was closed to us on account of our sin So that the church of God by this her separation and reception may, according to His Word, follow the previous separation and reception by God in heaven, of which the action of the church is only a proof and proclamation.

And since with God there is no respect of persons, therefore the church of God shall use this key of the Word of God aright, and, in punishing, spare no one, whether he be minister or brother, man or woman, but shall judge the small as well as the great after one rule and measure of the divine Word, according to the truth. And, as all disobedient sinners by consent of the church, with sorrow and sadness of heart, are excluded from the brotherhood, and referred to repentance and reformation; so also shall all obedient, penitent sinners with the consent and concurrence of the church, be received, by the bishop of the church. And, as men are wont to rejoice over the finding of a lost sheep, piece of silver, or son, so shall believers rejoice with all the angels of God over the repentance and return of their erring brother or sister.

How the minor sins, whether caused through weakness or ignorance, were reconciled by the priest with various offerings, read: Lev. 4·27; 5; Num. 5·6; 15:22.

But the open transgressors of the law were put to death without mercy under two or three witnesses Of this read Num 15·30; Lev. 24:14; Deut. 17:12; 19:15; Heb 10 28

In connection with this read also the words of the high priest Eli "If one man sin against another, the judge shall judge him; but if a man sin against the the Lord, who shall entreat for him?" (1 Sam. 2:25).

How Christ commanded the small offenses between brother and brother should be punished, read "If thy brother shall trespass against thee, go and tell him his fault between thee and him alone: if he shall hear thee, thou hast gained thy brother. But if he will not hear thee, then take with thee one or two more, that in the mouth of two or three witnesses every word may be established And if he shall neglect to hear them, tell it unto the church but if he neglect to hear the church, let him be unto thee as a heathen man and a publican. Verily I say unto you, Whatsoever ye shall bind on earth shall be bound in heaven; and whatsoever ye shall loose on earth shall be loosed in heaven" (Matt. 18 15-18; Luke 17:3; Gal. 6 1; Jas. 5 19)

"If any man see his brother sin a sin which is not

unto death, he shall ask, and he shall give him life for them that sin not unto death" (I John 5:16).

But open offending members Christ commanded to sever and cast away without exercising admonition, intercession, or forgiveness in regard to them, before the separation Read: Matt 18:8; Mark 9:42

Thus did also the apostles, according to the doctrine of Christ, deny eternal life to all known works of the flesh, condemning them to death, and in their assembly; delivered the Corinthian fornicator unto Satan, with the Word and power of our Lord Jesus Christ, without using the aforesaid admonition with regard to him (1 Cor. 5 3 Read also: 1 Tim 1:20; 5 20; 2 Cor 13 2)

"There is a sin unto death I do not say that he shall pray for it" (1 John 5:16; Num 15 30; Heb 10 28; 1 Cor 5 13; 2 Cor 13:2; Ps 1 5; 2 Tim 2 20; 1 Cor 6 9; Gal 5 21; Eph 5:5)

Article XXIX

Of the withdrawing from and avoiding of apostate and separated members, is confessed: As separation is commanded by God for the reformation of sinners, and the maintenance of the purity of the church; so God has also commanded and willed, that in order to shame him to reformation, the separated individual shall be shunned and avoided This withdrawing proceeds from the separation, and is a fruit and proof of the same, and without it separation is vain and unavailing Hence, this ordinance of God shall be practiced and maintained, by all believers, with the separated persons This withdrawing extends to all spiritual communion, as the Supper, evangelical salutation, the kiss of peace, and all that pertains to it. This withdrawing extends likewise to all temporal and bodily things, as eating, drinking, buying and selling, daily intercourse and conversation, with all that pertains to it

Thus, believers shall, according to the Word of God, withdraw themselves, from the separated in all spiritual, evangelical matters, as well as in all bodily and temporal things. And as in separation no persons may be regarded or spared, but must, by consent, be separated from the true members of the body; so also in withdrawing, extending to all spiritual and temporal matters, none may be spared or excepted, whether man or woman, parent or child, or whatever relation it may be, seeing we nowhere read, where God gave His church a general commandment or ordinance, that any members of said church was entirely exempted and excluded from such commandment; but on the contrary, it appears in many places, that the whole number, without exception, had to regulate themselves according to one rule set before them by God; hence this ordinance of God must be practiced and maintained by all the members of the body of Christ, without respect of persons, in the fear of God, to shame sinners to reformation, until the person punished is again received into the church

But as all divine ordinances must be tempered with Christian kindliness and discretion, these also must have their place in this matter of shunning Hence, the believers must conduct themselves with more discernment and equity with regards to separated persons, than did the scribes and Pharisees with regard to the Sabbath, who, as it appears would rather let men perish than that they should receive help on the Sabbath, thinking that the Sabbath should be broken thereby, though they themselves, in such a case, broke the Sabbath for various minor matters But, even as the pious followers of the law did not sin, nor break the Sabbath, when they, on this day, performed not their own, but only the works which God had commanded them, so the believers neither sin nor act contrary to the commandment of shunning, when they perform not their own works, but only the works which God has commanded them concerning separated persons; as, in case of necessity, to minister to their bodies with food and other needful things, and to their souls with the Word of God, as well as to assist them by virtue of the commandment of God, in case of danger from water, fire, and the like; these all believers are in duty bound to do; and they must thus, with great carefulness, seek that which is lost, and lead that which is erred, back to the right way, reprove and instruct them with the Word of God, where such Christian admonition may take place, according to the example of Christ; but in all human works believers must with all diligence withdraw themselves from the separated persons, until they have reformed and been united again with the church.

In order rightly to understand this matter, it must be considered that the people of Israel at the time of Christ were under the power and dominion of the Romans, and could not punish transgressors according to the law of Moses, hence they separated from their communion and avoided those who departed from the law of the fathers, and went over to the Gentiles, Samaritans, or open sinners. Concerning this, read. They regarded them as unclean, abhorred them, compared them to heathens and enemies, avoided all dealings and intercourse with them. Read also John 18:31; 4:9; Acts 10:28; 11; Gal 2:12.

This custom Christ also observed, and commanded that the disobedient in the church should be so regarded, saying "If he neglect to hear the church, let him be unto thee as a heathen man and a publican" (Matt 18:17).

This the apostles also practiced in like manner, according to the doctrine of Christ. Read: "I wrote unto you in an epistle not to company with fornicators yet not altogether with the fornicators of this world, or with the covetous, or extortioners, or with idolaters, for then must ye needs go out of the world. But now I have written unto you not to keep company, if any man that is called a brother be a fornicator, or covetous, or an idolator, or a railer, or a drunkard, or an extortioner; with such a one no not to eat" (1 Cor 5:9-11)

Here the holy apostle forbids us to company and eat with apostate brethren or sisters, which he did not mean or command with reference to the unrighteous of this world, but permitted it with them; else we would needs have to go out of the world, seeing the whole world lies in wickedness; hence it must necessarily be understood with reference to daily intercourse and eating, buying and selling, and the like. "A man that is a heretic, after the first and second admonition, reject" (Tit 3:10; 2 Tim. 4:15; 2 John 10).

"And if any man obey not our word by this epistle, note that man, and have no company with him, that he may be ashamed" (2 Thess 3:14)

How this withdrawing is to be observed by all believers with regard to all apostates, walking disorderly, without respect of person, read: "Now, we command you, brethren, in the name of our Lord Jesus Christ, that ye withdraw yourselves from every brother that walketh disorderly and not after the tradition which he received of us" (2 Thess 3:6)

Understand this withdrawing according to Scriptures (Gal 2:12; and the like), according to the spirit of the Gospel of Christ.

How believers must seek the lost, and not count the separated as enemies, but admonish them, as brethren. Read 2 Thess 3:15; Jas 5:19; Luke 19:10, 15, the whole chapter

Article XXX

Of the last day and the second coming of Christ from heaven, we confess· That the great God of heaven, who in the beginning created heaven and earth with all visible things out of nothing, also appointed a day and time, which cannot be known by the angels of God in heaven; much less by mortal men, but which shall unexpectedly overtake men, as the snare of a bird, and a thief in the night; at which time the Almighty God will destroy this whole visible, earthly, realm, and burn it with everlasting fire, except those of the human race who shall have done the will of God; these shall abide forever

In the last great day of the Lord the Son of God, Jesus Christ, who in the presence of the apostles ascended from the earth in a cloud, shall come again from heaven, in the clouds of the sky, but not in the humiliated form of a servant, as in His first coming into the world at Bethlehem For at this His second coming He shall reveal Himself in the clouds as a King of mighty kings, and Lord of lords, with the power and glory of His Almighty Father, and all the angels of God with Him, and shall thus, with the trump of God, and the voice of the archangel, peal forth an unutterable sound and shout; so that heaven and earth, all the mountains and islands, shall be moved; the sun and moon shall lose their brightness, the stars shall fall from heaven, and all kindreds of the earth shall weep and wail over themselves, for fear and expectation of the things which are to come; and all shall see the Son of man coming, with power and great glory.

Of this last day of the Lord, read. "And as he sat upon the Mount of Olives, the disciples came unto him privately, saying, Tell us, when shall these things be? And what shall be the sign of thy coming, and of the end of the world" (Matt. 24:3).

"The day of the Lord will come as a thief in the night; in the which the heavens shall pass away with a great noise, and the elements shall melt with fervent heat, the earth also and the works that are therein shall be burned up" (2 Pet. 3:10; Mal 4 1)

"For yourselves know perfectly that the day of the Lord so cometh as a thief in the night For when they shall say Peace and safety, then sudden destruction cometh upon them, as travail upon a woman with child" (1 Thess 5 2, 3)

"Heaven and earth shall pass away, but my words shall not pass away But of that day and hour knoweth no man, no, not the angels of heaven. but my Father only" (Matt 24 35, 36, Mark 13 31; Ps 102 27; Is 51 6)

Of Christ's coming from heaven, read "Ye men of Galilee, why stand ye gazing up into heaven? this same Jesus, which is taken up from you into heaven, shall so come in like manner as ye have seen him go into heaven" (Acts 1 11)

"For the Lord himself shall descend from heaven with a shout, with the voice of the archangel, and with the trump of God" (1 Thess 4:16)

"Behold, he cometh with clouds, and every eye shall see him, and they also which pierced him and all kindreds of the earth shall wail because of him" (Rev 1 7; Matt 24 30; Luke 21 27 Read also 1 Thess 1 10; 2 Thess 1 7; Dan. 7 13; Jude 14).

Article XXXI

Of the Death of the body and the Resurrection of the dead, we confess That, in the beginning, man was created immortal, but that through the envy of the devil and the sin of our first parents, death came into the world And as through the sin of Adam all men became sinful in him, so also through him, all men became subject to bodily death; so that in consequence thereof it is appointed unto men once to die, but after this the judgment; seeing this sinful, corruptible flesh and blood cannot inherit the eternal, incorruptible kingdom, but must be renewed and glorified through death and the resurrection, by the power of God.

And, even as, when a man falls into a deep sleep, his heart, soul or spirit does not entirely sleep, as the body, so also the spirit or soul of man does not die or fall asleep with the body, but is and remains an immortal spirit Hence temporal death, in the Scriptures, is called a sleep, and the resurrection of the dead an awakening from this sleep of death

And as a sleeping man cannot receive and enjoy any good gifts, either according to the soul or the body, much less any punishment, pain and torment, unless he be previously awakened from his sleep; so also, believers cannot receive the perfect heavenly existence, nor unbelievers the eternal death of the pain of hell, either in the soul or in the body, except they have first been awakened from the sleep of death, and have arisen, through the coming of Christ

Until this last day of judgment the souls of believers are waiting in the hands of God, under the altar of Christ, to receive then in their souls and bodies, the rewards promised them So also the souls of unbelievers are reserved to be punished, after the day of judgment, in their souls and bodies.

And as through the sin and transgression of Adam death came upon all men; so also the resurrection of the dead came upon all men through the Savior Jesus Christ, so, that, as in the springtime the sun, through his glorious radiance and brightness, draws forth all sweet scented herbs from the earth, as well as thistles and thorns, which are rejected and reserved for the fire;

so also shall Christ Jesus, the true Son of righteousness, in this great last day and hour, through His glorious coming and appearing in the clouds of heaven, draw forth from the earth, and cause to arise all men, the wicked and the pious; so that this great God, through His power and commanding voice, by which He spake in the beginning *Let heaven and earth be made,* and His Word was immediately a perfect work, and who created all visible things from that which was invisible, and made man of the dust of the ground; this same God shall, through His unchangeable power and almighty Word, in the last day, call all men who have been changed into dust and earth, and have been consumed by fire, birds, and fishes, from the dust, and cause each to arise with his own body, flesh, and bones, with which they have served either their Creator or sin

And, as a woman in travail, when her hour is come, cannot retain, but makes haste to deliver the fruit of her womb, so also shall in this last hour, death, earth, or hell and sea make haste to deliver up the great number of the dead which in them have become dust and ashes, and passed away These shall all arise, with their own bodies, incorruptible, which shall again be united with the soul and spirit, which through death had been separated from the body, and had remained immortal At that time the pious shall be glorified and changed from the mortal and incorruptible into the immortal and incorruptible, from the weak and frail, into the strong and glorious, being made like unto the angels of God, and the glorious body of Christ Thus shall also those who shall live and remain at this sudden second coming of Christ from the heaven, be changed and glorified after the image of Christ

Of the first or temporal death, which came by the first transgression, read "For dust thou art, and unto dust thou shalt return" (Gen 3 19, 25 33)

"And as it is appointed unto men once to die, but after this the judgment" (Heb 9 27).

"For since by man came death, by man came also the resurrection of the dead" (1 Cor. 15·21).

How at the second coming of Christ the dead shall rise through Christ, read "For the Lord himself shall descend from heaven with a shout, with the voice of the archangel, and with the trump of God: and the dead in Christ shall rise first" (I Thess. 4:16).

"Marvel not at this; for the hour is coming, in the which all that are in the graves shall hear his voice, and shall come forth, they that have done good, unto the resurrection of life; and they that have done evil unto the resurrection of damnation" (John 5 28, 29)

"I know that my Redeemer liveth, and that he shall stand at the latter day upon the earth· and though after my skin worms destroy this body, yet in my flesh shall I see God whom I shall see for myself, and mine eyes shall behold" (Job 19 25-27)

Read also Is 26 19; Dan. 12 13; Matt. 22 31; Luke 20 35, John 6 40; 11 25; 1 Cor 15 throughout; Ps 90 3

How in the resurrection of the dead, men's vile bodies shall be glorified, read "In the resurrection they neither marry, nor are given in marriage but are as the angels of God in heaven" (Matt 22 30)

"For our conversation is in heaven, from whence also we look for the Savior, the Lord Jesus Christ who shall change our vile body, that it may be fashioned like unto his glorious body, according to the working whereby he is able even to subdue all things unto himself" (Phil 3 20, 21; 1 Cor 15.42; 53).

Article XXXII

Of the last judgment; of hell, and the damnation of unbelievers, we confess. That in the last day, when Christ Jesus shall appear in the clouds of heaven, with power and great glory, all nations shall be gathered before his judgment seat, and he shall separate them as a shepherd separates the sheep from the goats, placing the sheep on His right hand and the goats on His left Over these Christ Jesus is ordained by His Father Judge of quick and dead, who will regard no person, nor need the testimony of any; for the heart, mind and thoughts of every one are manifest before Him as an open book This righteous Judge will judge the whole world in righteousness, and as the great Shepherd of the sheep, pronounce an eternal, irrevocable judgment upon them, rewarding each in his own body according to that he hath done. To all the believing, generated children of God who in this life, as obedient sheep, heard and followed the voice of Christ, He shall say, "Come, ye blessed of my Father, inherit the kingdom prepared for you from the foundation of the world " And to all unbelievers, who would not have Christ and His Word in this life, but, as disobedient, obstinate goats, rejected them, He will say, "Depart from me, ye cursed, into everlasting fire prepared for the devil and his angels "

In that last day of the Lord the righteous God will deprive this world of all good gifts; so that the sun, moon and stars shall lose their brightness, and all the light and glory of the world shall be changed into everlasting darkness In that time the earth, waters and streams shall be turned into burning pitch and brimstone, which shall burn forever and ever And, seeing this earth is called hell in many places in Scripture, and no other hell being anywhere mentioned, the same is regarded as hell and the place of damnation; in which fiery pool and outer darkness all unbelievers will finally have to suffer the burning of hell and eternal damnation; and thus they shall at last be punished and tormented with the visible things, which in preference to the eternal and invisible, they chose and served in this life

Into that place of darkness and fiery pool all unbelievers shall, after the resurrection, their souls having been united with their bodies, be sentenced by Christ Then shall be fulfilled that which is written concerning this last, sad day of separation; namely, that one of two shall be taken in the field, in the bed, and at the mill, and be caught up in the air to meet the Lord, but the others shall be left, and be sentenced into said pool of darkness, where they shall be tormented with the devil and his angels, burning, and suffering in all eternity, forever deprived of all grace and mercy from God, which is the second death.

Of the last judgment, and how the whole human race shall appear before the judgment seat of Christ, to receive each in His own body an eternal sentence, read "And he commanded us to preach unto the people, and to testify that it is he which was ordained of God to be the Judge of quick and dead" (Acts 10:42)

"Because he hath appointed a day, in which he will judge the world in righteousness by that man whom he hath ordained" (Acts 17:31; Ps. 7 11).

"For we must all appear before the judgment seat of Christ; that every one may receive the things done in his body, according to that he hath done, whether it be good or bad" (2 Cor. 5:10; Rom. 14:10).

"And I saw the dead, small and great, stand before God; and the books were opened: and another book was opened, which is the book of life. and the dead were judged out of those things which were written in the books, according to their works" (Rev. 20.12; Dan 7:10).

"When the Son of man shall come in his glory, and all the holy angels with him, then shall he sit upon the throne of his glory and before him shall be gathered all nations and he shall separate them one from another, as a shepherd divideth his sheep from the goats" (Matt 25 31, 32; 16 27; 26·64; 2 Thess 1 7)

Of hell and the place of damnation, read "For it is the day of the Lord's vengeance, and the year of recompenses for the controversy of Zion And the streams thereof shall be turned into pitch, and the dust thereof into brimstone, and the land thereof shall become burning pitch It shall not be quenched night nor day, the smoke thereof shall go up forever" (Is 34 8-10; 2 Peter 3 10)

"And it came to pass as he (Moses) had made an end of speaking all these words, that the ground clave asunder that was under them and the earth opened her mouth, and swallowed them up, and their houses, and all the men that appertained unto Korah, and all their goods" (Num 16 31, 32)

Read further concerning Sodom and Gomorrah, how they were overturned and condemned and made an example; and how the earth is called hell (Gen 19 24, Jude 7, Acts 2 27, 31; Ps 16 11)

"Your gold and silver is cankered, and the rust of them shall be a witness against you, and shall eat your flesh as it were fire" (James 5 3).

"For behold, the day cometh, that shall burn as an oven, and all the proud; yea, and all that do wickedly shall be stubble and the day that cometh, shall burn them up, saith the Lord" (Mal 4·1)

"The Lord knoweth how to deliver the godly out of temptation, and to reserve the unjust unto the day of judgment to be punished" (2 Peter 2 9)

Them "he hath reserved in everlasting chains under darkness unto the judgment of the great day" (Jude 6; Matt 25 30; Rom 14 10, 2 Cor 5 10)

Read further concerning the fearful and intolerable pain of hell (Mark 9:46; Matt 22:13; 24:51; 25:30, 41; Rev 19:20; 21:8).

Article XXXIII

Of the kingdom of heaven and eternal life, we confess That as there is a visible, perishable kingdom of this, which, though the sins and wickedness of men, lies in darkness, of which darkness, Satan, the spirit of wickedness, who works in the children of unbelief, is the supreme prince, who at last, with all his servants, shall be brought to everlasting lamentation and remorse, and shall perish; so also there is an eternal, immovable and invisible kingdom of heaven, of which Christ Jesus is King, Prince and Lord; in which all believers shall live with God forever in everlasting joy. To this glorious kingdom of heaven, God through His grace and goodness, from the beginning of the world, caused the fallen human race to be called; first through His servants, the prophets, and then through the Son Himself, who, leaving this His kingdom for a time came to preach, and to invite all men, to flee the shadow of this world, and to make haste to enter into this eternal rest For this end the fatlings are killed, and this glorious feast is prepared; so that men are prevented from making any excuse concerning the piece of land, the oxen, and the wife, but the way, door and gate, is open and well prepared

This glorious kingdom of heaven is typified and represented to us by a city full of good things, and the new Jerusalem, coming down from heaven, which is beautifully prepared by God, as the bride adorned for her husband; the streets of it are pure gold, and the gates and walls built of and beautifully adorned with manifold pearls and precious stones. In this city is the glory of the Almighty God, which neither Moses on Mount Sinai, nor the eyes of any mortal man were able to behold This brightness and everlasting light shall shine in this city for ever and ever. Here all sorrow and mourning, cold, nakedness, hunger and thirst shall be changed into everlasting, satisfying joy and consolation This glory and joy is so exceedingly great and unspeakable, that eye hath not seen, nor ear heard, neither have entered into the heart of man, the things which God hath prepared for them that love him; and into this heavenly state, which is beyond all praise, all believers and God-pleasing persons shall at the resurrection of the dead, when their souls, which through death had become separated from the body, and until this last time were preserved in the hand of God, shall be re-united with their bodies, be caught up from this earthly darkness, to meet the Lord in the air

And, as a bride is received by her bridegroom, so also shall all true children of God then be received with body and soul through grace, by Christ Jesus, and be admitted to this glorious joy, where they shall see God as He is, in His unspeakable glory, together with all the heavenly hosts Then shall their robe of mourning, or the mortal clothing of the flesh be put off, and the immortal be put on; and they shall be clothed in white, shining raiment, and together with all God's chosen ones, be fed by the Son of God, whom they confessed in the world, with the hidden heavenly bread, and shall eat of the tree of life, and drink out of the living fountain of water, and, being as the angels, shall, with joyful tongues and mouths, in gladsome voices, to the honor of the Lamb, their bridegroom, sing the new song, with unspeakable, glorious joy, which no one can take away from them; but they shall be kings and priests of God, and shall live and reign with Christ for ever and ever.

May the God of grace and mercy, and of all comfort, who has from the beginning called us to this His heavenly kingdom and glory, endow us unworthy children of men with His good spirit, make us worthy of Him, and draw us Him-ward, that we may follow and run after this high prize, and by grace receive the same, through Jesus Christ, and enjoy it for ever Amen.

Of the everlasting kingdom of heaven, and its King, read "Wherefore we receiving a kingdom which cannot be moved, let us have grace" (Hebrews 12 28)

"My kingdom is not of this world, if my kingdom were of this world, then would my servants fight, that I should not be delivered to the Jews; but now is my kingdom not from hence" (John 18 36).

Read further how this eternal King, Christ Jesus, at His second coming from heaven, after the dead shall have risen, and the eternal judgment been held, shall receive all the members of His kingdom in this His everlasting glorious kingdom of heaven, where they shall behold God in unspeakable glory. "Then shall the King say to them on His right hand, Come, ye blessed of my Father, inherit the kingdom prepared for you from the foundation of the world" (Matt 25 34)

"But the righteous live for ever more; their reward also is with the Lord, and the care of them is with the Most High Therefore shall they receive a glorious kingdom, and a beautiful crown from the Lord's hand" (1 Peter 5 4, 2 Tim 4 8; Rev 2 10; Jas 1 12)

"Then we which are alive and remain shall be caught up together with them in the clouds, to meet the Lord in the air and so shall we ever be with the Lord Wherefore comfort one another with these words" (1 Thess 4·17, 18, 1 Cor 2 9; 1 Peter 1 8; John 16 22)

"Beloved, now are we the sons of God, and it doth not yet appear what we shall be but we know that, when he shall appear, we shall be like him, for we shall see him as he is" (1 John 3 2; Phil 3 20, 27)

"When Christ, who is our life, shall appear, then shall ye also appear with him in glory" (Col 3 4)

"Thine eyes shall see the King in his beauty they shall behold the land that is very far off Thine heart shall meditate terror" (Is 33:17, 18).

Of all who from a true faith shall show forth the required spiritual virtues, and shall continue to the end in this divine calling, read "If ye do these things, ye shall never fall for so an entrance shall be ministered unto you abundantly into the everlasting kingdom of our Lord and Savior Jesus Christ" (2 Peter 1 10, 11)

Here is the patience and the faith of the saints (Rev 13.10).

finisher of the exploits of faith, of every age, will be more prominent than anyone else. Look unto Him and see Him! Declare from this time forward, 'We see Jesus, the finisher and perfecter of our Faith!'"

communications of the perfect will, which issues from the holiest court of all, shatter and break asunder your human arrangements.

Within the innermost court you become conscious that ' My thoughts are not your thoughts.' Then it is that the multitude is divided. Everyone turns his back, in spirit, upon the prophets who reveal the perfection which is My being; and the flesh always declares: 'Hard are his sayings; who can listen to him?'

The life histories of all of you will be found in the movements when they shall be unveiled. Submit to them willingly. Believe in the objects, which I am aiming at, to achieve; so that the elect whom you have not seen (even those who lie in the womb of purpose) may have a foundation for believing (when they read the biographies of My Gifts). I, the I AM, have been all things unto you, as I was unto your fathers, and through the elect I will carry out the pre-ordained operations of my movements.

If you abide in the outer court, you will see men only, you will only see the flesh. You must enter into the holiest of all to obtain a revelation of the pre-destination of purpose.

Fear not that someone else shall have more honour than yourselves. I have made an oath that I will honour all that honour Me. Nevertheless, the lives of the connecting links, in the chain of each age, must be manifest, and their lives chronicled for the purposes in view. 'Are all apostles? Are all prophets?'

Partake of this bread, so that you may be nourished. Hunger for My Word. I have those that will eat of My Word. Blessed are they, saith the Lord.

Remember this, the great initiator, object, author and

It must be borne in mind that, connected with those works which I perform, within the span of a generation, there are sent ones and chosen ones, predestined of Me raised especially at the right time for each age. They are the elect heroes of the faith realm.

You rejoice when calling to remembrance those heroes whose faces you have never seen; and you refer to them as worthy of acknowledgement – that they are gifts from the realm of light.

But at heart you are narrow-minded; and the discontented look on your faces plainly declares that you are not willing to chronicle the lives of My present 'gifts of men', lest they should be given greater honour than you are given. This selfishness has caused, and still causes, you to watch them narrowly; and if you come across a fault, or a blemish, how you chastise them!

..... 'You are my crown' said Paul. The eternal age will be spent in fellowship and harmony – each age meeting together in one, having performed the eternal purposes of My will.

The food of the divine will is dearer in price than daily bread. Whatever you eat, instead of doing My will, will leave you everlastingly hungry. You have never felt more contented than when, after knowing My will, you have performed it. At such times you have had peace in your hearts.

The measure of the depth of your faith, and the extent of your continuance in the vision, as far as the realm of prophets is concerned (when you believe them) is, if, and when something is given you, and when your own ideal arrangement (conceived in your own wills) is not crossed, but confirmed, by them! You do believe the prophets on such occasions! But the sufficient. Under the gaze of His eyes there is enough to feed the multitude and to feed the individual Elijah.

Job remained in the outer court when he was permitted to go through his tribulations and, because of that, he cried, 'All these things are against me.' But when he reached the inner most court, he changed his judgement and declared, 'Though He slay me, yet will I trust Him!' His end was better than his beginning.

In the outer court Peter said, 'I go a fishing!' He caught nothing. Those who have left off being directed by Him that dwells in the sanctuary of the holiest, always cast the the 'wrong' side, saith the Lord.

What of the conflict in which Mary and Martha found themselves? 'If Thou hadst been here!' said they, 'our brother Lazarus would not have died!' It was not a conflict arising from bodily needs; mourning, they could not eat bread. Nor was it a conflict in the realm of the soul – the Pharisees were there to comfort them! It was a conflict in their spirit. He besought them to enter the holy of holies that they might see the glory of God. 'Let us go, and die with him!' said Thomas. In the sanctuary where He dwells, no one dies, but lives, saith the Lord.

Hearken to the secret communications from the holiest of all; you shall put yourselves to the proof whether you are within it. I commanded in My Word that the posterity of all the children who have proved Me should know of My wonders, My mercies and My mighty exploits. How could that be made possible, unless they chronicled those exploits in scripture history, and in biographies so that the generations that should come after them might read them? One generation passes away and another comes.

time threatening woe upon Me if I do not walk, move and arrange things in the light of their altar fires. They contrive and arrange within it, and they expect Me to move according to their rules, and they seek to be quicker than I, by their cunning.

But let it be remembered that they do not dwell in the holiest of all. It's door is too small and narrow for ambitious self to enter.

I ask you, ought you to bend to My ways and order, or I to you? Your unanimous reply comes to My ears, 'We ought to bend to Thee!' Thus your boldness and presumption vanish when you come face to face with Me.

Nevertheless, you turn from Me and make attacks and secret assaults upon the prophets of Jehovah! In this matter the walls witness against you! Obedience is better than sacrifice. The mystery of the humbling (that I should come and speak to you) is too great to allow Me to be satisfied with anything less than complete obedience, saith the Lord.

'How wilt Thou be able to feed so great a multitude in the wilderness, so far away from the possibility of obtaining sufficient bread?' such is the question of the natural man, under a cloud, weighed down by the pressure of his present need. The reply came from the lips of Him who dwells in the holiest of all, 'Let the multitude but sit down and there will be enough and to spare!'

Those that walk according to the flesh must always 'see' and 'hear'; but those that know Him that dwells in the court of the holiest know also that which is in the hand of the 'certain lad' or the 'certain widow' is cause you to be unmindful of the authority of my Word. Support the feebleness of the weak!

Pride will make you to be independent of everyone, to be selfish, and unwilling to do anything, but, what from wilfulness, you do yourselves. Pride will make you uncontrollably independent in opinion and deed.

I would have you to understand the truth that, when the declarations are antagonistic to the revelation of My Spirit, to the commandments of My spoken word and to the light of My written Word, the cause is to be found, at all times, in the tyrannical strength of your proud spirit. For pride does not acknowledge authority and will cause everyone, at all times, to become haughty, and to secretly believe – even if they do not openly assert – that they are better than others.

...Receive My word and be possessed by the truth, 'He that glorieth, let him glory in the Lord.'"

A further example:

"There is no right of entrance into the court of the Holiest of all for those who live continually in the realm of natural bread, fearing that they shall not have enough. Take heed lest you be enticed by another, for another will come to sight who will satisfy the needs of a man's body. But let it be remembered that it is only by the word of My command that the sun ripens the harvest. Neither can those who live in the realm of their own meditations, bringing imaginations into being, and giving birth in the soul realm to schemes of self-interest, enter into the holiest of all. Being inflamed by the fire of their own self resolutions and, at the same ground of adoption. But it must be remembered that the child must arrive at full age before he can receive the inheritance in its fulness. I am warning you, so that the cancer of boastfulness may not eat away the nature received by adoption.

There are those who boast of their call into office, supposing, believing and proclaiming it aloud, that they have been called because of their perfection. What saith My Word? 'Make your calling sure.' Remember those principles which should be manifested to everybody, by virtue of your call into office, namely, sacrifice, effort, compassion, patience, suffering and love. See to it continually that you do not serve in order to draw the disciples of the Lord after you.

I need not remind you, 'Feed the flock!' That is the first thing you believe you ought to do, and of which you shout and boast on the ground of your calling, but I would remind you that you must have a revelation as to the nature of the food that is to be given to the flock. It should be nourishment to them. You are not to beat, depreciate, wound or despise the flock. Let the motherhood of your calling come to sight in acts of love…in order to keep, foster, comfort and safeguard the flock from every injurious pestilence that walks in the earth.

Be not blind to the dangers of prosperity and advancement. Receive my warnings; remain in the dust; then I will continue to work and to move in your midst. I will bring My judgement to victory.

Pride will make you blind to every need and to every responsibility. Pride will robe you of your compassion towards the weak and the weary and will

Boastfulness, as an invisible cancer, is eating into every vital strength that would enable you to remain faithful unto Me under every circumstance. Forget not My warnings! Cling to no one. Follow no party that boasts in things that will not stand the changes that will be brought about, and have been predicted, according to the roll of the Book.

Turning from the parties that are in the world, I will come nearer to you in the realms of the Spirit, into the realm of the new life. Take note of the word 'but' so that it may be read with emphasis: 'But he that glorieth, let him glory in the Lord.'

There are those who glory in their experience. The boastfulness of experience is found within My house, but it will not go far. It seeks to make its way into the heart of the believer, and to eat up his life, unless he is watchful. Some boast in the visions and revelations they have obtained. The visions are going to become a snare, if each personal revelation is not understood to be the inheritance of My people at large. Whoever will use it for his own exaltation and glory will find that he is using it for his own destruction.

Some boast in their calling. This vainglory has reached My sanctuary. Some make this empty boast, glorying in the flesh, in the General Church, that they have been called to be saints. But they despise the principles, which are connected with the life of all who have been called to be saints, namely, obedience, humility, a forgiving spirit and brotherly love.

I see and hear many of My people boasting aloud of their liberty, while, at the same time, in every realm, they despise authority. They would command me to do that which *they* will, and that which *they* desire, on the

the nations, despite the fact that the nations are concealing their power and their intentions, from one another. Although they conceal their purpose, vaunting stalks in the lands, and will reach its climax in every direction. Boastfulness comes to disaster in ever realm, in every government and in every kingdom. But the fall of boastfulness will be nothing like the disaster that will occur to those who have forgotten the pit from which they were dug, and from which they were raised, and the rock from which they have been cut.

The fall of that proud one (Lucifer) is not to be compared to the fall of these others. Nevertheless, their fall is equal to the depth and the height of his former honour and of his personality.

Boast not in your understanding. The wise boasts of his wisdom, but before the end it will be proved that his boasting is vain. Boast not like those in the world, in your strength (because you are mighty), for I declare plainly, the strength of every war-horse, and every cannon, and every engine of war, and every provision will cease in the day of the fall of pride.

Cities, nations and kingdoms, as great and powerful as those of today, have been brought to the ground. Why was Babylon seen in the dust? Why did Rome fall? Why did the walls of Jerusalem become a ruin? At the base of every heap, from the ruin of Babel's tower unto the ruin of the present age, at their foundation, I say, you will find pride and vainglory. I declare concerning every magnificent edifice, which is being raised up today, on the foundation of pride, its fall and its ruin will speak for itself. For there is nothing can survive every change, only that which is erected on the foundation: 'On this Rock.'

APPENDIX

Examples of Prophetic Ministry through W. Jones Williams

"I would have every member of My household, everyone among My people to understand and know that I am giving a word in order to safeguard and protect each one. The word is this: "*But he that glorieth, let him glory in the Lord*" (2Cor. 10:17) because vainglory strides up and down the land. Boasting with heavy footstep's, stalks abroad. Vaunting flies overhead on swift wings. The exaltation of self is taking hold of the mighty and My word comes as a warning beforehand.

The worm of pride is already eating at the root, and the actions of pride make a fall certain, inasmuch as a pit has been prepared for pride. I loathe the proud afar off. Many things will be seen and experienced, but this do I declare: all who have remained with Me will do so because I am their boast. You will know those who glory in themselves, for when you shall seek them in My temple, they will not be found. My Church, throughout the nations, will search for some persons, and it will be found necessary to say of them, 'Once we saw them mighty, flourishing and strong but today they are not to be found in the house of the Lord.' Why? Because pride hath gotten hold of them, and possessed them.

Boastfulness moves in every realm, moving into the thrones of the nations, moving in the governments of

The HUSBAND of the widow yet is faithful;
The FATHER of the orphan liveth still;
The BROTHER of the brethren is unchangeful –
We shall, one family, meet on Salem's Hill.

(Man's foul contumely turned God's gold to dross) –
Thou didst portray in words that, strong yet tender,
Exultantly proclaimed the Victr'y of The Cross.

And thou hast left us for thy better mansion,
Thy habitation knoweth thee no more;
And I am far from home, on pilgrim mission,
Longing for heavenly balm to heal my sore.

We parted with a handshake firm and hopeful,
Thy lips I pressed with holy, prayerful kiss,
Yet ne'er imagined – on yon shore delightful
We next should meet, 'neath purer clime than this!

'Twas not my lot in thy last hour to see thee,
Nor bid farewell when in the valley's night;
But we shall meet when morning dawns in Glory,
And sing God's praises on fair Zion's height.

Beloved prophet! – sleep! Thy work is finished!
Ne'er shall the virtue of thy labours end;
Enshrined in volumes they shall aye be cherished,
Generations shall to thee their tributes lend.

I've sought to hide the dankish sods that cover
Thy grave, with blooms, lest memory protest raise;
Death's valley conquered, soon we'll meet, my brother
The Lamb our fellowship, our peace our praise!

Belov'd – (your hearts with 'whelming sorry stricken)
Be not disconsolate, God's truth to us is blest;
Joy still awaits beyond the far horizon,
And Jesus is the Way – He knoweth best.

Earth's sheepfolds heard the heavenly Shepherd's voice,
That called unceasingly to follow fast;
Healed of sin's deathful wounds, hosts rejoice
That they, redeemed, were sought and found at last.
To wrongful wanderings, by vice enticed,
Fast held by mammon's thorny snares untold,
Freed by the precious, worthful blood of Christ,
They eat today the pastures of God's fold.

God's counsel thou didst ne'er to us withold
They brave endurance was thy strength and shield;
Though weaklings in the faith thy fall foretold
Thinking that thou thy sacred charge would yield.
Thy nature's fervency as fire surged
In ardent venturings and challenge met,
The lonely places found thy soul well purged
As though with cryings strong on Olivet.

Wert there where conflicts hottest waged and hard,
Thou knewest scorn, contempt and scar;
Unyielding in thy zeal, none could thee retard;
Watchful lest thou the unity would mar.

Reliant to the end, yet unreviling,
Assured fully of the merits of the blood,
How well we knew (thy gifts our hearts enthralling)
That 'neath thy feet the Rock of Ages stood!

The 'Fellowship of the Mystery' for the nations –
The 'Church of Christ' – Paul's 'Gospel' – blessed sound!
The whole essentials deep of faith's foundations,
God's 'Holiest' through thy tongue a channel found.
Th' infinite worth of Christ, the world's Redeemer –

Thine accents still reverberate in my ears,
They will remain when earth's foundations perish,
The influences wrought of God outlive the years,
Beyond the crack of doom, their worth I'll cherish.

Thy words were not the words of human weaving;
The tidal mind of God surged through our tongue,
And here upon our shores forever breaking,
Wrought wondrous descant, harmonies unsung.
Great thoughts and precious did thy lips set free,
Opening to view the folds of God's rich agencies;
Moved by their might, we felt the One in Three
In depths of peace reveal salvation's potencies.

Mere earthly trust climb cannot not o'erleap
The wall of doubt, nor to God's courts aspire;
Needful is faith, her glow divine doth keep
A white-hot ardour from the altar fire.

Obstacles unnumbered faced thy footsteps oft;
From prejudices of the day, and incredulity,
Thy faith untiring, fervent, soared aloft,
While serving God and our necessity.

Or day or night, they were but one to thee;
Thy labours soon became our proverbs sweet;
They shield rang true as steel mid battles' heat;
They faithfulness knit our hearts eternally.
And heaven's grave predicting words were keys,
Each continent wide opened to thy Lord,
And peoples, glad-hearing the prophetic word,
Came hand in hand, adored with bended knees.

Strange were th' initial tasks of thy high function,
For hidden are they ways of God's election;
The horn of sacred oil, with timely tilting,
Reveals the hand of providence, the gifts dividing;
The head was unctioned thus with God's anointing –
The Baptism of Fire thy call fast-sealing.
As o'er thy lips God's river-spates descending,
Th' attentive saints their music heard, enthrilled.

Strange were those days of tears and 'Hallelujah!'
When God was pleased to baptise praying Gwalia;
And miracles in her coasts tore hearts in sunder
As storms from heaven with lightening and with thunder.

Those were the days when love bedewed God's garden,
And every flower was crowned with gracious guerdon,
Thou also didst receive God's handsel graceful,
Sweet heaven's gift for future uses loveful;
He, quickening us His spoken truths to cherish,
Gave grace to heed His order – lest we perish!

We heard the secrets of th' Immortal Three;
God's purpose, as we scanned, her pages turned,
While judgement fearful at the threshold burned,
As though both earth and heaven had ceased to be!

Who there could not but feel the awesome sanctitude
Of words divine that searched the deeps profound?
The soul, to silence hushed by heaven's magnitude,
Yet, in their light, sustaining solace found.

LOVE'S ELEGY
To
Pastor William Jones Williams
A prophet and apostle of the Lord Jesus Christ in the Apostolic Church
A translation, by Ps. T. Davies, of the Elegy written in Welsh
By Ps. D.P. Williams

O Brother mine! fain would I in my tears
Bedeck thy earthy bed with myriad flowers;
With garlands beauteous hide thy grave from sight,
Lest its cold clods should ever gloom the light –
Praise God in meditation 'mid their fragrance,
As I recall thy virtues to remembrance.

Upon thee fell the lot of the Supernal,
Ordaining thee a prophet of th' Eternal;
The 'seventh' nursed in His cradle at Garnfoel,
Heav'n's voice revealed in time to point the goal.

No one had thought that, God's choice knowing not,
Thou, His own prophet, played around that cot;
The heavenly hand in morning council set
The Word-appointed-oracles unknown as yet:
Determinate heaven's will is ne'er defeated.

Thy soul was straitened in thee, one occasion,
Between Piahiroth rock and hard Baalzephon;
Thy lips licked then the dust of deep contrition,
But heav'n's God saw to thy due exaltation.

particularly special sense to his brother, Ps. D.P. Williams. The President, we know, will feel the loss in a double sense. First of all, his loss of a very dear brother and, secondly, his loss of one that has been with him through all his struggles as founder of the Apostolic Church and also being the mouthpiece of the Lord to His servant.

THAT as an Executive representing this far-flung Commonwealth of Australia, we feel that we can raise no better memorial to the memory of a great man of God, than to stand firm for the vision, and to continue to expand the vision that he so valiantly battled for, through the hard years of its inception. Our ardent wish is to be rejoined with him around the throne above, without shame, sorrow or loss to ourselves and the vision he loved so well.

(signed) James Turnbull

It may be added as significant, that, although the Lord calls His workers home, His ample provision was at the Penygroes Convention of 1945 shown by the following movements of His servants:

Ps. J.A. Tate (as prophet) to Australia.

Ps. Frank Warburton to Canada.

Ps. W.H. Humphreys to Ireland.

Ps. Vivian Wellings to be General Secretary at Penygroes H.Q. (with pastorate at Ammanford).

Ps. Evan D. Jones to undertake general Evangelical Campaign work.

AUSTRALIA'S TRIBUTE
To the Memory of the late Pastor W.J. Williams.

Pastor W.M. Humphreys (General Secretary of the Apostolic Church) related the following, moving testimony, in connection with the home-call of the late Ps. W.J. Williams. It was received by air-mail dated 27th July 1945 from the Executive Council of the Commonwealth of Australia and read at the Penygroes International Convention – August 4th – 12th 1945. The same was communicated to Pastor Dan in Canada.

MINUTE

THAT it is with the very deepest regret that this Executive has received the news of the home-call of Ps. W. Jones Williams on 15th April 1945. We were greatly shocked by the news, which came so unexpectedly, and just at the time when the Pastor was about to fulfil his call to the ministry in Canada.

As one of the Founders of the Apostolic Church in Great Britain we had come to look upon him as one of the principal pillars of the work. Our association with him as a fellow-worker, and servant of God, has become very closely bound with the progress of the Church worldwide, as well as that of personal friendship and fellowship.

The results of his faith and labours for the apostolic vision cannot be fully estimated, and we esteem it a great privilege to have been co-workers with him in the spreading of the vision, which he, with others, founded.

Our deepest sympathy and condolence goes out to his wife and family in their sad bereavement, and in a

"Come. My Father's blessed one
Receive thine inheritance"
(Matt.25:34 Weymouth)

Honoured art thou, blessed soul!
For when the Lord
A clean, illumined place would find
In which to place the Word
He looked on thee and said
'This one is to my Mind!'

And straight forthwith the utterance was given
That opened up the reservoir of heaven
And as God's plan and purpose came to birth
The Spring of Life upon the mountain height
Did water all the earth!

O here spirit! dauntless didst thou stand
Enough for thee that twas thy Lord's command
Fear could not make thee fall
Nor favour thee enthrall
All that thou had'st was his – voice, hands and feet
Until the trumpet sounded thy retreat

Blessed and loved and mourned indeed thou art
With tender memories our hearts low bow
The whole wide Church below (to furthest spheres)
Gives thanks for thee – albeit 'tis with tears

Thy fight was nobly fought, and nobly won!
And now thy soul is crowned with God's 'Well done!'

Lina Harding
Toronto, Canada

A vessel from the hands of God
A prophet from His throne
A channel whom before his birth
God claimed and sealed His own

A sinner saved by grace indeed
A soul that yearned for souls
A messenger whose heart and lips
God touched with burning coals

A man whose smile and sunny ways
Adorned the truth he spread
A signpost pointing every time
To Christ the fountain head

A servant of the Most High God
Of Jesus proud to tell
He's gone to see the One he served
And signals, 'All is well!'

Mourn not as those who have no hope
This servant of the cross
Will meet, when Jesus comes again,
The hearts that suffer loss.

The gift God gave He's taken too
(Bereavement is the story)
But lo! In wisdom God hath made
A further link in glory

V.E.R. Allen

IN MEMORY OF THE LATE PASTOR W.J. WILLIAMS

Called to higher service
A song of praise to sing
In the land of glory
Waiting on the King

Loved ones – they will miss him
Yet for them he'll wait
With a loving welcome
At the pearly gate

Loved ones – do not worry
Bear the cross and wait
Til the time of meeting
At the pearly gate

There the tie now severed
There the broken chain
Christ will gather closer
When all meet again

Called to higher service
A song of praise to sing
In the land of glory
Waiting on the King

Mrs E. Carne (Cardiff)

on the words, 'Only a voice'. It was an occasion never to be forgotten, to see many making their way to the penitent form in repentance and consecration. The candle went out, and his voice became silent as far as this earth is concerned, on Sunday 15th April. What a loss! Yet many of us have benefited spiritually, and eternally, through being in his company.

'You were willing to rejoice for a season in his light' – in the company of the messenger 'for a season'; in the company of the Master 'eternally'. Our responsibility will be great after being in his company for so long.

I will conclude by thanking God for lighting this candle and by reminding you that it is only for a time that we have the Light. Let us make the right use of the Light while we live. Let us pray that God will light more such candles in the world. What a grand thing to know that the Sun will rise soon; then there will be no need of 'candles'; we shall see and meet our blessed Lord, never to part again in the eternal light of heaven. 'Indeed, come Lord Jesus; Amen!'"

The following poetic tributes to the late prophet and apostle have not been published before, and express the sentiments felt by the whole church.

light to those around. The candle is indebted to another for its light. All light comes from the sun, and it returns to the sun. The candle burns itself out to give light to others. This speaks of sacrifice in the highest sense of the word.

At this memorial service, in remembrance of our beloved W. Jones Williams, we believe that these words are very fitting. It was in February 1911, at 'Brynteg' Gorsgoch Road, Penygroes, that the spirit of God fell upon Brother Ivor Thomas (who later married a sister of Ps. D.P Williams) telling Pastor Dan to repair to 'Disgwylfa', Waterloo Road, where two young men were talking about worldly matters. He was to command them, for the last time, to go to the meeting and surrender to the claims of the Lord. Pastor Dan went and found his brother, Jones, speaking to his friend, D, Henry Williams.

After a chat, the message was delivered, and the two young men wisely went immediately to the meeting, then being held at the Evangelistic Mission Hall, Penygroes, where they were converted and gave their hearts to the Lord. Then it was that two candles were lit; and the light and heat in both continued.

In the case of Ps. Jones Williams, he was privileged to carry that light into every part of the world. The revelations that passed through him as a channel of God at times, when preaching or prophesying, caused us to bow in worship and adoration before God. I look upon him, and his brother (the President), allegorically, as two wheels of a great divine chariot, carrying revelation, mysteries and purposes of God to the Church. But alas! Jones Williams has been called home to glory.

Many years ago I heard him preaching in Glasgow

c. Death in the pot (place of nourishment)
d. Deliverance from and in God, through His prophet.

Preceding Ps. Dawson, Ps. T.V. Lewis addressed the mourners and saints as follows:

"He was a burning and shining light, and ye were willing for a season to rejoice in his light." (John 5:35)

In the beginning of this chapter we read that Jesus healed a man who had been ill for thirty-eight years. The Jews persecuted our Lord for doing so, because it was the Sabbath day. Following that, the Lord took the opportunity to explain who He was. He gave the purpose of His coming into the world to be the Saviour of mankind, the Healer of mankind and also Judge of the quick and the dead. He speaks of a fourfold witness: John the Baptist, the works that Jesus did, the Father Himself and the Scriptures.

I believe it will be fitting in this memorial service to meditate on the words concerning John, as God's messenger.

i. The description of God's messenger – 'a burning and shining light.'
ii. The privilege to be in the hearing of God's messenger – 'you were willing for a season to rejoice in his light.'

Jesus calls John a 'burning and shining light' revealing the warmth and light of the gospel. In the Welsh version, the word we have for 'light' is 'candle' – 'a candle burning and shining.' The Lord had said that people do not light a candle to put it under a bushel, or a bed; but that it might be set in a candlestick, to give

His work is done. I can say from my heart that he is with the Lord. God is pleased to take to Jones to Himself. I would say strongly, 'The Lord bless you, keep you and give you peace. Amen.'"

Pastor John Lindsay closed this part of the service with prayer. He stressed that Ps. Williams had listened to the claims of the gospel with discipleship.

AT THE GRAVESIDE:
Ps. T. Vaughan Lewis voiced the Committal Service, while Ps. Rees Evans concluded with an affecting prayer.

The Funeral Hymn Sheet quoted Heb.12:1-2 and IITim.4:7 and the hymns sung were:
"There is a land of pure delight."
"Forever with the Lord."
"The King of love my Shepherd is."
"Dal fi, fy Nuw, dal fi 'mhob man." ('Hold me m God, hold me wherever I am')
"O Iesu mawr, rho'th anian bur." ('O Great Jesus, give your pure essence')
"Fel y mynnot, O fy Arglwydd, Dy Ewyllys yw fy ngrym." ('As you wish my Lord, your will is my strength')

MEMORIAL SERVICE
This was held on Sunday evening 22nd April 1945 at the Apostolic Temple, Penygroes. Pastor's T.V. Lewis and Hugh Dawson officiated.
Ps. Dawson ministered using the text: "O thou man of God, there is death in the pot." (IIKings 4:40)
a. Dearth in the land
b. Danger and death because of dearth

had ministered for between six and seven years in the Bradford District and called upon Elder Thomas Riley to address the service:

" 'Greater love hath no man than this, than that a man lay down his life for his friends.' I can confirm Ps. Lewis' remarks; I believe that our late brother, Jones Williams, has given his life for us. He was with us, at Great Horton church and we learned to love him and his family. Mrs Williams was a deaconess with us. We have pleasant memories of him, which will never leave us.

I represent Bradford Area this afternoon and I am here to express our deep love, our gratitude to God and our deep sympathy to Mrs Williams, the children and Jones' brothers and sisters in their great sorrow. We mourn with you and we weep with you.

We have heard many expressions of his work this afternoon, but what would be the expression of God if He were to speak of him? I would suggest:

> *'Speak through the tempest of the mourners' tears*
> *A still, small voice, like music low and sweet*
> *'I measure not man's life by years*
> *Time does not of itself make life complete*
> *Cut down so early in the midst of strife*
> *You see a broken arc – but up above*
> *You'll see the perfect circle of his life*
> *Rounded complete by sacrificial love*
> *You would have given your life for him, I trow*
> *With a like love he gave his life for thee*
> *Mourn not that he is crowned with glory now'*
> *And safely housed in paradise with Me*

to sing and rejoice. He could not get on with his message because the power of God came with it.

Above all, he was used in prophetic ministry in a mighty way and we mourn for him.

Pastor J.D. Eynon

"Memory is a very strange faculty. The moment I heard of the passing away of my dear brother there flashed back into my mind a mental picture of one of the first times I heard him speak. Strangely enough, I never thought of this instance until this particular moment. The message he was speaking that day was this: 'I know whom I have believed, and am persuaded that He is able to keep that which I have committed unto Him against that day.' As he stood in the pulpit the sun was streaming through the window, and his face lit up, and there was a halo over his head. As the message declared, He is able to keep his servant and He is able to keep His Church.

If I were to interpret the heart and life of Ps. Jones Williams aright in the midst of our sorrow, it would be to proclaim the truth that, 'He is still able to keep!' His servant who is with the Lord. He also is still able to keep us. This experience, however, is heavy to our hearts and memories.

On behalf of the pastors and saints of the Hereford Area, and the young pastors entering the ministry, we wish to extend to Mrs Williams, her family and relatives our most sincere sympathy and the assurance of our prayers. We pray that God will help them, comfort them and carry them through and that, in all things, God will be glorified."

The Chairman referred to the fact that the deceased

with Paul, 'For me to live is Christ.' Now that he has gone, we know all is well with him; absent from the body, but present with the Lord, for to be with Christ is far better.

I just want to touch on his work. Two things were outstanding; his pioneering abilities and the prophetic ministry through his lips. He had great pioneering abilities in prophecy. France seemed impossible to get into but, through the word of the Lord, God gave us the key through Jones Williams and that country was opened to the Apostolic revelation and doctrine. Not only was he used in prophecy, and told us what had to be done, but he himself went forth to many nations and laid the foundations of the work. He travelled to far countries and many came to see the truth.

We will never forget what he, and others, did to bring this church to the place that it is in now. Above all we will remember him as a prophet of the Lord (as we have heard) from Dan to Beersheba, not only in these countries in the homeland, but from one end of the earth to the other. God helped him to prophecy about these places.

We also praise God for his preaching abilities and ministry. One of the things I will never forget is when he came to Scotland at the beginning of our association with Wales, he preached at out Renfrew Hall, which was crammed to the door. As he ministered on 'the voice crying in the wilderness' the power of God came down in such a remarkable way that the people were falling down under the power of the words through his mouth. A few years ago in Penygroes, God came down in a wonderful way and Jones Williams rose and began knew he was seriously ill, but even then, when I heard what had happened on Monday night, I had a great shock, and I know it will come in a similar way to people in Scotland.

Having come once or twice in the early days to Scotland, they knew him very well. First of all way back in 1919, and many times with his brother Dan, he ministered the riches of God. Though we feel it very much, Mrs Williams and family will feel it much more. I am bringing the sympathy of the saints from Scotland in this hour of trial.

One thing that was outstanding in my brother Jones' life (I was very much with him in the earlier days) was his courage and convictions. He was a man of great courage. I used to admire my own father, and often wished for the courage that he had. I can say the same about Jones Williams; he had the courage to say what he believed – his convictions. God raises up different types of channels; Peters' as well as Johns'; Paul as well as Barnabas. God gave Jones Williams that courage in his calling as prophet. He would never have been able to be such a channel as he was, so wonderfully used in the Councils, in the Conventions and in the Church generally unless God had given him such wonderful courage in giving forth the message and the word of God.

Another characteristic was his love for Christ the Lord and the cross of Christ. I have been sitting beside him so often and heard him singing hymns about Christ and His Cross. His soul was exalted, his heart thrilled and bubbling over as a Welshman. Every time I sat beside him I knew, and realised, that he was rejoicing in the Saviour that he loved. He could say

I shall ever remember the prophetic words through his lips (as well as through the lips of other prophets). Thank God! He has other faithful channels in the Church. The words of God through His prophet have become part and parcel of my life. We have heard God and heaven's mysteries, through the divine oracles, break upon our wondering ears. We have memories that can never be erased. As a prophet, Jones Williams poured riches from the throne of God into our lives. The lips are silent, but we will, ever cherish the words that came through him, from the living God. The Church has been enriched, for something has come into existence at Penygroes in Wales, and in the nations, through the word of God, that came so faithfully through him. He, as Moses, saw the invisible God, and waxed strong.

I say with reverence, it is impossible to bury Jones Williams; we can bury his body, but his spirit and soul live on. His influence and ministry must live, because the God that took him up from the dunghill also lives. My heart yearns for thee, my brother; our fellowship together has been sweet and intimate. The Church has suffered a great loss in the passing on of William Jones Williams. Still we thank God for His elective grace, and that he has had, and is having, such men in these days. We attribute everything to the God of all grace, from whom cometh every good gift."

Pastor T. Napier Turnbull

"I must say that when I heard of the death of Ps. Jones Williams, it was a great shock to me. I was in London two weeks ago and went to his home; but he had been taken away to hospital. From what I heard, I whom he saw had the same verdict, 'Mr Williams you have killed yourself; you have driven yourself to death, and you have to pay the penalty', the penalty of constant faithfulness to the Master. Some have lived to eighty or ninety years, Jones Williams, dying at 53, has lived far longer than many who have lived to the age of ninety, because of the flame and burning passion in his soul, and his endeavour to meet the cry of many in this land, and among the nations, for the apostolic vision to be declared to them.

Not only had he travelled far geographically among the nations, and given us an example in service, but God alone knows the inward pangs he suffered, not only through the ministry of preaching, but in enduring the stones that the prophets of God must bare – those inward sufferings that the channels of God have to go through. No one knows the depths of that hidden suffering, the invisible burden that this man of God bore. He went far in the realm of service, and not only so, but he was a pioneer in prophetic realms. Everyone will not understand such a statement, but you Apostolic people, I am sure, will understand what I mean.

We have read of great men in the realm of science, and the amazing discoveries that have been brought to light. Other men have become great politicians in our land: but I venture to say today, as in the passage read to us from Jeremiah, that, as that prophet was chosen before he was born, and sanctified from the womb, Jones Williams also had been sanctified from the womb, ordained before the world was formed, as 'a prophet to the nations' to pioneer in prophetic realms. I may forget his sermons, and his outstanding preaching ministry, but fy Nuw, dal fi 'mhob man.' ('Hold me, my God, hold me wherever I am').

I do not know how far he had intuition of his pending home-call. Little did I dream that, in going over that and other hymns, which contain such a wonderful expression of heart longings for God, that he was coming to the finale, in giving the utterance of his soul through these hymns. 'It is a wonderful hymn' said he, of 'Dal fi, fy Nuw!' I am mystified. On the one hand, I cannot realise that Jones has gone; yet he is still with us somehow. I cannot realise that Jones Williams is dead, and that his body is here.

Jones had travelled very far, in more ways than one. First of all geographically. He spoke in Kennington a little while ago, and gave a most interesting account of his travels from the beginning – marvellous experiences. If my memory serves me aright he mentioned that he had been in seventeen countries preaching the gospel, and carrying the banner of truth, as we have heard today, as a faithful preacher and minister of God's Word. Only God could have enabled him to do so. What a transformation! Especially when we remember that, in the early days, he thought much of the art of boxing and of other worldly things. But God, through the channel of prophecy used at that time, sent Pastor Dan to fetch him, and his friend (D.H. Williams) - you may have heard the story - God not only saved him, but changed him, and made him a channel for His predestined purposes.

Jones travelled very far also in sacrificial service – he has died a martyr for the Word of God. He told me that he feared to go to the doctor; but subsequent events compelled him to see a Specialist. Each of the doctors service to be accomplished here, and to be continued beyond 'the glen of the gloom'. May your sentiments and our association with you in your sentiments today, invade the Apostolic Church, and all the branches of the Christian Church in this locality, and elsewhere, so that we may go on to fight the good fight of faith, to believe in the God whom our brother believed in, and of whom he preached.

Thank God for the service he has rendered in various spheres according to his light and convictions. May God raise men and women to hold the lamp of truth and the banner of spiritual verity of life, as set forth in the gospel, and the survival of human personality, redeemed by the grace of God. Our brother has gone; his sunset while it was yet day, but the natural sun, though it goes down, rises on another continent. Though the sun of his life has gone down comparatively early, he has passed through the gloom, beyond our vision, he has risen and is shining beyond the shadows. ' Henffych i'r dydd y cawn eto gwyrdd!' ('Hail to the day we may meet again!').

Pastor W.H. Lewis

"Apart from relating my 'Internee Camp' experiences last October, this is the first time that I have been privileged to speak in the Temple since coming back from my long internment in Germany. Little did I realise that almost my next opportunity to speak here would be at the funeral of Ps. Jones Williams. I saw him a number of times lately and had many a heart to heart chat with him, most intimately. We had many a prayer together. He was exceedingly fond of the hymn, 'Dal fi, perhaps had not heard, as yet, of the passing over the 'great divide' of his dear younger brother.

There was an affinity and intimacy in spirit which could not be discerned with the reason and could not be conveyed, between kindred spirits such as their departed friend, himself, and those who has spoken already, and his brother the President currently in America. "May the anguish which accompanies this separation be very soon transformed in the experience of the widow, and children and all the relatives.

When I visited our departed brother in London, little did I think at that time that I would be present at his funeral so soon. I have very vivid memories of his kindness when visiting him at Cardiff and elsewhere, and the conversation in regard to the book written by him already referred to. I mourn his loss along with you; to worship God and thank Him for calling our brother into the work, and for anointing him with the oil of gladness above his fellows. If he died in London, he will never die in Penygroes, as witness this assembly and the representatives from various parts of the country here today.

Well, he is buried today. No! He cannot be buried. You cannot bury the soul of a man on fire with the divine. You can bury the body. Let us remember that in these days of secularity and unbelief, when the Gospel of immortality is challenged. May God bless this solemn occasion to deepen our sense of the reality of the life that is by faith in Jesus Christ. There is nothing more romantic than an individual Christian, a man of faith, who goes forth not knowing where he is going, yet knowing to the full that there is 'a land that is fairer than day', and a service that is better than any secular ago. He was called to the full-time ministry and also called to go to China and Japan through the prophet declaring the will of God in that respect.

Since leaving Plymouth for London he had co-worked with Jones and had received much hospitality at his home. He was with him at his home in Edgeware and visited him in the hospital. "I saw Jones through the window last Sunday and would have gone in, but was stayed because he was so ill. I am a better man today because of him. Again and again I have exclaimed, 'Well, well!' as I have listened to words divine through his lips. I am glad that I have been privileged to see and know him, perhaps most intimately these last few weeks. He has gone from us, but we will meet again one day. "Blessed is his lot; he is resting from his labours, and his works do follow him."

Rev. L. Berian James (who with Rev. Brynmor Thomas, 'Mynydd Seion', Rev. Handel Turner, 'Calfaria' and Rev. Henry Evans, Pontlliw, represented the local denominational pulpits).

As minister of the oldest church in Penygroes, and a friend of the departed, and his family, whom he had known for many years (and who had received instruction in the Christian religion at his chapel, culminating in the call to the ministry of Pastors Jones Williams and D.P. Williams), he wished on behalf of his church, and his brother ministers at Penygroes, to express their sympathy with Mrs Williams and family. Also with the brothers and sisters that remained and, in particular with their brother and friend Ps. D.P. Williams who had crossed the Atlantic, and who changing years' a friendship was formed in unique circumstances. They had been prophets together (not in the general sense accepted in the religious world) but called as channels in the Apostolic Church. Jones was saved a month before the speaker and, one year later, the Lord commanded him to go to Llwynhendy. They had been praying for three weeks that the Lord would reveal Himself in the 'apostolic fashion.'

By an audible voice the Lord spoke to Omri Jones saying, "*Thou shalt pray no longer; thou are the man*", for they had asked God to send them a prophet who would lead them into 'higher realms.' On the following Sunday Ps. Jones Williams, and his brother, D.P. Williams, came to Llwynhendy and separated Omri Jones as a prophet in the church, under the instruction of the Holy Spirit. A bond was thus formed between them. "We shall miss him; a faithful friend and servant of God." The loss was a personal one for they had lived and loved through many changing years.

Pastor C.C. Ireson (London)

"I was preaching at Kennington last evening on the subject of 'tears', and I almost feel them coming. I do not want to weep, or add many tears again to those who have been weeping since last Sunday evening when the news was conveyed of the passing of this great man. I am (despite the 'becloudment' in the spirit) reminded of the words of Jesus, "What I do thou knowest not now, but thou shalt know hereafter." "Blessed are the dead which die in the Lord....their works do follow them.""

Ps. Ireson was present because of prophetic words through the lips of Jones Williams almost twenty years mourning, and were following one who had 'gone before'.

God had knitted his heart to the departed as the hearts of Jonathan and David and, in losing 'Jones bach' he had lost a great friend, brother and fellow-worker who had been in most of the Overseas Missionary Council meetings. Overseas there would be a sense of loss of a dear brother, a pioneer, a faithful servant and a prophet of God. He was 'faithful unto death' who, though dead, yet speaketh. He was one of those who died in faith, not having received the promise, but having seen them afar off, was persuaded.

Jones Williams, though his life was finished here, still lived. They rejoiced that someday they should meet face to face.

Pastor D.T. Rennie. (Chairman of Ministry Committee)

Ps. Rennie referred to ICor.15:13 "But now is Christ risen from the dead." This was not the end; if it were so, they would have no hope; but they had a glorious hope. The morning would soon dawn when they should see their dear beloved brother and be with him in the presence of the Lord. On behalf of the Ministry Committee, and the Sunday Schools of the church throughout the world, he extended to Mrs Williams and family the deep sympathy which was felt by all for each one concerned. The Lord would fulfil His promise to be a husband to the widow, a father to the fatherless; to whose sustaining strength he commended them.

Pastor J. Omri Jones (Llanelli) had lived with, and loved, the prophet Jones Williams. 'Through many which they were congregated, was due to prophetic utterance through the lips of the deceased. In the dark days of 1940 God spoke through him, "*I will give you (Britain) the victory*". Despite opposition, he still gave out the divine word.

He was also a great preacher. Many would remember his sermon on "The Four Hallelujahs" of Revelation. The speaker would never forget the impression while Jones discoursed on the verse, "This is a faithful saying", and his reference to our Lord "dying from home" (Jesus leaving His home in glory to die for humanity).

He was also a great pastor. A Cardiff friend had written to say that a wreath should be bought on behalf of the Cardiff assembly, and added that it should bear a card, with the inscription, "In cherished and loving memory of a great little shepherd."

Everyone who had the privilege of sitting under his ministry and pastorate knew that to be so. The 'great little shepherd' had lived, for the last few years, in the 'blitzed' city of London. He (the speaker) had visited him, and found Ps Jones Williams more concerned about the saints than about himself. Whether Cardiff was blitzed, or London, he went out of his way to see that his flock was all right.

Very sweet was the thought that he would lie in ground, forever sacred, because it had come to being as 'God's acre' through a word from God spoken through himself as a prophet.

Pastor Herbert Cousen (Chairman of the Missionary Committee, Missionary Centre, Bradford) voiced the feeling of all connected to the missionary work, in an expression of love and sympathy, with those who were mean, but I have not the time, but I will read a portion of the poem on the last page: -

> "*Servant of Christ stand fast amid the scorn*
> *Of men who little know or love thy Lord*
> *Turn not aside from toil, cease not to warn*
> *Comfort and teach, trust Him for thy reward*
> *A few more moments' suffering, and then*
> *Cometh sweet rest from all thy heart's deep pain."*

So, to Ruth (who, being so young, does not understand), Mark, May, Omri and all those who were dear to him, and as one who loved and admired him, I would say that this booklet, not only photographs the outward man, but is a record of his inward man. Fearless and faithful, loyal and loving, 'Jones bach!' ('Little/ loved Jones' – Ed) we love thee, and wait to see thee again!

Pastor W.M. Humphreys (General Secretary) referred to a letter received from Ps. Frank Hodges (another pioneer) as representative of numerous letters and telegrams received expressing sympathy, extolling the deceased for his ministry and prophetic utterances as international prophet. The speaker referred to the history of Samuel the prophet as typical of that of Ps. Jones Williams, who had, at a past funeral, expressed his desire that, in his own (too-soon) funeral, Jesus should be exalted with a "Hwyl" (not an easy word to express in English – 'a depth of feeling in exuberance' - Ed), nothing mournful.

The A.C. saints realised that, as a prophet, God had spoken through him. The existence of the Temple, in

Our hearts go out to the President (Ps. D.P. Williams), brother of the departed. What this will mean to him, perhaps not one of us will ever know, but his Father in heaven knows, and He will comfort him, I am sure. For it is not only a severance only of brother from brother, but from us, members of the same Body of Christ. We believe in the divine ordination of God.

We sorrow also with the six brothers and three sisters, and the rest of the family. This pile of telegrams and letters will give you some indication of the esteem with which our dear brother has been remembered and held. No doubt there are many more to follow. I want to dissociate from its context part of a verse in ITimothy 4:6.

"*If thou put the brethren in remembrance of these things, thou shalt be a good minister of Jesus Christ*" etc.

Of the deceased it can be said, "Thou hast been", but also, "thou shalt be", because his position is assured by what he has done here upon the earth. These words were used by Ps. Jones Williams himself, in the title of the booklet published by him, when a pastor at Cardiff.

The highest possible testimony that I personally could give is what he wrote in his book, "A Good Minister of Jesus Christ" (which is of the very highest standard), and what he himself endeavoured to be. Can I give him a higher testimony than that which is found in the pages of this book of his, which exalts the responsible ministry of the servant of Christ to such a high standard? I do not think I can.

This booklet carried with it not only a photograph of the outward man, but a record, I believe, of the inward man. I would dearly like to quote to you passage after passage, to prove and to emphasise what I was no surprise to his numerous friends to hear the medical opinion that his 'journey's oft', and care for the flock in the Kennington, London district, had hastened the end. Very moving were the tributes paid but space will allow only for a few summaries. The usual funeral sermon was set aside so that those colleagues might express their appreciation of the services which this true servant of God, had rendered to His cause worldwide.

After a short service at 'Mispah', Bryn Road, Penygroes, under the charge of Ps. T. Vaughan Lewis, appropriate scriptures were read by Ps. Thomas Davies (scribe) and prayer was offered by Ps. Wm. I. James. On the roadway, outside the house, Ps. John H. Hewitt gave a hymn that was sung by the large concourse; afterwards proceeding to the Temple.

After opening the service in prayer, Ps. Hugh Dawson (A.C. Vice President) said: -

"Dear Mrs. Williams, Ruth, Mark, May, Omri and friends. We have met today with great grief in our hearts. Visiting Penygroes on previous occasions has meant much joy to me personally, because of the time of rejoicing in the House of the Lord, the ministry we have received in God's House and in this village of Penygroes. We are joined in this grief by many Apostolic members whose number will, as the news is flashed to the uttermost parts of the earth, join with us in conveying to those, who are mourning at this time, such a wealth of sympathy and such a message of love, as only can be put in the hearts of human beings, by God Himself. We are beginning to understand how to mourn with those who mourn. We sorrow today with those who are sorrowing.

A REPORT OF THE FUNERAL OF THE LATE PASTOR W. JONES WILLIAMS

One of the most progressive churches in the land, as well as overseas, has sustained a severe loss in the decease of Pastor W. Jones Williams, born at Garnfoel, Penygroes, Carmarthen aged 53. A convert of the Welsh Revival, he left his work as a coal-miner at the Emlyn Anthracite Colliery, Penygroes and, with his brother, Ps. D.P. Williams (presently in U.S.A. and Canada preaching in the Apostolic assemblies), pioneered, at first with the Apostolic Faith Church (Pastor Hutchinson) and afterwards founded the Apostolic Church, which has made phenomenal progress in the five continents.

The late Ps. Jones Williams had visited twenty-seven countries in the course of his travels in the Apostolic cause. He maintained by his ministry the fundamental truths of the Bible and, especially, the truth evangelical and the early order of church government as known to St Paul.

At the Apostolic Temple, Penygroes, a last tribute was paid to the memory of the deceased on Friday last, 20th April 1945. Supported by Pastors T.V. Lewis (Temple, Penygroes), W.M. Humphreys (Ammanford, General Secretary at Penygroes H.Q.) and representative ministers, Vice-President Hugh Dawson (Glasgow) gave presiding guidance. A congregation of over a thousand people filled the edifice.

Death occurred from cardiac trouble while deceased was a patient at St Andrew's Hospital, London and it

The strenuous labours of the servants of God, away so often from home, unable to give that attention to their offspring which they would desire, has brought, to many of them, much anxiety. Ps. Williams hearth was successively under the supervision of two understanding mothers. Of both he declared, 'A virtuous woman rejoiceth her husband, and he shall fulfil the years of his life in peace. A good wife is a good portion, which shall be given in the lot of them that feareth the Lord.' In the cause of the Lord, such women, tested and tried, have proved their worth.

In this respect, the words of William Cowper (the writer of the 'Olney Hymns', and other exquisite verse, as well as letters of much charm) express the thoughts of many a thankful Christian husband: -

> *What is there in the vale of life*
> *Half so delightful as a wife*
> *When friendship, love and peace combine*
> *To stamp the marriage-bond divine?*
> *The stream of pure and genuine love*
> *Derives its current from above*
> *And earth a second Eden shows*
> *Where'er the healing water flows*

William Cowper.

time, Mrs Jones Williams was very ill, and the doctors warned the household that he could offer no hope of recovery.

In the circumstances, the fortitude and faith of the mother shone with much lustre. Her words, to her distracted husband were "Jones you must go, the Lord has called you *I have never said, 'No!' to His will during all these years and I will not say it now. If he takes me while you are away, then all will be well.*" (The event is recorded earlier in the book – Ed).

The week after the family moved to 'Kapi Oki', Ammanford Road, Llandebie, and for a year and six months, Mrs Williams was sustained of the Lord to enjoy her husband's company. There it was she died much to the sorrow of all that knew her patient and cheerful person.

Ps. Jones Williams second wife (whom he married on 1st March 1938) was the daughter of the much esteemed John and Rachel Evans of Crossnant Farm, Capel Isaac, Llandilo. She was the widow of Mr Daniel Davies of Nantyffin Farm, Capel Isaac, to whom she bore a son. While in charge of the assembly at Cardiff, and during his many visits in the Pontypridd Area to other assemblies, from March 1938 to 1943, her domestic and spiritual help was invaluable, especially during the German 'blitz'.

Later, at Edgware, London (from April 1943 to 1945) those trying times proved the wisdom of the pastor's choice of a helpmeet, Mrs Williams' loving care and forethought being of much comfort and consolation. Of the union, there is Ruth, who is progressing in stature and grace, while David Omri, of Mrs Williams' first marriage, is a true disciple of the Lord.

April 1945. His body lies interred with that of his first wife.

The strain, disappointments, encouragement's and progress of the servants of God could hardly be borne were it not for the help, comfort and wise counsel of their wives. Ps. Jones Williams first wife was Mary Ann Evans, whom he married at Llandilo on January 25th 1912. She was the youngest daughter of, the godly couple, Mr William and Mrs Mary Evans of Pantcaemelyn Farm, Penygroes, who reared a family of boys and girls noted for their firm, and conscientious, after-lives. Two other daughters were Jane, the wife of Deacon Tom Jones (who accompanied the two brothers on their Australian tour in 1934/5, at his own expense), and Sarah, wife of Overseer John Evans (later to be Pastor of Carmel, Pontardulais and the A.C. assemblies of Australia).

These three daughters lived honourable lives and were of strength to their husbands in the faith. All three lie in the Temple Cemetery, Penygroes, awaiting a triumphant resurrection.

Mrs Mary Ann Williams bore the prophet two children; the present Mrs John Evans ('May'), whose husband is now pastor of the A.C. at Porthleven, Cornwall, and Mark, who married Lois (daughter of apostle A.H. Lewis, London and one time Superintendent of the church in Denmark).

An indication of the sacrificial spirit of Mrs Williams can be deduced from the fact that, during her husbands public ministry, only one Christmas (that of 1936) did he spend at home, such were the calls for his help at home and abroad. The brothers Williams left these shores for Australia on September 12th 1934. At that *and your minds by bringing burdens and sorrow concerning this, that and the other. But remember that he has taunted, 'If Thou art the Son of God, save Thyself and us!' It was not by giving obedience to that gibe that salvation was procurable. The salvation to the 'us' (that is, to you) – and to all – was to come by His refusal to save Himself.*

.... But He made no effort to get free. For what purpose? Because in His bondage, and in the fulfilment of what the bondage would bring forth, He defeated them without 'saving Himself'.

It is for you now to remain in His freedom and realise that the satanic host is outside of you and they shall not touch one of you.... Remember that I am within you and, as I am within you, I am stronger, greater and better than he who is without.

Therefore, there is no need for you to fear them that are without.

Realise that I have the keys of death and hell. Rejoice in this truth and say, at all times when under oppression, 'The Lord is within, and He will preserve me eternally.''...

But God's hour came for His prophet to be called home. It can be said of Pastor William Jones Williams, as is written of Elisha the prophet, "Now Elisha was fallen sick of his sickness whereof he died" (II Kings 13:14).

Doubtless, the strain of his early collier life (straining on inclined headings had brought on varicose state in the veins of his legs), and labours oft called a halt to the courageous heart while a pastor among the London assemblies. The change came after a hot bath, which weakened the heart's action, and, finally, brought that faithful pendulum to a stop.

Entering the hospital, he received all that modern medical skill could muster, but the end came on 15th

CHAPTER 18

THE HOMECALL

How little of a life work can be contained in a volume such as this! We have been unable, because of the exigencies of space and cost, to delve into the diaries, for 1918/19, of the late Pastor Jones Williams, and reconstruct a tapestry depicting his early and late labours with his brother. The latter, it is hoped, will be the subject of a later volume.

The willingness of the prophet to help others, by a timely word from the Lord, won the hearts of all sincere enquirers in the early years. The writer of this chapter remembers the meetings held in Bradford when the Missionary Movement came into being.

Satanic oppression was heavy and we returned very late from one meeting, soon after midnight on April 18th, 1922, to our lodging at Ps. H.V. Chanter's Manningham house. The Lord was sought for a word of enlightenment and guidance for the scribe (Pastor T. Davies) whose privilege it has been to accompany the two brothers, since July 1919, during the first 28 years of church progress. The principle of action given in the word is worth noting: -

"You have seen before you arrived here how the enemy has raged and opposed. He has done his worst to try and break upon the peaceful plan of my purpose but he has failed. Victory has been achieved. Now you need to remember, though this has taken place, that he will trouble your spirits

of a memorial, this great and growing spiritual movement, belting the globe, is an acknowledgement to the great spiritual forces that visited our nation in 1904/5.

The transforming power of the glorious Gospel, when it is followed by an obedience to the will and ways of God, to be seen so clearly in the Word of God, is the Lord's way of building His Church – the Church which is His Body, the fullness of Him that filleth all in all.

We can never be grateful enough to God for such a Revival.

"*Remember the words which were spoken before by the holy prophets*" (II Peter 3:2)

> *When the lamp is shattered*
> *The light in the dust lies dead*
> *When the cloud is scattered*
> *The rainbow's glory is shed*
> *When the lute is broken*
> *Sweet tones are remembered not*
> *When the lips have spoken*
> *Loved accents are soon forgot*
> (Shelley.)

Calabar, and the surrounding area, are upwards of 200 churches with 26 African pastors, 28 paid workers, 18,000 members and about 18,000 adherents.

Gold Coast

This country, once a "white man's grave", and now enjoying self-government, has 21 African pastors, 30 ordained overseers with 352 churches (having a membership of over 17,000). In 1940 the Annual Easter Convention attracted about 100 visitors and in 1953 over 20,000 Africans attended these services.

In addition to this weight of evidence, the Apostolic work in Denmark is of such a size and strength, that they are responsible, as a Missionary Advisory Board, to help the work that is steadily developing in the continent of Europe. They, with our help, have established in Berlin, 200 miles behind the iron curtain, a chain of 5 churches that are in constant contact with visitors from the eastern zone.

An established work in Germany, France, Italy and Switzerland, with interests in Norway and Sweden, has necessitated the forming of a European Apostolic Council, which meets twice per year in Switzerland, Denmark or Great Britain, according to the need.

Child evangelism, Youthful witnessing and active evangelical efforts, in every church, couples with a great zeal for ministering the Word of God from an open Bible, constitutes a fellowship which is deep, strong and true.

The Temple in Penygroes was dedicated to the memory of the Revival of 1904/5. The new Convention Hall will also be dedicated in the same way, but far beyond any earthly structure, raised by way baptism in the Spirit, and kept alive down the years by the continual seeking after His enabling power, has resulted in a most remarkable passion for missionary work amongst coloured people. So much so, that Apostolic missionaries have gone to Japan, China, India, New Guinea, New Hebrides, the Aborigines of Australia, the Maoris of New Zealand, the Bantus of South Africa and the various tribes in West Africa.

Some details of the growth of the work, in these rapidly developing countries, will serve to illustrate the great spiritual vitality that is still existing:-

Lagos, Nigeria

In this most important city, and the immediate surrounding country, in 1953 we had 15 African pastors, 42 paid workers, 7 men in training, 120 churches with 2,256 members and 4,794 adherents.

Ilesha, Nigeria

It is here that we have established an Educational Training Centre, supported by the Government, which prepares Africans for the ministry as well as giving a measure of secular education. We have in this area 10 African pastors, 35 paid workers and 150 churches with 8,000 members.

Ibo, Nigeria

In this large area we have 11 pastors, 35 paid workers, 150 churches with a membership of 6,835.

Calabar

To many of us the name is so familiar, reminding us continually of the life and service of Mary Slesser. In formulated for the building of a Convention Hall to seat, at least, 3,000 people, which also will be dedicated to the memory of the Revival.

If the continual, developing activities, in this country of one of the products of the Revival can be said to testify to the great blessing, received during those far away days of 1904/5, what can be said of the overseas and missionary activities, some of which I am able to give you in this broadcast?

The two monthly periodicals published, entitled "The Apostolic Herald" and the "Riches of Grace", carrying in them home and missionary news, doctrinal articles and prophecies in Welsh and English, slowly began to reach many countries overseas. Many small groups of Welsh folk, starving for news of their own beloved country, with their inborn desire for the things of God, both in song, sermon and Welsh 'Hwyl', eagerly read these publications, and found themselves in agreement with the moving of the Spirit of God.

Other groups of English speaking emigrants, and seekers after truth, read and believed until today the Apostolic Church is established in Canada, Australia, New Zealand, South Africa and U.S.A., having sent ministers from Wales, Scotland, Ireland and England to all these countries.

Even though there are only a few remaining ministers who remember the soul-stirring time of 1904/5, yet our present ministers freely acknowledge the debt we owe, as a Church, to this country of Wales, and those people living here in those days, who heard, believed and received the message of God.

The intense evangelical fervour manifested in the Revival, communicated to whoever experienced the basic salary with extra allowances for children. This community of interest amongst the salaried ministers, coupled with the fact that all salaries are paid from the central fund in Glasgow, has been the means of the strong helping the weak, and the forging of a strong link of fellowship between all the churches.

In the village of Penygroes, the Apostolic Church Bible School has been built (loaned to the County Council for an Isolation Hospital during the Second World War), where students from Denmark, Switzerland, Italy, Germany and South Africa, along with students from Great Britain, have been trained and sent out to minister in many lands.

The influx of visitors to the Convention at Penygroes, held every August Bank Holiday, from many overseas countries, as well as Gt. Britain, has necessitated the building of a campus extending over an acre, where hundreds are accommodated. Visitors from Norway, Sweden, Denmark, France, Germany, Italy, Switzerland, Australia, New Zealand, Canada, U.S.A., South Africa and West Africa often take part in these great gatherings, where the Missionary offering last August (1954) amounted to £2,700.

Meals are served form a most up-to-date kitchen, in a dining hall seating 300 persons. This year, during the nine days of the Convention, over 10,000 meals were served and about 800 visitors were accommodated, both on the Church campus, and in houses in the village, with bus-loads coming daily from many of the Welsh valleys. The large Temple, built in 1933 at Penygroes, in memory of the 1904/5 Revival, is unable to accommodate the crowds, even with a temporary marquee erected for the occasion, so plans are being a great flood of light upon some Scriptures that had heretofore been as closed as a book. The Headship of Christ, both towards the Church, and of the Church, began to take new meaning when it was realised that the Father had given His Son to be Head of the Church, that is, organic Head of an organism and not an organisation. The Son, after His ascension and arrival on the Throne, had given, and was giving, "...*apostles, prophets, evangelists, pastors and teachers for the perfecting of the saints, for the work of the ministry, for the edifying of the Body of Christ, till we all come to the unity of the faith, and of the knowledge of the stature of the fullness of Christ*", and that the Holy Spirit was willing to give severally, as He willed, the nine supernatural gifts enumerated by Paul; educational, operational and oral.

Thus, the Apostolic Church was brought into being – a direct product of the 1904/5 Revival.

With roots 1937 had established deep down in this great visitation of God, this body of people, with its vision of the Headship of Christ, in nearly 300 churches in Great Britain. The principle of central government had been established in Wales, Scotland, Ireland and England with a 'Constitution and Guiding Principles' registered in the Supreme Court of Judicature, London.

Penygroes had been established as General Headquarters, Glasgow as Finance Centre and Bradford, Yorkshire as Missionary Centre, with the British Isles divided into Areas and Districts.

With the principle of tithing established from the beginning, in the hearts of the members, there was never any necessity for recourse to secular means of raising money. With the belief that they should have all things in common, all the ministers are paid the same

Although this great blessing was first experienced in Wales, many other countries and peoples benefited, in an increasing way, as the news spread, until today it is possible to contact older people, in almost every Christian country, who speaks in terms of deep respect and thankfulness to God for such a visitation.

The reading of historical records, dating back 50 years, may be inspiring to the few but the more thrilling story, of some present day activities, resulting from such far away happenings, will surely interest and inspire many more. So, we come to speak of the Apostolic Church and its relation to the Revival.

In the hill-village of Penygroes, Carmarthenshire, from which a glorious panoramic view of the Amman Valley, backed by the Black Mountains, can be seen, this great Revival fire burned brightly, and hot, for many months. As people continued to meet for prayer, testimony, ministry of the Word of God and fellowship, the Holy Ghost fell on them, as it is recorded in the book of Acts. Many spoke in the unknown tongues mentioned by Paul in his epistle to the Corinthians. This, indeed, was so unorthodox that some refused to believe such experiences were for the twentieth century. Many others, through searching the Scriptures, were led to believe both through the Word of God and by their personal experience that this baptism in the Spirit was that which was so urgently needed by all Christians.

Very soon the news, of this further visitation of the Holy Spirit, was carried over the hills and down the valleys of Wales until groups of people were tarrying, in many places, for this baptism of power.

With this baptism in the Spirit there came, as it were,

CHAPTER 17

THE APOSTOLIC CHURCH
1904 – 1955

Copy draft of intended broadcast
by Pastor Hugh Dawson
President of the A.C. Council.

BBC Cardiff, slightly modified from the following script made broadcast on Thursday 25th November 1954 from 10.00 to 10.15am:

"To many people, the striking manifestations of the Holy Spirit amongst the fervent Welsh folk, particularly during the years 1904 and 1905, are only a matter of history.

Much has been written on the subject by journalists, who flocked to the Principality, to report for their daily papers on the extraordinary happenings of those days; By critics, who condemned the religious fervour as unseemly; By curious visitors, some who travelled across continents and seas to see this new thing; and by religious leaders who recognised such a visitation was the 'Revival' for which so many people had been praying so long.

It is not at all surprising that, to many people, this tremendous spiritual upheaval became associated with Wales, and was, and is, often spoken as the Welsh 1904 Revival.

Sound the Gospel of grace abroad
There's life in the risen Lord
Spread the news of the gift of God
There's life in the risen Lord
God above desires it
Sinful man requires it
Tell it around, let it abound
There's life in the risen Lord

Saints, apostles and prophets, all
Published with one accord
This deliverance from the fall
This life in the risen Lord
Glory be to Jesus
Who from bondage freed us
Tell it around, let it abound
There's life in the risen Lord

P.P. Bliss

"Cry out and shout, thou inhabitant of Zion: for great is the Holy One of Israel in the midst of thee"
(Isa.12:6)

"Jerusalem, Zion, is not only a place of bricks, stones and mortar, but the souls of men regenerated by My Spirit."
(Prophetic word, summarised, through Ps. Jones Williams)

"I will use every device and invention of man to proclaim the Gospel of redemption by blood"
(Prophetic word, summarised, through Ps. Jones Williams)

"But His word was in mine heart as a burning fire shut up in my bones, and I was weary with forbearing, and I could not stay. For I heard the defaming of many, fear on every side....But the Lord is with me as a mighty terrible one."
(Jeremiah 20:9-11)

Climax — Gal.3:13 'He was made a curse for us'.
Consummation — Rev.22:3 Curse removed. New heaven and earth.

The rightful Heir to the eternal throne ascends.

'Worthy the Lamb' who died to save us
'Worthy the Lamb' let is sound through earth and sky
'Worthy the Lamb' sing the angels in chorus
'Worthy the Lamb' our redemption draweth nigh
Worthy of honour from highest archangels
Worthy of glory of the universe around
Worthy of majesty, pow'r, adoration
'Worthy the Lamb' the loved and lost are found

banished. Daily duties forgotten. John the Baptist the best man; friend of the Bridegroom.

8. The Light of the Lamb – Rev.21:23
   There is a common expression regarding many a person. 'Was he not good and kind? He was the light of the company or home.' Ours, after all, is borrowed light (John 18:12).
   "I am the Light", "The True Light", and "The Light of the world" is Jesus.
   Stars glitter, the moon shines but still its night.
   Sun rises, day comes.
   The Lamb's light is greater than all. No night there.

   To my blessed Lord and Saviour as He walks before me Here
   I am getting nearer, nearer every day
   And He says I shall be like Him when before Him I appear
   And I am getting nearer, nearer every day

9. Throne of God and of the Lamb – Rev. 22:3,4,11. Genesis 34 :
Commitment	– Disobedience and unbelief brought disaster. Calamity, loss, suffering and death. Curse on Creation, beast and man.
Continuation	– Matt.3:9 'Ye are cursed with a curse'.

A mightier host here, our of every kindred, tribe and nation, people and tongue; saved through the blood of our Lord Jesus Christ (the Lamb of God), from sin's pollution, power and presence.

See the contents of the song. What substance!
Great and marvellous Thy work. Great, just and true, Thy ways. King of Saints. His wealth.
"How marvellous, How wonderful, and my song shall ever be!"

6. The Marriage of the Lamb – Rev. 19:9
   Of happy days, the happiest in a man's life is his wedding day; else there is something radically wrong.
   'His wife hath made herself ready.' Hallelujah! Rejoice and be glad! (All saints are not in the bride, otherwise there would be nobody to rejoice at the marriage).
   The elect are chosen by Him, We claim the right of choice. Will we deny Him this privilege of choice?
   The redeemed of all ages will benefit, eternally, when this marriage will take place.
   Preparation – Communion – Union (II Tim. 2:2)

7. The Supper of the Lamb – Rev. 19:9
   "Blessed are they which are called (invited) to the marriage supper of the Lamb."
   All are invited. Unlimited happiness and joy (Ps. 45:12)
   There are a mighty host of guests. Long faces

Mark the change (v14-17):
Serving God day and night.
Shall hunger and thirst no more.
They refused to worship the man of sin. They starved; were naked, without covering etc. Greta tribulation for them.
But what a mighty ransomed host, washed in the blood. 'It is the blood that maketh atonement for the soul.'

4. The Book of the Lamb – Rev.13:8
   The Registrar General
   The Registry Book
   The Registered Names

   Every child born is registered and parents receive a Certificate of Birth. National privileges are ours on producing certificate.
   If you want to get married – certificate.
   If you want old aged pension – certificate.

   The Great Day- dividing line is coming. (Rev.20:15) – Portion
   The Great Day- warning (Rev.3:5) – Possibility
   The Great Day – Hour – but watch (Luke 10) – Position.

5. Song of the Lamb – Rev.15:3 (Exodus 12)
   Song of Moses and the Lamb. The mighty hosts of Israel celebrating their deliverance, redemption and salvation from Egypt's bondage and Pharaoh's cruelty, through he blood (envisaged by the blood of the Passover Lamb).

'Tis so sweet to trust in Jesus
Just to take Him at His Word
Just to rest upon His promise
Just to know, "Thus saith the Lord"

"Rejoice and be glad! for He cometh again
He cometh in glory, the Lamb that was slain"

3. The Blood of the Lamb (Rev.7:13,15,16)
   His love brought Him down.
   His life pleased the Father.
   His blood atoned for our souls.

   The blood of the Lamb of God is not like our blood.

   Questions put:-
   'Who are these?' – Note of admiration and wonderment.
   'Whence came they?' – New type and kind of humanity.

   Answers given:-
   'These are they who have come out of great tribulation'

   Question: Will there be any saint's left to go through the great tribulation? (read v9).
   Multitude which no man could number – triumph of the gospel.
   Representation of East, North, West and South.

v.9 The first triumphant note in glory – the worth of the Lamb. "Thou art worthy to take..and open the book."

The book of redemption and restoration of ruined humanity is opened. "Thou wast slain."

When none was found to ransom me
He was found worthy
To set a world of sinners free
He was found worthy
Oh the bleeding Lamb
He was found worthy

2. The Wrath of the Lamb – Rev.6:15-17

   We see clearly in these verses that He is not a respecter of persons. Those that have not, do not, and will not acknowledge the worth of the Lamb, will have to bear the wrath of the Lamb.

   We are glad to say that salvation is free to all – 'God loved a world of sinners lost' – but 'be it known unto all people'. Position, power and place will not exempt us from the wrath that is to come. Kings, great men, rich men, chief captains, mighty men, bond-men and free men shall be calling on the rocks and mountains to fall upon them, to hide them from the face of Him that sat on the throne and from the wrath of the Lamb.

   His coming will bring fear and terror to the unsaved but it will bring joy and gladness to the hearts of the redeemed. "Even so, come, Lord Jesus!"

   (Rev.22:4; I Tim.1:1)

iii. Proclamation (angelic) of Truth
Source of Divine truth (Lord God) – Prophets – Angels (v6)
Saviour to Worship – (v8) Not through a Pope, Priest, Idol, Shrine, Angel – No! (v9) 'Worship God!'
State of mind in the eternal world. - No purgatory, no second chance, no promise of deliverance.

Wonderful book, pregnant with divine truths.
Satan uses his craftiest strategy to hinder us from reading, saying, 'You cannot understand it' etc. There is a promise for its readers and its reading (ch.1-3); read in the light of these thoughts:-
Sin and Satan exposed.
Satan and sinner's final doom.
Saints singing song of salvation saying, "Thou are worthy... Thou wast slain... Thou has redeemed us."

Well may this be called the Lamb's book. Twenty six times you will find the word in it. The Lamb is all the glory of Emmanuel's land.

1. The Worth of the Lamb – Rev.5:9
The book of redemption in the purposes of God is sealed.
Humanity is doomed, dead, damned.
Widespread consternation: 'No one in heaven or earth able to take the book and open it.
v.3 Weeping is the lot of humanity. Weeping and gnashing of teeth for rejecters of the light.

i. In Genesis we have the promise of the Saviour. (v7)
What force of inspiration there is in His Word.
Three sayings:
- I will send the Comforter – Did He fulfil it? Yes!
- I will build My Church – Does He do it? Yes!
- I will come again.
   Compare the statements of certainty – v7, 12 & 20
   'I will come again'
   'Behold I will come again'
   'Surely, I will come again'

Then we have the solemnity - 'Blessed is he who keepeth'
Something to know – Something to preach
Something to believe – Something to keep

Compare again Genesis and Revelation:
a. Living waters – Pure water from under the throne.
b. Tree of Life – Leaves of the tree cure the nations.
c. Paradise lost - Paradise regained.

ii. Paradise Restored – vv1-6.
Perfect deliverance – No more curse v3
Perfect protection – Throne of God v3
Perfect service – Servants shall serve Him
Perfect holiness – His name on their foreheads v4
erfect day – No night there
Perfect light – No candle/sun; the Lord God giveth light v5

Towards Sinners – Lost. (illustration of mother dying but save; son unsaved)

Towards Satanic host – Rule of the great whore – the Roman Church. Cry of religious circles today (all religions and creeds, except the saints that contend for the true Faith) How can we amalgamate, how can we unite etc

3. Alleluia of Worship

They fell down. Isaiah fell down. John fell down. Job fell own. All these fell down and worshipped God. Not shouts, emotionalism or temperamentalism. Not 'bags of wind'.

4. Alleluia of Reigning

"The Lord God Omnipotent reigneth."

Refer to the martyrs, James, Stephen, Peter.

Later martyrs of Latimer and Ridley. (1555)

Farrar of Carmarthen and Nicol of Haverfordwest (both publicly burned for heresy i.e. Protestantism – by the Roman Catholic authorities under the reign of Queen Mary (the bloody); John Knox; John Penry etc.

Persecutors: Herod, Nero, Hitler etc.

Revelation 22:17

Principles or Truths revealing what our attitude should be in face of His coming.

Our walk of life – Keeping the soul. v7

Our work or duties – Working; the body. V12

Our watching or attitude – 'Even so come Lord Jesus'; the spirit. v20

It is interesting to compare Genesis and Revelation:

Note the contrast: -

Genesis	Revelation
Sin brought	Sin abolished
Sorrow, sighing, pain	No more sorrow
Curse came	Curse removed
Death came	No more death
Paradise lost	Paradise regained
Satan appeared	His final doom
Promise of Redeemer	Everything redeemed
Sun, moon & stars	No night there

When seeing these sights, John heard the Alleluia Chorus. The singers are not shouting for the sake of shouting; they have substantial reason:

1. Alleluia
   Salvation is of the Lord. All that are in heaven are attributing their safe arrival to the Lord. No boasters, not one. They are there by, and through, no merits of their own, but because of the merits of the Lord. They are able to realise and comprehend the force of the word of truth, 'Savation!' Salvation from the guilt of sin, from the power and from the presence of it. "For there is other name …"etc (Acts 4).
2. Alleluia of Judgement
   "True and righteous are His judgements."
   Towards Saints – Judgement began in the house of the Lord.
   a. Baptism.
   b. Tithes

You've carried your burden,
You've carried it long;
Come take it to Jesus....

v. Jesus Christ the Hope of the Soul
"Behold! He cometh."
The One that loved me, and washed me – he cometh!
His coming will be a grand one in the splendour of His glory, with clouds.
  a. The Manner – with clouds.
     Emblem of majesty, ensign of power; sign of storm.
  b. The Certainty of His Coming
     It will be a literal coming.
     Publicity of His coming – "Every eye shall see Him."
  c. The Effects of His Coming.
     Waiting to execute judgement.
     Drama of Calvary; those who pierced Him shall see Him.

Revelation 19:1-6

John, banished to the island called Patmos for the Word and his testimony, suffered much. Satan, making this world as a boiling cauldron, is alert. The man of God is immortal till his work is done. There John is in fellowship with the Alpha and Omega. On the divine canvas he sees living pictures, from Him Who was, is, and is to come.

iii. Jesus Christ the Enobler of our souls
He maketh us kings and priests unto God. The cross gives dignity and royalty. He elevates the filthy, down-trodden sinner from the depths to the heights of the throne.
He gives dominion over:
The world — its attraction, allurements, bewitching with its phantasmagoria, illusion and lies.
The flesh — victory over the flesh.
What does it mean? Much is said in these days, in pulpit, press and parliament regarding divorces, birth control and morality. What will solve the problem of the flesh in its baser sense? Is it laws, codes of rules, commandments, parliamentary legislation or the Pope's authority? No! The flesh, the self-life in its entirety can only be conquered by reigning grace through our Lord Jesus Christ, by dying to sin and self enabling us to wield the sceptre of self-control, making all things subservient to the moral advancement of our souls.
The Devil — Yes! We are kings over his wiles and devices. The power with which the Lord endows his sons and daughters hath made us free (not will make us free) and free indeed; kings and priests to the Most High.

iv. JESUS CHRIST
The hero of our souls: "Unto Him" is the inscription.
The heroes of the football field, following a bag of wind — how empty of all substantial joy.
Satisfaction is found in Jesus, He is our challenge to the impossible. Nothing is too hard for Him.

i. Who Loved Us
   Jesus the lover of our souls. The word 'loved' carried with it the blessed truth of past, present and future – the reality of His eternal love.
   a. Absolutely unmerited – nothing in us to draw Him to love us. Have we been moved by this truth? If not, we have not seen ourselves; we don't know who we are. Our pedigree, our ancestry. God might have given up humanity (the Adamic race), ruined by the fall. Not one clean spot, but he loved me in my filth and shame.
   b. His love was practical not natural – He gave Himself for me; the love that Jesus had for me.
   c. His love was a forgiving love – "When we were yet sinners, Christ died for us" – the ungodly. Not when we were in sympathy, but when we were in open rebellion. This love passeth knowledge.

   Oh twas love, twas wondrous love,
   The love of God to me,
   It brought my Saviour from above
   To die on Calvary

ii. Cleanser of our souls
   He loved us before washing us. This is a revelation of the intrinsic value of the blood. "What can wash away our sins? – Nothing but the blood of Jesus."
   He loosed us and delivered us, setting us free; severing our connection from hell's power. Can you wonder why it is I love Him so? "He breaks the power of cancelled sin."

iv. The Lamb Praised
Rev. 5:11-13
Universal adoration for eternal duration, throughout God's creation, "Worthy is the Lamb that was slain!"
   a. Who praise Him? – Living creatures. The chorus is full of life. The dead cannot praise Him.
   b. United praise – "Singing with a loud voice."
   c. Reverential praise – They fell down before Him, 'lost in wonder, love and praise.' What do they sing? Truth! – Not pretty poetry.
   d. The Deity of Christ – "Thou art worthy to take the book."
   e. Authority and sovereignty of Christ – "To open the book."
   f. Sacrifice; Redemption through Christ – "Was slain ... and brought us back to God."

Redemption is an inexhaustible theme. The praise is contagious in its inspiration. Heaven and earth take up the strain.
Universal Redeemer – the Lamb slain.
Universal song – heaven and earth, the sea, angels and the whole creation take up the strain (v13).
Universal in acknowledgement – "Worthy is the Lamb."

Rev.1:5-7
Source of the Revelation – God
Purpose – God's will
The Person – Jesus Christ – No time to deal with the Persons of the Godhead, but with the Person the Lord Jesus Christ.

Duncan, King of Scotland, spent a night with Lord and Lady Macbeth in their castle and retired to sleep. Macbeth, instigated by his wife, walked softly to his room, and plunged a dagger into his heart. Lady Macbeth followed, and smeared the sword of a drunken, sleepy guardsman with the king's blood, to make it appear that the soldier had murdered the king. Walking in her sleep, Macbeth was heard to mutter:
"*Here's the smell of blood still; all the perfumes of Arabia will not sweeten this little hand.*"
Water from the Atlantic Ocean cannot wash it — guilt of a stricken conscience.

>Not all the blood of beasts
>On Jewish altars slain
>Can give the guilty conscience peace
>Or wash away the stain
>
>But Christ the heavenly Lamb
>Takes all our sins away
>A sacrifice of nobler Name
>And richer blood than they
>
>Believing, we rejoice
>To see the curse removed
>We bless the Lamb with cheerful voice
>And sing His bleeding love!

iii. The Lamb Preached
John 1:29 "Behold the Lamb of God."
The efficiency and efficacy of the Lamb of God.
   a. He satisfied divine justice.
      God raised Him from the dead as a proof of the acceptance of His sacrifice, and not only from the dead, but far above all, and gave Him a name above every other name. Now sitting down at His right hand invested with the insignia of universal royalty.
   b. His sacrifice satisfied the longing and absolute need of humanity.
      Jewish sacrifices brought sin to their remembrance every year – accumulation!
      Now, no more, no more, my sins are remembered no more! Not only the guilt, but the power of sin taken away – of inbred sin removed – by tradition, by the fathers. Heredity handed down; birthmarks that have so disfigured the human race.
      Advertisement in papers – 'Ten days trial of cure for drink and smoking habit! – FREE (and yet later charged for).
      This cure is really free to all. Also instantaneous, not after 'ten days'.
      David Brainerd, North American missionary, was asked by a native boy how one Lamb of God could settle the sin of the whole world?
      Answer: One gold sovereign is equivalent to 240 copper pennies. Christmas Evans said, Christ lifted the 'ten turnpike gates of Sinai' off their hinges, and suspended them by the nails of His own cross (Col.3).

ii. The Lamb Proved
I Peter 1:19
It must be without spot or blemish, absolutely sound, inside and out. The incarnation was an act of infinite condescension, but this was not the atonement. Voluntarily, He emptied Himself; He came, He gave Himself.
The Jewish Passover Lamb was to be a year old, to be tested, after going through the four seasons, spring, summer, autumn and winter.
He went through – tested, tempted and tried.
In Him was no sin – Immaculate Conception (I John 3:3).
Did not sin – immaculate life (I Peter 2:22).
Knew no sin – immaculate completion of life (I John 3:5).
Listen to the report – the result of the testing: -
Pilate said: "I find no fault in Him" (John 18:38)
Judas said: "I have betrayed innocent blood." (Matt.27:4)
Thief said: "This man hath done nothing amiss." (Luke 23:41).
Centurion: "Certainly this was a righteous man." (Luke 23:47).
Devils confess: "I know whom Thou art, the Holy One."
Christ Himself: "Who can convince me of sin?"
"The prince of this world cometh, but he findeth nothing in me."

God said: "In whom I am well pleased."

wonderfully helped him to deliver the message in his weakness that night."

About the same time, selected portions of the message was preached at the Temple, Penygroes, much to the edification of the congregation. It was noticeable that the servant of God had weakened much in strength, physically, though the delivery lost none of its vitality and spiritual unction.

Behold the Lamb of God
Meditations on the Book of Revelation
Gen.22:8, Ex.12:5, I Peter 1:19, John 1:29, Rev.5:11-12

The message of the scripture is "Without the shedding of blood there is no remission of sin." Sin is a fact in the history of the world. There is not much benefit in arguing how, when and where it started, and how to cope with its effects. The Church can reveal the remedy. Sins wounds can be cured, its effects destroyed and its power broken forever. "Behold the Lamb of God!"

i. The Lamb Provided
    "Foreordained before the foundation of the world"
    a. It implies a plan; in the unfathomable depths of the divine mind there was a plan found, eternally conceived, to rescue sin-doomed, damned humanity.
    b. Calvary is an embodiment of God's eternal thoughts, not afterthought. Ordained before the foundation of the world.
    c. In eternity there was an ordination service; three Persons present in the beginning of eternity, when One was set apart for the ministry work of Redemption (Y Cyngor borau).

here; nothing grand about us here; but the air by and by! (1Thess.4:17) I had an experience of going up in an aeroplane and the command came that we were not to take any luggage with us when going up, at all. I was glad of the experience of proving, for myself, whether I was willing to leave everything here and go up!

If there are any burdens upon you, or if you are grabbing at anything, or if you are not willing to let go of everything you have got, you will not be 'caught up'. Only those that are ready and willing – with no luggage – will be taken up to meet Him in the air.

Look at John's food and raiment – locusts and wild honey was his food. But by and by the marriage feast, the 'custards' prepared in the glory for those that will meet Him there. Camel's hair for dress, but by and by we will be able to say, with John:

"With our wedding garments on
We shall meet the loved ones gone
At the great marriage supper of the Lamb"

This is our hope this afternoon. The soon coming of the Bridegroom. May God bless His word! Amen!"

The following outlines of Pastor Jones Williams's last meditations will enable readers to know how thoroughly he prepared his addresses. His daughter (Mrs E.M.M. Evans, wife of Pastor John Evans) in forwarding the same, wrote, "I treasure the manuscript very much, this being the very last sermon I heard Dada preach at Pontardawe, just a few months before his death. It was a wonderful meeting, and the Lord hated by some, was feared by others and followed by many. Above all, he was commended by Jesus. Jesus said, "Among the children of men there is none like John the Baptist." Whether we will be hated, feared or followed or obeyed, the only thing we crave is the commendation of Jesus.

Think also of the contrast between his present life and his future. Our present, light, affliction is nothing to be compared with the glory that shall be revealed. Also, as John said that Jesus was coming – which refers to His first coming – we affirm that Jesus is coming again soon. Praise His name. We are waiting for Him.

I understand there is a man in the streets of Copenhagen distributing messages that Jesus is coming again on 6th February 1924. We do not know when Jesus is going to come (it may be tonight, it may be tomorrow, it may be on 6th February, we have not got the date of His coming), but this we are sure of, He is coming.

I should like to say this (as someone has said here, that the man I have mentioned looks like one who has quarrelled with his wife and with his home, and that he is glad of his future hope that he is not to return to them), I think there would be very little hope for a man who has quarrelled with his wife, or anybody else, who is not right with his brother, to be caught up to meet Him, for when He will come He will take the pure in heart to Himself.

John the Baptist will be coming with Him. He will not be in the Bride, but he is the friend of the Bridegroom; he will be the 'best man' at the marriage.

Think of the difference between John, then, and also between us now and what we shall be then. Wilderness

Another phase of his character it humility. When all Jerusalem came out to the wilderness, the priests and levites came to ask, "*Who are you, John?*" It is here we get an explanation why God sent him to the wilderness at the beginning. The Lord knew that it would be impossible to have a building large enough to hold the crowd that would come after him, so He said, 'Go to the wilderness, there is plenty of room there.' John did not tell the crowd what a wonderful man he was, or what a wonderful preacher he was, or what influence he had over the people – 'everybody runs after me!' No! The question was "*Who are you, John?*" "*I am the voice of one crying in the wilderness.*" 'I am a candle' (if we may put it into John's mouth what Jesus afterwards testified of him), 'burning and shining at the same time'.

When we see a candle burning and shining, you remember that the candle is always decreasing. "The one who is coming after me is greater than I; I am unworthy to loose the latchet of His shoes." That was John's testimony. Are we in this position today when God is moving? Or are we taking the glory to ourselves? John was there to speak about somebody much bigger than himself and that is our ministry today. We go here and there to speak, not of our own sacrifices and our own work and prosperity, but to speak of the wonderful Christ and His glory, whom God has raised from the dead and has exalted far above all.

It would be well to touch on the fact of the effect, the outcome or the influence of his ministry and message.

Owing to the principles that he preached, he was

in the daily newspapers concerning healings etc. If anybody else does so, all well and good, for God's miracles will stand the test of a critic, without our boasting of them. The tendency is to say, if one is saved, that one hundred have been saved. If I am healed of a little pain in my side, it was appendicitis or something very painful. We are always exaggerating the work of God, but there is no need. It will stand the test of a critic that may come along. All we have to tell you, of the work of God in our land of Wales, is come and see!

Pardon me for saying just this, the last sister of mine at home, who was unsaved, was saved and healed miraculously on the very same night. In the morning I had seen my sister ill in bed, but when I came home at night, she was dancing because of the healing God had wrought in her soul and body. I shall never forget the scene. She has been well ever since.

I would like to say this, we are not following the Lord because of healings or blessings; we are following Him because the truth of God has taken hold of our innermost being. We praise God for everything He is doing and we know that He will do wonderful things yet. But we want to have this word of commendation, that everything we say is truth indeed. Everything that this man, John, said was true and it is grand, is it not? To have that commendation made concerning one.

His character was composed of two opposites, humility and boldness. Righteous indignation against sin is not inconsistent with humility. John had no home, no support, no followers (at first; later he had disciples) no one upon whom he could depend, but he rebuked king Herod on his throne. He could not compromise with sin at all.

clothing and his language or words. We are to absolutely separate from the world in every sense.

The child of God is not mastered by his appetite – it did not master John. We have in the scriptures, God saying regarding some people, 'whose God is their belly.' We need to realise that we have been called to a separated life and that our bodies, and bodily appetites, are not to master us. We are to live a single-eyed life for God's glory. Think of John's dress or clothing. He was not following the 'Paris fashion' of his day. Think of how much is done in this direction in our days. We can truly say that there is more sinning, because of the fashions of the day, than anything else we can think of. We ought to ask God to give us grace to live a separated life and not be carried away by the fashion of the day. I know I shall not be a popular preacher by preaching this but, after all, we must preach the Word of God. John was not thinking of the opinion of people regarding his dress and food.

Another fact in his character, which we notice, is his truthfulness and his accuracy of statement. He always spoke the truth. The Word of God says that he did not do many mighty miracles and wonders, but everything that he said of Jesus was true. I believe we can take a lesson here as God's saints. There is a tendency in us, by nature, to make things bigger and greater than they are – to exaggerate. I do not think you have heard us saying so as regards what God has done for us in Wales, and we can keep you for a long time saying how God has been moving. That is not our purpose here. Our purpose is to give the Word of God, as it is written here, for the benefit of every soul gathered in this hall.

I do not believe there is any need to publish about us

He has shown it at Calvary. But remember that He is just also.

I was holding a week of special mission work in a certain place recently and, at the end of the service, a man came to me and said, "*Mr Williams, I am coming forward to tell you that I am lost and that God does not love me. I am going to hell with no hope and I have been failing to sleep for seven nights. If I am unable to sleep again this night there is nothing to come of me and I must make an end of myself.*" I smiled in his face and, as soon as he saw the smile, he said, "*Are you laughing?*" "*I am smiling*", I said, "*because what seems to you to be hard, unkind and unfeeling, it is there I can see God's love. You think that God is hard and unkind, and that He does not love you, and is not allowing you to sleep because you are unsaved. I believe that God loves you so much that He is keeping you awake for seven nights so that you may see that you are not saved.*"

As soon as I said these words he began to smile and said, "*Well, there is hope for me then?*" "*Yes!*" I replied, "*and if you are ready to be saved, He will save you now.*" Down on our knees we went and he went home with his face shining with the glory of God.

How glad that we are able to say that 'Jesus saves', everywhere, anywhere, and everybody who wishes to be saved on this earth: but He never saves in hell. Today is the day of salvation, but if you neglect a great salvation, while you are here on earth, how shall you escape?

Again we see the habits of John the Baptist. You will remember that his place of mission was the wilderness. His message was 'Repent', 'Behold the Lamb of God' and a warning. He is an example to us in his habits. He was separated from everything, in his appetite, his faces, in sackcloth and ashes, crying for forgiveness; and He, our Saviour will come to our rescue.

It has been made very plain in these meetings that, by nature, we are all lost and on our way to hell and, whoever goes there, there is no way out from there. Man is very clever, and I am sure if men could invent a way from hell today the myriad's of lost souls, that have gone to eternity without a Saviour, would rush to such a door of hope. But there is no way out!

But thank God! We are sinners saved by grace and, like John in the wilderness, we can turn our faces to men and women and shout, "*Behold the Lamb of God which taketh away the sins of the world!*" It is there we find a place where we can have deliverance from sin and its tyranny, and from the enemy of our souls, and be ever free from its clutches. 'God so loved the world that He gave His only begotten Son," because He does not want to see any one perish, but that everyone should come to Him and return to Him.

As John was telling the people they were to repent, and then showing them the way of deliverance – the Lamb – and the consequences that would follow if they did not comply with the condition, he said to the Pharisees and Saducees: "*Who hath warned you to flee from the wrath to come?*" You may ask us, 'Where are you standing, as God's people in the Apostolic Church; do you believe in the second chance or no? Do you believe there is a second chance in the other world, the hereafter?' We very definitely say, No! We are exhorting every man today to repent, and to turn to the Lamb of God, while it is called today, because this is the only chance sinners will get. 'God is love', you say. Yes! And *should have stayed in bed all my life, because it was there that I was saved!*" (The Danish audience, which filled the hall, having a capacity for 2,000 people, to whom this sermon was interpreted, showed their appreciation of the humorous sally by much hearty laughter).

We note that John's message in the wilderness was, 'Repent!' Take the truth in. See a man, by himself, in the wilderness (with no other man near him), shouting at the top of his voice, 'Repent!' Surely the people would say, 'God has made a mistake; John has made a mistake – going to the wilderness to preach and no one there!' No! John gave obedience to the will of God and to the wilderness he went, to preach, with no one there. He proclaimed repentance in the hearing of no one then present, and without asking what of the future, and without knowing anything of the future. Here we see that the Word of God is effective and creative.

Once you leave the Word of God, by faith, go out from your lips, then it does the work whereunto it was sent. That is the first message the Apostolic Church has for the world, here, there and everywhere: 'REPENT! that your sins may be blotted out!' I believe we ought to be very careful lest we make the way of salvation too simple, and too easy, for those who listen. Jesus preached repentance; His disciples preached repentance; and we are preaching repentance, declaring, 'Except also ye repent, ye shall likewise perish.'

We have experienced this truth, that when we have sinned against God, there is no need of coaxing people to come to Jesus then. When we will see the grossness and heinousness of sin, and our condition through sin, and through the fall, we will repent prostrate on our believe, after all, that we are 'God-sent' to the people at this hour.

Another thought that came to my mind. The reason why God would not send John to the religious people was, the Lord knew what He was going to do through him and, if he had been accepted by the priests and the levites, and the religious people of the day, they would take the glory and the credit for that which would take place. But when God does a thing through a channel, such as John, there is no chance for anyone to be puffed up at all, because John must (and every 'sent of God' must) give the credit and honour to God alone.

The question has been asked in our days: If God gave you light in the chapel or the church, why didn't you stay in and let your light shine among them? A question was asked, here yesterday, if it was possible for a child of God to stay in his or her own place and not 'come out from among them' and not be separate'? The question was asked whether he or she should comply with the will of God in water baptism. Such a question was asked at a certain place of worship. The answer that was given was that if such an obedience was given, then that congregation would not desire that person there anymore. That is a real sign that God wants us to give full obedience to His will and Word at all times.

I remember my father (who is today in the Glory, because he believed God) was once in a company of people. They were asking this question and one person in the company said, "*I believe that you are saved, and that you have had this blessing and the other blessing, but what did you want to go out from the Chapel for? I believe that everybody should stay in the place where they had the 'light'.*" My father answered and said, "*If that is logical and right, I*

I should like to deal with the character of John, as a type of what every Christian should be, and what the Church of God should also attain to. We can have comfort when we read that he was sent of God. We are called to day 'fanatics' and 'extremists' and other names, because we say that we are sent of God; but if we can believe this truth, that we are here in God's will, sent of Him, then we can do something in His name.

You must remember that in John's day there were plenty of people to be had, but *he* was sent of God, the only 'sent' one among the children of men. The meaning of his name is 'the gift of God', and it is very appropriate to what we are teaching, and what has been said through the meetings. It runs parallel with the teaching: "He gave some apostles, some prophets..." etc. (Eph.4:11).

You notice where God sent him – to the wilderness. Surely, there must have been something wrong, before God needed to send a special gift like this, because there were plenty of priests and levites in Jerusalem at the time and much religion. But God sent John outside the walls of religious formalism to the wilderness, alone. God did not send him to the priests and levites; they would not have accepted him.

He did not look like a preacher at all with his raiment of camel's hair. They surely would say, "*Where have you had your schooling from?*" "*You have no knowledge, or vocabulary and no grammar. You are not a 'degree' man. What do you want with us?*" But God spared them the trouble of refusing His 'sent one'.

We are sure that he is doing the very same today, for if we are to go to some places, claiming that we are sent of God, they would show us the door very soon. We

CHAPTER 16

PREACHER

Pastor Jones Williams as a collier, and as a preacher, had one thing in common; underground, he had one object at the 'face' and that was to get coal at any cost physically.

As a preacher he had a knack of getting at the truth and placing it, uncompromisingly, before his congregation plainly, naturally and without any attempt at oratory. One was left with the unadorned substance of truth in one's possession, conveyed in language easily understood, and driven home by illustrations that were simple, illuminating, often humorous but never dull.

He preached the following sermon at the Evangeliehuset, Copenhagen on Friday 1st February 1924. A deputation, consisting of Pastors D.P. Williams, H. Cousen, W.T. Evans (Evangelist), W.J. Williams and T. Davies (scribe), at the invitation of the Danish brethren, visited Denmark. Encouraged with the "God speed you" of the A.C. Council in the homeland, the deputation were honoured of God to persuade some seven hundred of that Pentecostal congregation to decide to throw in their lot with the Apostolic Church of Great Britain.

The Character of John the Baptist
Text: *"There was a man sent from God, whose name is was John."* (John 1:6)

"*Whereupon O king Agrippa, I was not disobedient to the heavenly vision.*" (Acts 26:19)

> *In his duty prompt at every call*
> *He watched and wept, he prayed and felt for all*
> *And, as as a bird each fond endearment tries*
> *To tempt its new-fledged offspring to the skies*
> *He tried each art, reproved each dull delay*
> *Allured to brighter worlds, and led the way*
>
> (Goldsmith)

> *Two brothers freely cast their lot*
> *With David's royal Son*
> *The cost of conquest counting not*
> *They deem the battle won*
>
> *Now they join hands once more above*
> *Before the Conqueror's throne*
> *Thus God grants prayer, but in His love*
> *Makes times and ways His own*
>
> (Newman)

possessions, but allow the holiness of your personalities (as you abide before me) to raise you higher, and be conscious that I am dealing with you.

Let it be understood that the penny that bears the inscription of Caesar is of little value in such a meeting. I must have your 'wills' I must have the inner man to respond, "Here am I."

Father and Son, we are one in essence and in that unity there was manifested the sacrifice in mutual co-operation, in order that the need of humanity might be met.

There was no other one to call unto me, "Withhold your hand!" (Gen.22:11-12) There was neither thicket nor ram near me. The thicket of mankind's need was myself and the peace offering of sufficiency was found in myself.

I could have given many things to mankind but, if I did not give 'ALL', I should not be giving sufficient ...When you are face to face with these facts in the presence of the altar, you, yourselves are answering your own cries, very often, by the nature of your own gifts. When you reply, "Here am I" I give a promise. The promise is this, "Ask of me, and I will give you an inheritance."

The First Missionary Meeting
(Prophetic ministry through Ps. Jones Williams)

"Believe, yes, believe! I do not desire you to ask of me unless you believe. You can accomplish a great work in a missionary meeting. Its importance is not appreciated as it might be. 'It is only a missionary meeting', you say, 'It does not matter.' A missionary meeting was the first important meeting that I ever held. At such a meeting you perceive the worth of a soul. In this meeting you come to see your connection and relationship with mankind. In this meeting is revealed also your responsibility in face of the value of the soul and your relationship thereto.

"Who will go for me?" That was my question, and my work, in the first missionary meeting. You think of, and pray for, one country at a time. That is good, for you are unable to deal with every country; but I have not chosen one more than another.

Humanity as a whole is the 'country' of my missionary operations.... "God will provide Himself a lamb for a burnt offering." That missionary meeting cost me something but I do not repent of it.

Many have refused to attend missionary meetings because it costs them something. It means sacrifice to be present. It costs something in effort and in giving but I bore all the cost myself...I gave to satisfy the need of the whole world.

I held that first missionary meeting in order to give. I would have your missionary meetings to be so apostolic in character that you will realise that you cannot have meetings without giving. Do not suppose that I am pressing hard upon you in order to obtain your material reached your shores. The promise has been given that "He shall see the travail of His soul and be satisfied." I would have you to perceive, and know (with that knowledge), that what I am doing is to honour labour, labour, labour! And without 'travail' I cannot satisfy.

Some of you are too idle. Plenty of effort in the natural! Plenty of effort in planning for your own profit! But your schemes contain none of the plans needful to be devised for the deliverance of others. Take the lesson to yourselves.

You rejoice that you have been called to be co-workers. Always believe that there are unending possibilities to that which I have commenced. Do not measure at any time my work by a comparison with *your* power but with the power, which is in my being saith the Lord.

I have foretold that I would send peace messengers and, while making peace through the ministry of their words, they shall sweat blood and sink to their graves. While this happens, you will be judging wrongly if you judge that I am subverting, or dealing unjustly, with any man in his cause. If two obtain life eternal through the death of one, is that worth while? The promise is, "He shall be satisfied!" yes, "He shall be satisfied!" and this promise is also given to all who go forth on my work.

I declare, there is a life to be lived, my people; a life to be attained unto; a life to be possessed; a life that is satisfied with nothing less than the fruit of dying. With this knowledge, I would have you again to realise that herein you have materials for rejoicing, in that you have been saved to do my will, saith the Lord."

the promise of my lips, saith the Lord. Sufficient for the disciple to be as his Lord.

You rejoice when truths are laid before you, the substance of which conveys the possibility that you shall do greater works than He did. ...In the hearing of a truth such as that the hopes of everyone of you glow brightly and there is an increase of inward desire to do those *greater works* – for that is the characteristic of man always, to achieve greater. But the other aspect has been made known also: "If they persecuted Him, they will persecute you; if they refused Him, they will also refuse you."

"It is a privilege to be called!" you say, "It is a great joy to teach others!" As of old, so today man sees the privileges of those who cross the seas on missionary journeys but, at the moment the ship sails from the harbour, they see not "the two seas" (Acts 27:41) they are not on the horizon, they are far away!

There are some of you who imagine that a life of voyaging aboard a ship is an easy life but there is no perception that there are hidden rocks ahead. Some declare also that, because of my choice and calling, I am bound to keep alive all those that go and no ones vessel must strike against a rock. They say that I must turn back the onrush of every "two seas" lest they touch the missionaries. You must know that something is going to come to sight when the missionaries are escaping and surviving on planks.

...Of a truth, the purpose of sending forth will be accomplished in the lives of all that are obedient. I want you to understand the nature of the divine sendings. "Who will go?" I asked. I prepared a vessel (a body) for that 'Sent One' to make His voyage. In the effort He joy solely to be experienced by myself. Truly, I do rejoice, for it must be remembered that it is I too who have sown. The only seed that I possessed I have sown. But the wind of persecution was not allowed to blow it upon the rock of unfruitfulness neither were the stones of obstruction, which were in humanity allowed to prevent Him from dying. Sown was He!

Who sowed Him? ...It was I that sowed Him. Willingly I sowed my 'last' Seed. I turned my back on the field and the Seed, in His own realm, cried after me, "*Why hast Thou forsaken me?*" I declare, while turning my back upon Him I did not turn away in despair but in my own realm I was glad and rejoiced exceedingly.

"*From this Seed and abundant, immense harvest will come; Buried there, lies the substance of every surrounding soil of faith.*"

...Go ye to the field. Remember, if you have bled while giving the promise assured. Do not sow in this world in order to have the blessings that shall perish. Some have covenanted with me for earthly blessings in that manner: "I give if I shall obtain a return!" I have indeed given in return on the basis of a covenant and condition; I have acted in that fashion. But it depends upon you to what realm you look for fruit. I desire you to reap the fruit of a profitable harvest where I eternally dwell and where you shall come to dwell.

...If the gift (or the sacrifice) should cry after you because it has brought suffering, "Why has thou forsaken me?" do not turn again to the gift but let it die there on the altar, so that through its virtue you shall receive abundant fruit in the future according to

Bradford in October 1922) there follows a prophetic exhortation through Ps. Jones Williams.

The Father's One Grain of Corn

"You must needs believe, says the Lord, in the presence of the invisible movements of the laws of nature. The various realms direct your understanding to a grasp of the realities, so that you discern that there is, behind all, a cause before the effects can be observed. Sowing goes on in ever realm, by everybody, all believing that there is a harvest to follow soon. The sower turns his back on the field of his labours in humility. He does not question within himself whether fruit will come; neither does he doubt whether it will come. He looks forward expectantly and watches the seed from the earth coming to sight and, when he sees it, he rejoices.

I would have you to realise, in truth, that in the realm of the seed, my word, there is fruit. If, because of the obstacles preventing the life in this seed coming to view, you feel disheartened at times, do not, for lack of realisation, turn your backs upon the field of your labour, but in the strength of inward faith, turn therefrom with a sure consciousness that fruit will come to sight on the morning of the third day that is to dawn upon you.

Is it the farmer only who rejoices when he sees his barns full? Truly he is the first undoubtedly. But if the granaries be not full, those who are not farmers tremble because of the future. It is they who first declare that the deficient harvest is such than mankind will suffer in the days that shall come.

I would have you to remember that the joy arising from the fruits of the harvest, which is to come, is not a should go into hospital. After Jones had prayed, the Lord spoke through him, in Welsh, and this is the translation: "*I have given you faith. I will tell you something incredible. You do not need to go to the hospital but take a glassful of the fruit of the lemon tree with water and my servants will come to see you towards evening.*" After I had thanked the Lord for His word Jones asked me whether I believed it. I said, "*Of course, I am going to walk on the word.*"

Reaching home, my wife made me a jug-full of lemon essence and water, which I took from time to time, while laying in bed. I felt a release in the appendix and soon the pain increased as the contents made their way through the intestines, and stomach, enabling me, at last, to spit it out – a greyish mass, which had probably accumulated since childhood; like the soft roe of a herring. Since then I have had no pain.

What added point to the relief was that I had been reading a book by an American author, which stated on the first page, that it was an insult to the Lord Jesus to 'use means' (i.e. herbs) and ask Him for healing. He said that the great Physician had in His Word indicated the means to use.

During my attendance at the 'Babell' Apostolic Hall, Penygroes, during the years 1922-1933, I had proof abundant of the comforting, guiding and exhorting ministry of the Godhead through the prophetic channels. One didactic prophecy, which has left a lasting impression on my memory, is produced below. To illustrate the persistent word concerning the A.C. Missionary outlook (which culminated in the establishing of the A.C Missionary Movement at

Occasionally, individual members, who might desire a word of counsel, enquired of the Lord. There came to Penygroes, from Treherbert, an interesting man by the name of Thomas Martin. He was one wealthy man who, in younger days served in a cavalry regiment, against the Matabele. He, with his wife, prospected for diamonds, kept and Ostrich farm in South Africa, had been converted and was, thereafter, very generous in his monetary giving. At Plymouth Hall, Swansea, Jones Williams prophesied and told the Welsh apostles, "*Here is a man; ponder over the word and see if you can fathom my meaning when I say 'Here is a man.'*" Evidently, the Lord meant, as in the poem, 'Abou Ben Adhem' by Leigh Hunt, that brother Martin was counted as, 'One that loved his fellow men.' He paid the fare of one Bible School student (W.J. Davies) to India and was always ready, according to his restricted means, to assist every good cause.

Brother Martin wished to know from the Lord who was right in the keeping of the Sabbath, the Seventh Day Adventists, the Jews or the Christians? The reply of the Lord, through the prophet, was noteworthy and lifts the service of God to the perfect level: "*Rest not in a day, but rest in me and make every day holy.*"

It may not be out of place to refer to my own personal enquiry of the Lord when I suffered from chronic appendicitis from 1924-1928, by which time the pain had become unbearable. At midnight (after a Sunday of great pain) I went to 'Ramah' Waterloo Road, and knocked at the prophets door, who came to the window and, hearing my request, opened the door.

Entering, and kneeling before the kitchen fire, I made my case known and I needed to know whether I

The atmosphere of the meeting was tense but, happily, light dispelled the gloom as Pastor Dan brought to mind the example of the prophet Elijah, who was told of the Lord, outside the cave of his depression, that he was to anoint Jehu as king of Israel and Hazael king of Syria. Did Elijah do so? No! He was taken to glory in a chariot. Who carried out the divine injunction? It was an unnamed prophet, at the command of Elisha, who anointed Jehu king of Israel, and that under peculiar circumstances.

Elijah must have told Elisha of the divine command and thus passed on the obedience of it to the unnamed prophet. That could not be called 'wire-pulling' but a delegation of authority for the divine purpose to be fulfilled.

In the case of Hazael, the actual anointing, delayed, and apparently not actually fulfilled, even by Elisha, who simply intimated to him his destiny to occupy the throne of Syria. The elevation of Hazael to the throne remained in abeyance for years to come, despite the divine revelation to Elijah.

Thus did Pastor Dan meet the charge of the so-called unbiblical word from the prophet in calling the two brethren to the apostleship and much edification was obtained by the illustration from the Old Testament.

Jones was alert to add to his library from time to time. In order to acquire further volumes he would either give away or sell items from his theological shelves. I was able to verify that his reading was judicious and helpful. His own sermons were systematic, interesting, fundamental and inspiring both in English and in Welsh.

the basis of the guidance which would be given to both brothers in the future.

Pastor Dan was told to study the life of David, and of the men and women who were in that king's company. He should study the victories and defeats, the joys and the sorrows etc. for, like David, various associations in the spiritual warfare of the church would chequer his own life. This exhortation was acted upon and both brothers were well equipped in knowledge of the written Word. Readers of past 'Riches of Grace' will vouch for this for prophetic ministry and its exposition, through the mouths of the prophet Jones and Pastor Dan, remain a valuable contribution to the doctrinal and exhortative teachings of the church.

One example of this scriptural knowledge found an instructive avenue of light when the Welsh assemblies met at the Wesleyan Chapel, near Swansea, during a May Day Rally. Jones had been used of the Lord, at Skewen, to tell the assembled Welsh apostles that he would call Ps. W.H. Lewis and T.V. Lewis to be apostles at the forthcoming convention in Tonypandy. This use of a prophet to tell another prophet what to prophesy was challenged as being unscriptural, indeed a mere 'wire-pulling' to get things to happen, a tempting criticism that may have assailed others.

The Tonypandy convention had passed and Pastor's W.H. Lewis and T.V. Lewis had been duly called through, through Ps. J. Omri Jones to the apostleship. Procedure having thus been challenged it lay with the chairman of the meeting, Pastor Dan, to both vindicate his brother's prophecy as being on scriptural grounds and, also, to the obedience of Ps. Omri Jones in obeying the prophetic command of the Lord.

occasions, of the long English word instead of the short, easily understood synonym. During a visit to Copenhagen, Denmark in February 1924, at the invitation of Ps. and Mrs S. Bjorner and Ps. Carl Naeser, it was Jones's turn to speak. The previous day he had collated some extracts, which were to prove useful, some of which he read out to me. I implored him to set aside the long words and substitute easier ones, but the rolling periods sounded well and the orator was unwilling to discard them.

When the moment came to preach Ps. Naeser stood at the side of Jones to interpret the 'grand' sermon. All went well and the congregation, of Danish and Swedish saints, followed with understanding, zest the truths that were being expounded. But to the speakers confusion, the interpreter was not interpreting stretches of arid English, however well spoken and beautiful, but simply said, in English, an impatient '*Go on!*' This was exasperating; but presently simpler English, from the mouth of the oracle, made it easier for Ps. Naeser and the congregation voiced with 'Amens' their wonted appreciation.

Knowing the warning I had given, I rather enjoyed Jones's words of comment and disgust on his own performance, "*Davies that was the worst sermon I have ever preached.*" Jones's discomfort with the 'long English word' rather heightened my personal enjoyment for he was ever on the alert to put one on his mettle, human traits that made him all the more engaging as a companion. His constancy as a friend was often tried and found reliable.

Early in the career of both brothers, the word of the Lord, to them personally, was to study the written Word first and foremost for the contents of its pages would be way', which was true. Jones said to me one day, at the office at 'Brynteg' Gorsgoch Road, Penygroes,

"*Davies, you are about the only one with a grasp of English, among us at present; tell me how I may learn the language.*" I advised him to learn some English sermons by rote; memorising them, and using extracts until both meaning and style had been assimilated (making of course suitable acknowledgement). He set about in earnest to do so, with the result that, as the years unfolded, his knowledge increased, and soon the Lord used him in prophecy (or 'prophetic ministry', which were the words ordered of the Lord, through him, should be used instead of 'The Word of the Lord') and that in English.

His mastery of Welsh was adequate enough and one of the wonders, among spiritual 'settings' and 'gifts', was to hear the Lord moving in depths profound through his set prophet. In this regard the earlier volumes of the 'Riches of Grace' ('Cyfoeth Gras') contain testimonies to the manner in which the divine utterances brought, through the Welsh language (especially at the earlier conventions) stores of thought before such as could understand their native tongue. The English translations, and expositions by Ps. Dan, illumined both doctrine and precept, strengthened with apt Biblical and other illustrations, and remain transcendent in their worth.

This marriage of the prophetic ministry to the apostle's setting was, and remains, a marvel during convention time when the saints at Glasgow, Bradford, Hereford and Penygroes sit to unequalled spiritual repasts from the spoken and written word.

Not without its humour was Jones's use, on

gwr bychan' or '*y dyn bychan*', that is, '*the man of small stature*', in terms of endearment and love. Such was his determination not to yield to physical weakness, which might prevent him from carrying out any planned journey or duty, that any reasoning with him was of no avail.

On one occasion, when he was very ill, accompanied by the beloved Ps. Caleb Morgan (then Treasurer of the Welsh section before unity was achieved), we visited Jones at his home in 'Ramah', Waterloo Road, Penygroes. The Lord spoke to him advising him not to rise from bed but to rest that day (Saturday) over the following Sunday. Such, however, was the patient's determination, that he sought to test his strength, rose from bed Sunday morning, only to find that the Lord had a little more knowledge of his condition that he; for he failed to carry out the task which he had desired to fulfil.

This strong will to overcome physical, and other, obstacles may have been hereditary, for one of the last injunctions of the blind father, William Williams, to his two sons was, '*never give in.*' Where mere mental power was ever necessary, the parental command must have enabled both brothers to overcome, where others would have failed.

Yet, apostle and prophet knew how hopeless it was to attempt any task except in the power of the Holy Spirit who was their mainstay in all their arduous work.

This persistency and doggedness, which distinguished the two brothers Dan and Jones, enables them to overcome their ignorance of the English language. Dan could declare that he had 'picked up English on the

(American courtesy was quick to observe the need and many cars were offered to them) while Ps. Hodges remained with Jones to see that any damage was put right, after which they returned to join the others. What might have been tragic and fatal, proved to produce an element of humour.

'Andrew' wished to enquire of the Lord why He had allowed such a happening to occur, the reply through the prophet was chastening: "The one amongst you who has had the greatest damage shall make his complaint against me now." No one was anxious to make such a complaint so the word proceeded: "Did any of you ask your heavenly Father for protection this morning? No! You took it for granted. You should not take anything for granted, but humbly petition the throne for the guidance and protection which, as travellers, you need. Nevertheless, my rolling hand was in the rolling chariot!" ended the Lord, to the sound of thanksgiving and praise! All present had experienced a miraculous escape and the temporary, physical, shaking had become negligible under the healing hand of God.

Jones's work underground as a collier (coal-miner- Ed) during which time he often undertook more than his share of the work (In order to spare his brother, Dan, from overstrain at the same job), left its affect on him. Owing to the steep gradients upon which they had to stand, while cutting coal, the varicose state developing in his legs was severe, although he seldom complained. Treatment with iodine did little to relieve this and the strain imposed by this malady must have intensified his personal anxieties during his labours often.

The Lord would refer to Pastor Jones Williams as '*y*

illness or otherwise, and his motor car was always at the disposal of any urgent case. Being a deft driver, the work of the Lord was considerable furthered in the numerous journeys that were necessary in those early days of pioneering the apostolic vision.

On one occasion a broken axle might have brought on a serious accident, careering down the steep road from Hirwaun to Neath. The occupants of the car, made aware of the danger, called upon the Lord to intervene, and providentially the speed of the car was reduced at last by a rise in the roadway, enabling Jones to turn it into the ditch without damage to the passengers.

On another occasion, faced with a child standing in the path of the car (suddenly and without warning) Jones deliberately turned towards the steep hedge/bank, cleared it, and came to rest in the field behind, but not before an angry crowd had expressed their resentment was he free to leave. It dawned upon them, when explanations had been given, that he had risked his own life to save that of the child.

A car accident in the U.S.A., when Pastors Andrew Turnbull, D.P. Williams, Frank Hodges and Jones Williams were on their way to San Francisco, over the concrete road, brought forth a useful lesson for the children of God everywhere. The run was commenced in high spirits but at a particular right angle turn, the sun being in Jones's eyes (so he related to me); he did not see the bend in time. The sudden call on the mechanism of the car resulted in a topsy-turvy summersault, with the apostles and prophet beneath the car. Other car drivers on the road soon took Pastors Turnbull and Williams back to their starting point

CHAPTER 15

REMINISCENCES

By Pastor T. Davies, Penygroes

I met Ps. W. Jones Williams first in July 1919, when I was invited to take a course of lectures on 'The Way of Salvation' ('Ffordd Iachawdwriaeth') delivered at 'The Babell', Penygroes by Ps. Dan in the Welsh language.

My stay at 'Ramah' Gorsddu Road, where Jones then resided, brought his loving, fatherly, qualities before me in his care for his little daughter May. He related to me the crisis he was in when Diphtheria broke out in that district, and the agony of mind resulting from hearing of deaths of infant children in the neighbourhood. His own daughter had contracted the dread ailment and was facing death.

Led of the Lord he asked the doctor in attendance to take any risks that would follow and operation. As a tracheotomy was the only available means of cure, the doctor immediately proceeded to his task, which proved successful, and led to many children being successfully treated in the same manner, and their lives being saved. Immunisation by injection has now brought about amazing results and prevented the havoc wrought in past years by this epidemic.

One characteristic trait of Jones was his immediate response to the call of neighbours in distress, whether

THE PRIESTHOOD

But the holy men of God such vessels are
As serve Him up, who all the world commands
When God vouchsafeth to become our fare
Their hands convey Him, who conveys their hands
O what pure things, most pure must those things be
Who bring my God to me!

Wherefore I dare not, I, put forth my hand
To hold the ark, although it seem to shake
Through th'old sins, and new doctrines of our land
Only, since God doth often vessels make
Of lowly matter for high uses meet
I throw me at His feet

There will I lie until my Maker seek
For some mean stuff whereon to show His skill
Then is my time

George Herbert.

running to the building to find shelter. The vestry had a galvanised roof and the shrapnel was literally sliding off it.

Our evening meetings were well attended in spite of the blackout and during special meetings the pastor would call for the saints in turn, as many as his car could hold, so that we could share the good things of God. He strengthened the belief of the saints that God had His guardian angel for each of them, drawing on the Scriptures and showing how Jesus Himself was mindful of Peter in prison and Paul during the Euroclydon storm when he declared, "Fear not, Paul...wherefore sirs be of good cheer: for I believe God, that it will be even as it was told me."

Jesus was Himself the guardian angel in these two cases and had He not declared, even of his 'little ones', 'In heaven their angels do always behold the face of My Father which is in heaven.' "Ps. Jones Williams was a man who understood the movements of the Holy Spirit in the meetings, was led by the Spirit and never spared himself in the service of the Master." Such was the testimony of the Sisterhood.

viii. The Christian must be expert in the use of the offensive weapons of the Spirit, the shield of faith, the helmet of salvation, the sword of the Spirit with all prayer.

It may well be that it was the faithfulness of the few in the Spirit that extracted from the Lord the promise contained in the prophetic ministry quoted above.

During the 'blitz', Ps. Jones Williams was in charge of the Apostolic assembly in Cardiff. Overseer F. Atkins writes of that period, "He was a good minister of Jesus Christ in every sense. While staying at Cardiff the saints were truly blessed. His Christ-like character left an influence and his ministry truly edifying.

In the period of national emergency the pastor proved himself a true shepherd. After every evening raid, by the German planes, he was to be found visiting the saints, ministering to their need both spiritually and naturally. The older folk cannot speak too highly of him and those that were 'bombed out' can only speak of his devotion to them as members of the flock.

Although his own home (not far from Llandaff Cathedral, which was completely demolished in one raid) also suffered by enemy action with part of the roof being blown off and windows and doors being blown out, yet he was concerned about the saints under his charge. Only eternity will reveal the extent of the service rendered by our beloved pastor during his term in Cardiff.

The Lord spoke through his mouth one night and told us that nothing would come nigh us in the house of God. This came to pass during the heaviest blitz; even those living in the vicinity of the church were

Remember that that Kingdom is not everlasting. The earthward kingdom that shall be seen, fruitful in all its aspects, shall bring honour unto my name as Sovereign over all kingdoms and realms, but that kingdom is not eternal.

The spiritual is eternal. The Church must live with me, for I have loved the Church and given myself for it...."

This chapter may well close, having shown in this volume and in the general literature of the Apostolic Church, the part played by the faithfulness and obedience of the prophetic channels, before and since the unity of the various homeland sections (Welsh, English, Scottish and Irish). The remarks made by D.P. Williams in the issue of "Riches of Grace" already mentioned, take the headlines:

i. In the spiritual conflict the Christian must be free from every sin.
ii. The believer must know his position in Christ through the death-union with Him.
iii. The believer must be free from the trammels of the world.
iv. The Christian believer must take his stand in his position with Christ, in His dominion as Lord.
v. We must not underestimate the power of the enemy.
vi. The attitude of every Christian warrior must not be merely passive but aggressively standing against a fierce foe.
vii. The Christian warrior must be fully equipped with defensive armour.

definite word regarding the war that is going on – as for victory, I will give victory to your country. Now, where is faith to believe and where is the test of the prophetic ministry regarding the future in the most difficult time in history? Disaster pending, blackness and darkness gathering, clouds hovering, the nations trembling and thrones shivering? Yes, I am declaring now in your midst, few as you are, as for victory, victory will come but not because of virtue, not because of merits. No truly, but I am telling you that, according to my movements in the unseen realm, from country to country and from nation to nation I am moving, brooding, destroying and removing out of the way those things that are in the way, so that I may establish that Kingdom that must come earthward.

Do not say that there is no need for you to do anything now. Do not ask what is the purpose of doing anything when you know what is to take place. Surely you are spiritual enough to understand those things that are written in my word, "Before you ask I know." I am giving you the privilege of asking so that you will become operative, pliable in my hands, so that you may be channels to the end that you may know my eternal purposes on the earth....

"And He gave some Apostles." Watch that the strategies, struggles, difficulties and earthward movements do not bring you down. They have brought you down to organisation, as I have warned you and the conflict is to bring you down to that place. But I want you to function in the heavenly realms with me....I want to bring victory and to bring about my purpose in the three realms I have mentioned, but not from the earthward up through the spiritual to the Church.

That is your ministry, the highest, the foremost, the perfection of your function at this time. The need is not earthward, not nation-ward but spiritual. For is it not written that you have been given for that purpose of building, edifying and perfecting that Body? You are privileged to do this, but I am Conqueror. The gates of hell shall not prevail.

There is a spiritual kingdom. I want you to know that there are divine and holy principles, even attributes, which belong to the eternal Deity, that are to be incarnated and born in the spiritual Kingdom to then end that, in my eternal will, the Kingdom spiritually shall not be demolished, nor diminished, nor destroyed forever.

I want you to remember this, that even the spiritual Kingdom does not depend upon or belong to those that say, 'I must have my way!', for it is 'Thy will be done!' There is a will that must be incarnated in the spiritual Kingdom, that is born from the womb of the eternal Godhead, so that the ages to come may know of the realities of righteousness, and of those attributes that are existing, and have their home in the eternal Deity, that they may keep the eternal future in safety, and in preservation, from the powers of the infernal that are appearing on earth.

There is a spiritual Kingdom that will function eternally in the ages to come to display that which man lost because he did not come under the sway and sceptre of Him that blessed him in paradise. Yes, the spiritual Kingdom will function and will be in existence, parallel with, that Body the Church which must be presented to the promise given in my Word.

There is a natural kingdom and if you would like a

Prophetic Ministry through Ps. W. Jones Williams.
"Mark my word, my servants, and let faith be tempered with that which I am giving unto you. For I declare that there is a church,

that there is a spiritual kingdom and that there is a national kingdom. At the very outset the eternal Son of God concerning the Church gave the declaration of victory. Yea, definitely the promise was given with the declaration that that the gates of hell shall not prevail against it.

Think not that this victory (the completion of that eternal Body which has been predestined and chosen in the heart of the eternal God) is by your might and your merits. There is no might nor merit that can be compared, nor presented in the conflict in which My Church is found. The eternal Son, the Christ, the Head of the Church will triumph over all.

What a defeat there would be if it depended upon morals as when Ananias and Sapphira tried to deceive the Holy Ghost! What if I would apply the same principle and truth to the position found in your midst, not as regards money, but as regards the virtues of life? But your merits, your power, your credentials….that all who count themselves as such will not be found in the final consummation and victory of that eternal edifice that I am building, My Church. I am throwing stones aside as I am building and I would have you to remember that the declaration has been given that the gates of hell will not prevail against it.

If you would have yourselves in this building…I am giving unto all the opportunity of presenting themselves so that they may be pliable in the hands of the Builder to the end that the Church may be completed.

ii The sins of the nation in general, including its desecration of the Lord's Day, in the pleasure seeking sense, and its forgetfulness of God.
iii The need of the whole world in respect of its iniquity and its state of alienation from God.

Then a strong petition to God:
i For the Church – that the power of God may come back to His people in all its fullness for the saving of souls, the bringing back of the backslider, the outpouring of the Spirit with pentecostal signs following and the gathering together of the elect Body of Christ throughout all the nations of the world.
ii For the Country – that God may turn the hearts of the people towards Himself and miraculously intervene on behalf of our beloved land.
iii For the World – that the gospel may be preached as a witness to all nations, in order that the purposes of God may be fully brought to pass in readiness for His Second Advent.

Acting on the minute (of which a part only is given here) prayer was asked and made throughout the whole church, with deep intercession and supplication to God, that His hand should move.

A special promise through W. Jones Williams was given to the Executive and, through them, to the church in general on Tuesday afternoon 11th June 1940 (The prophecies at this time, which also came through T.N. Turnbull and J.D. Eynon, were made known to the whole church through the medium of the magazine "Riches of Grace No.7 of Volume XV August 1940")

Truly as of old, God spake and it came to pass.

foretell victory on the lines referred to in the prophetic message reproduced below.

The General Executive met at Wem, Shropshire from 11th – 14th June 1940. Those present were, Pastor's D.P. Williams, Hugh Dawson, D. Caleb Morgan, W.A.C. Rowe, T. Vaughan Lewis, John Lindsay and Jacob Purnell. The prophets were W. Jones Williams, T. Napier Turnbull and J.D. Eynon with the scribe, Harold C. Jones.

During the deliberations the prophetic ministry was, as might be expected, timely, Illuminating and strong. Summarising the same, minute 12 of the Wem Executive Report shows the alertness of the members to the need of the hour in obedience to the exhortations of the Lord. The said minute read as follows:

"It was moved, seconded and unanimously carried that the following is, in our judgement, the synopsis of the prophetic ministry received at this Executive meeting through Ps. T. Napier Turnbull. The principles mentioned therein are to be the special object of prayer of the church in general, and of the individual members, to whom we, as called out servants, should give a very definite and spiritual lead.

First, our identification with:

i *The sin and failure of the Church of God in general, and ourselves in particular. A repentance, humbling and confession of our lukewarmness, unbelief, rebellion and iniquity, for 'We have sinned, and have committed iniquity, and have done wickedly, and have rebelled, even by departing from Thy precepts, and from Thy judgements (Daniel 9:5).*

feared might develop into a stalemate, was dissipated and, again, bad weather turned out to be an ally.

The foregoing are only a few of the many blessings that indicate the victory was of the Lord. General Anderson's words are as appropriate to the whole war as when spoken at the conclusion of the campaign in Tunisia. He said, "Sometimes we are apt to take credit to ourselves for our accomplishments and not to thank the Almighty enough for His part."

We thank Rev. James McWhirter, and the editor, for the above inspiring article and we echo the concluding words with their fervent desire:

"We shall thank God best by proving ourselves worthy of the victory of arms. If we do, a great national repentance from sin and selfishness will cleanse us for service in the ushering in of the kingdom of God. That is the purpose for which we have been preserved, not to further any political or social cause, except in so far as they are compatible with theocracy – the goal of history: when the kingdoms of this world will have become the kingdoms of our Lord and of His Christ (Revelation 11:15).

HE SPAKE THE WORD

The extremely anxious period of the Second World War did not prevent the members of the General Executive and General Council of the Apostolic Church from meeting at the prescribed times and places. The Lord spoke through many prophetic channels in the assemblies of the church exhorting, comforting and warning. Some channels were used to

"Thou preparest a table before me in the presence of my enemies" found so complete a fulfilment.

Undoubtedly, the goodness of God led many to repentance, for a marked resurgence of spirit was experienced in Britain. But was it commensurate with the blessing? Is the question we should be asking today.

The story of the miraculous element in our progress to victory can be merely hinted at. Commanders and war correspondents have witnessed to the 'miracles' of the weather during the landings at North Africa and Sicily, which proved as important factors in advance as they had in retreat.

To superficial observers, the favour of the weather was reversed just before, and on, D Day; whereas the facts were as follows: "Because German weather experts were wrong, the Allied landings in Normandy found many enemy troops without officers and other coastal units were on exercises. 'S.H.A.E.F.' (The Supreme Headquarters Allied Expeditionary Forces – Ed) revealed yesterday that a day or so before June 5th, the German commanders were advised by their meteorological service that there could be no invasion in the period, including June 6th, because of continuous stormy weather. The invasion, however, was made during a brief break in the windiest month in Normandy for at least twenty years."

Weather conditions, apparently adverse, in the immediate post D Day period, influenced the decision of the German High Command to throw their reserves into the battle of Normandy, which, when the weather suddenly cleared, gave the R.A.F. its greatest opportunity of the war. A situation, which many observers phenomenon unknown in the lifetime of south coast dwellers.

About the weather let this be understood; Britain experienced its unusual favour at times of great crisis and emergency. Generally speaking, she had to cope with nature's ways which without respect of persons. At times, foul weather, when it was punctuated by sudden changes, proved to be our good fortune e.g. when the big offensive was launched in Libya on 18th November 1941. While the bad weather was not heavy enough to hinder us, it turned the sand of a coastal belt into a morass, which clogged the counter moves of two German divisions and waterlogged their aerodromes.

In New Guinea, during March 1942, after the national day of prayer throughout the Empire, the floods drove the Japanese back to their bases giving General MacArthur time to rally his forces and prepare the defences of Australia. The first time that a day of national prayer fell on weekday was September 3rd 1942. Of it, Canon Ottley of Canterbury, wrote, "…the tide definitely turned after the last day of national prayer. Observed on a working day, as an act of penitence and faith….it has received its answer in the stupendous events since, in Egypt, North West Africa and Russia."

Perhaps never in our long history was the Harvest Thanksgiving so real as in the autumn of 1942. The Minister of Agriculture, in a broadcast, said: "Some power has wrought a miracle in the harvest fields this summer, for in this, our year of greatest need, the land has given us bread in greater abundance than we have ever known before." Never had the words of Psalm 23:

asking. In a few weeks the Feuhrer's answer came, and the Battle of Britain was on, as a prelude to invasion.

For our defence we possessed 50 tanks and 200 field guns only, and the L.D.V. (later the Home Guard) had armlets!

Commenting on that fateful period, A.J. Cummings, in the 'News Chronicle' wrote, "…by all the rules of logic, by every military and political omen, we were doomed to invasion, defeat and prolonged subjection." Heaven ordained otherwise and the decisive factor is acknowledged by the Chief of Fighter Command: "I pay my homage to these gallant boys…but I say with absolute conviction that I can trace the intervention of God…but for this intervention the battle would have been joined in conditions which, humanly speaking, would have rendered victory impossible."

But for a sudden change in the weather in Europe, on the night of 29th December 1940, Hitler would have lit a bigger fire in London than Nero did in Rome. The city and dockland were ablaze with incendiaries, but the heavy bombers could not perform their follow-up task because of the weather.

The next phase of the war, on the home front, was the heavy night bombing during the dark winter of 1940-41 while the threat of invasion still hung over us. In the war of nerves one of the principle invasion dates, played up by German propaganda, was mid September 1940 during the full moon and when the sea is normally calm. At that time, however, it was the roughest in living memory.

The other date was November/December of the same year when their coming would be concealed by winter fogs. But no fogs came that winter – a

Those most qualified to answer said that, at the most, 20,000 would get away. Lord Gort was given permission by the War Office to surrender if he thought fit to do so. He did not. For, as the stars fought in their courses against Sisera, so the elements combined to defeat the foe. This is what happened.

To impede the enemy's progress the dykes were opened in the low Countries. Then the wind blew in from the sea helping to flood the land. When the rescue ships arrived – that superb saga of the sea – the wind changed and, during five out of the seven days of the evacuation period, the wind blew from the land, making possible the embarkation in small boats.

As a heavy storm swept to the mouth of the English Channel from the Atlantic, the wind changed and diverted it in the nick of time up the west coast of Ireland, and the armada of little ships, which might have foundered, carried on an exceptionally calm sea. A spell of wet weather and fog (which was unseasonable as unexpected) blanketed the scene. As a crowning mercy, the dense pall of smoke from burning Dunkirk helped to hide our men, who were lying on the open beaches.

The final result, of an epic story, was that, instead of only 20,000 escaping, the grand total was 350,000. This was acclaimed as a miracle by high authorities conversant with all the facts. The miracle was in answer to prayer. On Sunday 26th May 1940, when the withdrawal was in progress, at the call of the King, the nation, representatively, went to prayer.

How long would the barrier of the channel halt Hitler? That was the question the whole world was

This also shall never be forgotten, but for God's help, England would have fallen and, with her, many nations would have been enslaved. Because God was with England, they, and we, are celebrating victory – the victory of God. His intervention was the deciding factor.

As the story of Israel's exodus from Egypt is still told so all men recount the stories of Dunkirk , the battle of the Atlantic, the Arctic and Mediterranean convoys and on and on until that long, dark sea of years – "blood and tears and sweat" – was crossed.

With the thrill of escape still catching our breath, let us think for a moment, and thank Him, but for whose mercy, the rule of cruelty would have conquered; and the hell of Dachau and Belsen spread across the face of the earth.

Our first cause of thanksgiving is for the fact that the disaster of Dunkirk became a miracle of deliverance. With the collapse of France, the B.N.F. (British National Forces) had fought a creditable withdrawal against great odds. With the capitulation of Belgium all hope of making a stand had gone. Hemmed into a narrow salient fifteen miles wide by ten deep, were a quarter of a million British troops and one hundred thousand French.

What were their chances with depleted equipment against the swelling surge of the 'Huns' with their converging supply lines?

The Channel was infested with enemy craft. The town of Dunkirk was ablaze, and its docks and water supply rendered unusable. There remained only the harbourless beaches, barren of everything but death. What were the chances of escape?

CHAPTER 14

"HE SPAKE THE WORD" (Ps. 105)

One of the greatest crises, which might have brought unspeakable disaster to this island, was the Second World War with Germany under Adolf Hitler's leadership as aggressor. Desiring an 'overlordship', affecting all nations, he was apparently going from strength to strength and adding conquest to conquest (beginning with Poland) when the word and hand of God, signally, put an end to his ambitions.

We do not propose to detail either his successes or disasters, which ended with his death by suicide at Berlin, but we gladly avail ourselves of an article by James McWhirter (Ex-officiating Chaplain to the Forces) which appeared in the B.S.B (The Bible Speaks to Britain) magazine, edited by Hugh Redwood.

It is No.1 of Volume 1, June 1946 of that edifying periodical, under the heading:

The Decisive Factor of Victory

"*Nothing before equals this. Men will tell how after Warsaw, Vienna, Prague, Oslo, Copenhagen, Amsterdam, Brussels and even Paris, had fallen, the City of London still stood and retained hope for all others that fell. One country stood alone that will never be forgotten by free men.*

In Stockholm, June 1945, I heard different nationals express their gratitude in moving words. This was typical: "When all the lights were going out in Europe, one hope remained – God and England."

THE PRAYER OF THE HUMBLE IN SPIRIT
(Ecclesiasticus 35:16-20)

He that serveth the Lord shall be accepted with favour, and his prayer shall reach unto the clouds.

The prayer of the humble pierceth the clouds; and till it come nigh, he will not be comforted; and will not depart till the Most High shall behold to judge righteously and execute judgement.

For the Lord will not be slack, neither will the Mighty be patient toward them, till He has smitten in sunder the loins of the unmerciful, and repaid vengeance to the heathen; till he has taken away the multitude of the proud and broken the sceptre of the unrighteous.

Till He has rendered to every man according to his deeds, and to the works of men according to their devices; till He has judged the cause of His people, and made them to rejoice in His mercy. Mercy is seasonable in the time of affliction, as clouds of rain in the time of drought.

A new development during the past months has been the increasing interest in the work shown by the Swiss saints who have supported the work financially.

It is well that the increasing blessing on the Continent should be watched and provided for, as regards the supply of workers, by the European Council of the Apostolic Church who have the missionary's interests at heart. The day of small things is moving forward under the blessing of its Giver.

the assemblies in Grosseto and Castellamare, with many healings, 20 persons testifying to recovery.

In the south of Italy, Castellamare, Di Stabia, Gragnane, Vice Equense, Peggiomarine. Torre Annunziata and Casola, all testify to the spread of a widening influence for good despite Roman Catholic opposition. In Vice Equense, Ps. Wellings and Ps. Thomas were told by the Chief of Police that two thousand Roman Catholic priests, virtually, ruled the district.

Ps. Ulivagneli was ordained and set in office as an apostle, being Italy's first apostle in the Apostolic Church. How good it is to read that the Lord, through a prophet (Bro. Santino), by the same Spirit as stirred the spirit of the late Ps. Jones Williams, said that He was smiling upon the flock there. It was a smile as the sun shining upon His church, His garden, bringing the fruits of apostleship and prophet-hood to fruition. The seed of early sowing has indeed burgeoned under God's smile.

To show the rapidity of the advance since the first visit to Italy, we quote from a recent report of Ps. A.H. Lewis (The Missionary Board Secretary):

Grosseto Region
There are 41 assemblies and 1,100 members.

Castellamare Region
There are 9 assemblies and 340 members.

Syracuse, Scicily
One assembly and 15 members.

Italian apostle Marshal Ulivagnoli serves these, 4 recognised prophets 5 pastors.

the flock. In the will of God they were stationed at Grosseto where, in due time, a splendid hall was built.

At the inauguration Pastor's A. Turnbull, F. Hodges, W. Jones Williams and Dr. Carl Naeser officiated. Many souls were saved and bodies healed.

Though the Italian converts were poor, circumstantially, their fervency of spirit was blessed of the Lord and many were the enquirers. Other centres were also visited and the Lord worked with signs and wonders in each place.

In 1933 Ps. W.R. Thomas (a redoubtable footballer in his youth) consecrated his powers of mind and body to the Lord's work in Italy and, at this time, he, and his family are doing a grand work with substantial numbers of citizens joining the various assemblies.

In May of the same year, a further visit of delegates (Ps. D.P. Williams, H. Croudsen (Missionary Board Secretary) and Prophet Jones Williams took place with good results. At that time in Rome, under the nose of the Pope, a small company of believers gathered and it was felt the time had come to set the assembly in order. From the private house where they had been meeting they moved to a small hall attached to the American Episcopal Church (rented at low cost) and here, in New Testament fashion, the church was set in order, and elder and deaconess being set apart.

Escaping the ravages of the war, Ps. Thomas and his family, providentially warned, came home; but the Lord raised up a shepherd in the person of Marshal Ulivagneli and the work went on apace.

In February of 1953 Ps. Wellings reported (after visiting the Italian field) 21 souls saved while visiting timid souls from venturing as missionaries to countries dominated by Papal rule. Such craven fear has not hindered the A.C. missionaries however.

In the year 1909, a Christian gentleman went to Florence, Italy where he held meetings in a dwelling house, and preached the baptism of the Holy Ghost for believers. Two members of a Baptist church were obedient to this vision and were filled with the Holy Spirit.

In 1914, a young Baptist pastor, who had just finished his training, returned to Florence to commence a work there, heard about the baptism in the Holy Spirit, held tarry meetings according to the scriptures, and there a young man named Alfredo del Rosso was baptised. This young man later became the first Apostolic pastor ordained in Italy, eventually taking charge of the A.C. work.

By invitation, on the 21st February 1927, Ps. D.P. Williams, his brother Jones Williams, Ps. Sigurd Bjorner (A.C. Copenhagen), and Dr. Carl Naesser visited the Italian assembly, or rather, the saints whom Ps. del Rosso had gathered in several homes. There at Civita Vecchia a hall was hired, del Rosso was ordained a pastor and two others appointed deacons.

At Grosseto a group of believers intimated their desire to be considered to join the Apostolic church and two brothers were separated as elders.

After a visit to the August Penygroes Convention of 1929, Ps. del Rosso returned to Italy as the chosen of the Lord to superintend the Italian field accompanied by Ps. & Mrs B. George Evans. Their aptitude for languages helped them and soon the Italian language was mastered sufficiently to enable them to speak to and a great deliverance, for the Welsh nation). The difficulties are but a stepping-stone for a further revelation of His glory.

God has declared that His great steps in the convention, and in the Body of Christ from the very beginning, is in counteraction to the great Babylon, towards the woman who is going to be drunken with the blood (she is drunk already with wine, the wine of pride and of all kinds of things) with the blood of the saints.

"*Have you realised that I am preparing you to meet that woman who hath the cup of blood in her hand, which shall be drunken by her in the future? In my Church the declared mission to the heathen, although I will move towards the heathen by the means of my people, for I desire that none should be ignorant, but should hear the Good News. I desire you to understand that where my Spirit finds a place in my Body in these days, to fulfil the perfection's, purposes and movements of my Spirit in this age, it is essential that my Body should go forth against that Babylon, of which it shall be said some day, she is fallen!*"

And we will be able to cry with joy in that day, we who will have had a great part in this great step of His word. Her beauty will be so great and her breasts will give supply, for they will be so attractive that they will give sustenance to the nations to draw substance from her heart.

"*But inasmuch as I have separated you to have a part with me in this respect, when she will be ready to drink the cup of blood, and murder the saints.... Never the less, as it is declared in my word, I will fight her with the word of my mouth. I would have you to understand, as you move ahead with me, to know and acknowledge that I am the Lord.*"

Prophetic utterances of this nature might dissuade

If we look to the directions where our missionaries have been already sent, and also where those who followed the first pioneers, we find that William Philips (A.C. Superintendent in N. Ireland) and Evan Jones were sent there to the heart of Roman Catholicism. Ps. Hollis and D. Morris were sent to Argentina, a stronghold of Romanism (Other subsequent sendings were Ps. & Mrs. W.R. Thomas to Italy, Ps. Noah Evans to France and also, more recently, Ps. S. Scholes, while Ps. W. Gummer, after a period in France, was sent to the French speaking province of Quebec).

The Lord continued, "*Some, have been asking how it is that they are not sending their missionaries to uncivilised and uncultured nations, just as others are. They are asking that because they have not seen the mission of the Body of Christ at the end of this age. I have other people that I will send as missionaries to the uncivilised nations, and I will use them; but inasmuch as I have you, and have given to you a revelation directly of my will from the throne in these latter days, I am revealing to you that my battle is against the great Babylon, the great whore at the end of the age.*"

South America is under the spell of Roman Catholicism, and of superstition. The Lord has also opened the doors of France to our hearts, so our young brothers must be prepared. This is but a beginning.

Read the movements of the past, read the movements of the Baptists, the Independents, the Methodists and the Presbyterians. Do you think they moved without difficulty in their home and missionary enterprises? Read the account of Daniel Rowlands and Howell Harris, two godly men (they misunderstood each other on certain points, but all the same, God brought out of the difficulties and misunderstandings a great revelation,

"Then when the multitude is on the mountainside, wanting bread to eat, the word is needed there."

Some of you have felt the moving of the Spirit within you during this convention, that you ought to be at liberty; and as you march forth to your assemblies, you must be more prepared than ever to open your being for Him to work and to bring forth His word. He declares that this battle depends on the word of His mouth. It does not depend on preaching, that is, sermonising. Of course we must not forget that it does depend on preaching the gospel, divine revelation and understanding in the Book of God.

This is the foundation of the Church and we combine the spoken word and the written word together, because they are one.

But this great battle does not depend on sermonising and eloquence, because there are better preachers outside in other denominations. I tell you; this is the ground of victory of the Apostolic Church in the future. Let us remember to have faith in the word of God. Every elder that will fail, he will fail because of unbelief in the word of God and he will consequently fail in the plan of God for this day. It is a special aspect of the divine revelation to have faith in the word of God in order to move ahead.

Then the Lord moved on in regard to the Missionary aspect of the convention. If you noticed, you Welsh friends, the Lord said…

"In my Body, and in my movements in the church, I am not moving you to the uncivilised world, in regard to the missionary cause. I am making a direct move in the body of the Apostolic Church, through the prophets from the beginning, towards and against the great Babylon."

has is for other nations also. We are to live to others in the Body of Christ and be absolutely willing to sacrifice for the sake of everybody else.

The individual is to sacrifice for the assembly and the assembly to sacrifice for others (for the nations and so forth) and the nations to show the same principle.

"*You have heard in this convention of my word. I declare unto you that this is a battle of My word. It is by this implement I am going to conquer in the battle and at the end of this age it is the word of my mouth that will give the victory.*

The channels that I have been using could have been more obedient and yielded to me – yet they have reserved and held back because they have been snared, entrapped and fettered by the fear of man. It is no wonder that there is a battle now and that the forces of darkness from the pit are raging in this battle at this time against the spoken word. Satan knows that he is going to be conquered at the end of the age by the word of My mouth"

We read in the Book of Revelation that the word of God travels.

"*The enemy would seek to have the councils, the overseers, the elders or the apostles meeting, in every aspect of the divine government of the church, to annul and to break down the power and authority of the word of God through the oracles, and to get you to put this sword in its sheath. But there is no sheath big enough to place this sword in. This must be out of the sheath whether you are among the beasts in the wilderness, or whether you are in the storm when the shipwreck comes along.*"

This last reference is to Christ having victory over the Devil, or perhaps Paul on his journey to Rome and the angel of the Lord appearing to him when he said, 'Not one would be lost,' because he believed God.

living to ourselves. Now, dear saints, let is remember this fact, there is no benefit or blessing that we inherit, intended to separate us from the Body at large. Perhaps this phrase is not very apt, but I will use it. We may make 'pet dogs' of our experiences. I may have a special blessing, or a special experience, and perhaps condemn you because you have not got what I have got. You can then become narrow-minded, selfish and puffed up with spiritual pride.

"*But when I give a blessing, or an experience to an individual, I am not giving it to arrange things in private, in that person's corner and for themselves, but for the benefit of the whole Body at large.*"

Then I am not my own; I am glad of you, and you are glad of me. So let us beware that our blessings will not drive us to a peculiar, personal and selfish state, but rather that they should broaden us and make us more open hearted in order to convey the substance to others.

"*Although you are in the feast, the spirit of the age is upon some people. There is a possibility for one individual to be possessed with that spirit, and to live to himself, because he has some unique experience. There is the possibility for the same spirit to possess an assembly; and the same spirit to possess a nation.*"

Suppose the Lord would give to the Welsh assemblies some revelation, something special, in the will and purpose of God. It would be selfish on our part to think that we are better than some other assemblies, or some other nation, because of that. If the Scottish, Irish or English received such a revelation, or some aspect of the truth, to keep it to themselves would be selfish.

There is only one Holy Ghost, only one Lord, only one Faith and only one Body and whatever a nation

The prophetic word in the instances given is in Italics with the exposition, by Ps. Dan, following:

The Purpose of God in this age

"*It is my presence that makes your hearts to burn when I am drawing near to speak to you. Not only my presence, when I was speaking to them, but when I was unfolding to them the great fact of the plan of the ages in the scriptures in conversation.*"

'Now, the word that we have heard covers a great ground. I will try to be brief, and condense it, and get the substance of it into our hearts.

Referring to the time when He drew near to the disciples on the road to Emmaus. As you remember, Jesus drew nigh unto them and they did not recognise Him at first and He asked them why they were so downcast. He then upbraided them for their unbelief saying how foolish they were to forget what was recorded in the Psalms and Prophets about the happenings in Jerusalem, namely, the Crucifixion.

It does make our hearts warm! When He opens up the hidden meaning and the mysteries of the plan of the ages to us in regard to His divine will.

"*I would have you to go from the feast separated from the spirit of the age. The spirit of the age is fighting for his own justification and for his own righteousness. But I would have you to leave here and fight, not for your own righteousness but for my righteousness: the righteousness of His Kingdom. I would have you to lose yourselves in the future; lose yourself in the general need and benefit of the Body at large*"

That is another aspect of the spirit of the age. We may be blessed, and partake of a certain blessing, or blessings, that will make us narrow-minded, selfish and

CHAPTER 13

THE CONSOLIDATING WORK OF APOSTLE AND PROPHET

A feature, noticeable to those who have attended Apostolic Church Conventions, is the use made of the spoken word of the Lord through the prophets, in exposition to the congregation, by the Apostle in charge of the convention (usually the convenor). Some of our readers may never have had occasion to read such expositions, much less to hear them. A specimen, or two, are here given in order that the happy union (which has been referred to by the Lord as a 'marriage' between the two gifts of Apostle and Prophet) may be seen; although this 'marriage' applies more conspicuously to the handling of the spoken word in church administration. Conventions at various times of the year made such expositions possible where both ministries were present.

Drawing upon his thorough knowledge of the Scriptures, Ps. D.P. Williams would comment upon the prophecy (given in the Welsh language) to the evident edification of the listeners.

The expositions that follow are taken from reports issued of the 1925 Penygroes Convention, and deal with truths of constant value.

In more recent years the words given were in the English language eliciting much scriptural, illustrative wealth.

HERO OF FAITH

(II Timothy 4:13)

Bring me from Troas that cloak of mine
Dank was the prison and chill
My bones wax old, yet the Sun Divine
Is my ardent comfort still
His shining rays illume my night
Cheer my heart in this hired room
Filling my spirit with hope and light
Despite hell's threatening gloom

Felix and Festus, Agrippa great
I warned with words of power
And fear gat hold of those lords of state
As I spoke of God's judgement hour
Would that I could have persuaded them all
To seek the birth new-given
Preferred they the fasces Roman pall
To the cross and the Christ of heaven

The books and the parchments will solace my soul
While I wait Nero's regal frown
I have finished my course and soon at the goal
Shall receive a victor's crown
I have fought a good fight I have kept the faith
And clothed upon by love
A cloak immortal untouched by death
Will be mine in the home above

Thomas Davies
Beth-Horon, Penygroes.

reaching out to Ahmednagar and Kolhapur. Information was gathered which has since enabled further strides to be taken by the Missionary Committee. Converts were baptised and three believers ordained to be responsible for the work.

Miss Harvey and Miss Davis-Colley afforded much help. Ps. Hurst (Australia) ministered for a term; Ps. Collwyn Powell, Mrs. Powell and family subsequently filling the breach.

In 1956 the work is in charge of Ps. & Mrs. J. McCullough with H.Q. at Madras. There are 86 members at Vepery, Perambur and at Thacker st., an Anglo-Indian Sunday school of 41 members with 150 members at Tamil S.S.. Groups of Pentecostal saints are keenly interested in the A.C. work and expansion is prayed for in this interesting but slowly productive field.

hall. Three times he went on his knees but he was too agitated to remain there, rising and crying, "*He cannot save me; I am damned already; I am going out, but where shall I go? – To hell in the end!*" I asked him, "*Who is your mother?*", "*She is a deaconess in the Apostolic Church; I could not bear her prayers; I ran away*" said he, falling again on his knees, weeping and helplessly weak.

Suddenly, a change came, and saved he said, "*I have never had this joy and peace before; but now I am starving and there is no work for me in Australia, what shall I do?*" I said, "*The Jesus that saved you is able to find you work*", and gave him some money to buy food and procure lodging. Later he came back saying, "*I am glad to tell you I have had a job to do, work that I used to do, driving a lorry.*"

At that time a Missionary Advisory Board for Australasia was established, and interests affiliated to future mission fields in India, China and Japan (also the New Hebrides later).

A visit was also paid to New Zealand and a royal welcome given by Ps. & Mrs. A.S. Dickson, Ps. & Mrs. A.L. Greenway and the saints of the many assemblies. The work commenced by Ps. John H. Hewitt and further by Pastor's Cathcart and McCabe, with their helpers, was found in a flourishing condition. The word preached through the ministry of both brothers, as well as prophetic ministry through Ps. Jones Williams, strengthened the hands of the presbyteries; they in turn desiring more servants to be sent out from the homeland.

Guided of the Lord, a visit was also paid to the mission field in India where Miss M. Clark and lady helpers had centred at Poona, a slowly advancing work, consolidated in Australia and New Zealand, many able pastors and evangelists assisting in the work.

Ps. Jones Williams, in his autobiographical account 'From Pit to Pulpit' has given the facts relating to his visit to Australia along with his brother. They sailed from the homeland on September 12th 1933 and travelled in 1934 throughout the land, visiting assemblies widely apart; and including a part of India in this tour. Pastor Dan reported in his survey, on returning home, that they had covered 40,000 miles, slept in 70 beds, often on the floors of homes where beds were not available and voyaging in 9 different liners; no mean physical ordeal for the two brothers who kept constantly preaching the Word to hungry and expectant congregations.

A prior visit by Ps. Tom Rees (Tygwyn, Llanelli) and the unwearied efforts of Pastors John Hewitt, Joseph McCabe, John Evans (formerly of 'Carmel' Pontardulais) and very many Australian preachers and evangelists, had borne much fruit.

The years 1933-4 saw the celebration of the Australian Centenary that coincided with the visit of the two brothers. The last Sunday of the convention at Melbourne saw a great demonstration of the Holy Ghost with remarkable healings and many souls saved. One outstanding case was that of a man who sent a message by a deacon that he wished to speak with the visitors. This is what happened:

"If there is a God to be had" said the stranger, "this side of eternity, tell Him to save me; I have been living in sin." "My brother, I will show you the way to get peace", said Pastor Dan. *"Do you think He can give me peace?"* said the stranger. He was led through the back door into the

Africa saying, "What are you doing in my country?" and the conflict would be appalling. Meantime, what needs to be done is to redouble every effort evangelically so that the harvest of the redeemed from darkest Africa may be as large as possible. Also, in facing the future, God's blessing will richly endow the servants, handmaidens and native Christians of that Continent, but His devoted missionaries there.

Australia

'*He that goeth forth and weepeth, bearing precious seed, shall undoubtedly come again with rejoicing, bringing his sheaves with him*' (Psalms 126:6). The glory is the Lord's, however, for it is He alone that gives the increase, though other's sow, and with tears waters the good seed.

The work in Western Australia commenced through the happy thought of someone taking over there a copy of the A.C. magazine, 'Riches of Grace', which opened the eyes of a recipient to the perfect church order that was intended, not only for Perth, W.A. but for many towns cities and villages of Eastern and Southern Australia.

Deaconess Marshall of Perth was among the first of three persons to form the nucleus of the A.C. there. Membership grew and the homeland church was asked to help. Brother Glyn Thomas of Maesteg, Wales was much used at the commencement of the work in Australia.

Volumes would be required to narrate all the doings of God through His servant Ps. Wm. Cathcart and his devoted wife and family after their arrival in Australia. In four years, 37 assemblies were established or prophets and workers, whose chronicler must be found amongst their own people, helped Ps. & Mrs. Albert Seabourne.

This was also the case in N. Nigeria where Ps. S.G. Adegboyega (apostle) and I. Sakpo (prophet) are outstanding names among the native apostles and prophets with their fifty-two evangelists and 23 pastors. Surely West Africa has a cherished place in the hearts of Apostolic saints where Ps. Wm. Taylor (Kaduna) and Ps. W.E, Rhodes lie buried. More recently Ps. W.H. Grabham (who, with his wife, now returned, and Ps. R.J.J. Lewis, laboured in the Ibo Area of Nigeria) buried at Enegu in December 1955, has a cherished place in the hearts of the saints.

The labours in the Calabar area of Pastor's L.J. Derry (N.Z.), J.L. Ashwood, G. Parry Selby with their wives, helped by 8 native apostles, 3 prophets, 21 pastors and 40 workers (without mentioning in detail the ever increasing number of assemblies and members) is some indication of the marvellous progress of the gospel under the unction and power of the Holy Spirit.

The night is far spent and the hours of the day of evangelistic need call for unremitting, vigilant labour and sacrifice not only in the Gold coast and Nigeria, but also in Rhodesia and South Africa where the A.C. flag waves over an increasingly profound and complicated situation.

The word of the Lord, through the late Ps. Jones Williams, sends forth a terribly tragic note for the future generations. At one of the earlier conferences of the General Council at Bradford the Lord said, that at a future day, the children of Ham would turn upon the children of Shem and Japheth who would then occupy part of Nigeria, whole-heartedly embraced the apostolic vision, desiring to affiliate themselves with the Apostolic Church in principles and practices.

To the Gold Coast

Very much space would be needed to tell of the development of the work in Nigeria from the period of this first visit, while an incidental call at the home of 'black David' (a friend of Ps. Andrew Turnbull to the Gold Coast in those early days) has brought great expanding blessing. While some of the succeeding missionaries left the field for various reasons, honourable mention may be made of all.

Under the superintendency of Ps. George Perfect at Lagos, aided by Ps. Idris Vaughan, the work spread to Calabar (Ps. Vaughan taking charge) and he later did further pioneering work with his second wife (a nurse from Llanarthney, Carmarthenshire). Others who have done giant's work are Ps. And Mrs. C.H. Rosser (who in troublesome times after the visit of an American 'Latter Rain' delegation consolidated the work on a still stronger basis, eliminating many erroneous views that had found a place among the natives. Ps. Vivian and Mrs Wellings also did pioneering work strengthening the hands of the native pastors.

At the Elementary Training Centre of Ilesha Ps. Vernon Wood took up the threads of work previously attended to by Ps. And Mrs. Elton (whose secession was keenly felt).

Ps. Noah Evans, after much good work at Calabar, left for another mission field in British Guiana. The Gold Coast has been well served by Ps. & Mrs Sercombe, Ps. & Mrs. H.L. Copp and native apostles, connected with this body of native believers was undertaken including Yaga where many sought for, and were given, healing of the Lord. Clergymen and native Bishops also sought anointing and went away rejoicing, the campaign in this town sweeping everything before it, 400 people being saved.

On Saturday 17th October 1931, the visitors left for Ijebu Ode amid scenes of grateful acknowledgement for the blessings received and with hearty wishes of 'God speed!'

Welcoming them was a long procession of choristers singing appropriate anthems. With the help of an interpreter, the gospel was preached in power, some 300 anxious enquirer's being dealt with.

At Abeokuta, about 150 people attended the reception and later an audience was given them by the native king (the Alake of Abeokuta) who, when attending the coronation of King George VI, wrote (through his secretary) regretting his ability to visit the A.C. Bible School at Penygroes owing to a host of prior engagements. At the revival meeting held the same evening, the Alake, and his court, with over a thousand of his subjects, formed the congregation.

Journeying thence to Ibadan, the Holy Spirit blessed the ministry of the visitors. Many other towns and districts were visited, and a mighty outpouring of the Holy Spirit showed that the favour of God was with the visitors in a special way. After this tour, the delegation, together with the native brothers, sat in council, and matters of doctrine and government were discussed over an open Bible. Many questions were satisfactorily explained by the visitors, with the result that the whole of this native body of believers, in that

Nigeria

"*Thou shalt stand before kings*", said the Lord through prophetic ministry at the Babell, Penygroes to the subject of our biography. Soon, Ps. Jones Williams discovered that the kings would include the ebony coloured chieftains of Nigeria. Correspondence with coloured brethren at Lagos, Nigeria, during 1931 eventually led to a request for a delegation of leaders in the A.C. from the homeland to visit Nigeria. The Lord chose Pastor's D.P. Williams, Andrew Turnbull and Jones Williams to take the apostolic vision to that land.

On 9th September 1931 they left Liverpool for Lagos, Nigeria, sailing in the Elder-Dempster R.M.S. "Adda", arriving on 23rd of the same month, after an uneventful voyage.

On their arrival a reception was held, when Ps. D.P. Williams gave an address on the circumstances attendant upon their visit.

Revival and Divine healing meetings were held in the following days and it was reported that 800 people received salvation, healing and baptism in the Holy Spirit.

The Spirit's power was so felt that men and women in the church were swept off their feet and baptised immediately with unction from on high. Many wept; others rejoiced and praised God. Halls were crammed with enthusiastic congregations and, in spite of the great heat, the delegation was able to minister in freedom and power.

At the end of the three weeks mission in Lagos, another building next door to the mission hall had to be hired to accommodate the great multitude of people. After these special services, a tour of other churches mouth of the prophet (J.D. Eynon) at the Penygroes International Convention of 1948 that, in the future, offences would come, the schisms caused by certain leaders of the 'Latter Rain' movement in Canada and America, although much deplored, have but strengthened the saints and officers of the A.C. to continue steadfast to the end.

The prophecy referred to, as far as certain of the exhortations are concerned, were these:-

"*Therefore you can expect in the world around you rebelliousness; even in your own life's experience, you may expect the temptation to be rebellious, but let your lives find grace in my sight that you may humble yourselves before your God.....some indeed who will hinder the movements of my Spirit will be dealt with by my hand....but I will put the same principles to work in them, because I will shake the Body from one end to the other, and I will shake in and I will shake out and I will shake together, saith the Lord, for the day of reunion, the day of meeting, the day when your Head (the Glorious One) will gather to Himself a perfect Body.*"

The fact finding tour of Ps. Hugh Dawson (as President) and Prophet Evan T. Edwards did much to help the saints to judge what had occurred in the proper perspective and with a right appreciation of the motives involved. It is this help during 1954 that makes the year 1955 full of hope that those who have been misled will progressively return to their first love.

The tour of Ps. Idris Vaughan Lewis in 1955-6 shows that the breaches are closing and a consolidation of effort going on apace.

Ps. Gummer (the Maesteg convert, who learned French in the Danish restaurant in Paris) has for some time been conquering Quebec with the gospel, a feat undreamed of when General Wolfe fought for the heights of Abraham.

Invitations from friends of Pastor Hodges at Woodstock brought an opening, and from there the four pioneers motored to Toronto, where they were met with a welcome (already given by correspondence with Penygroes) by Bro. Benjamin Fisher. Many meetings followed, the Lord blessing each one.

The preaching of the written Word was instrumental in the elimination of many schismatic notions, and from giving a too exalted place to spoken word (prophetic) at the expense of the written word, balanced views were established, especially through prophetic ministry, Ps. Jones Williams being much used in this respect. At Toronto, such was the reception of Spirit-given messages to the believers that the Lord declared the flame would burn in that city.

November 5th 1922 (their last Sunday in Canada) brought a manifestation of the Lord's favour and power, and the contacts then made have since developed. The arduous labours of succeeding servants brought much edification to the saints and the work shows evidences of the blessing of God. Servants such as, Pastor J. Larkins, B.J. Noot (President of the autonomous church in Canada), B.G. Evans, W.J. Evans with his friend Bro. Nally and later strengthened by the pastorates of W. Gummer (France), Jacob Purnell, F. Warburton, George Purnell, Kenneth Whitehall etc. with other resident pastors such as Verge Card of Nova Scotia.

Having been forewarned of the Lord through the

the homeland visited France and strengthened the hands of the brethren.

The Second World War found Superintendent S. Scholas and his family labouring with zeal and success; but the devastation that followed the track of war brought a sigh of relief to the saints that Pastor W. Gummer, his wife and child, had escaped by the skin of their teeth to the homeland from the seething cauldron which France was fast becoming. They had preserved, in a large measure, the lives of the saints of the A.C. assemblies in the villages, towns and cities. Ps. Scholas and his wife were among the internees but later released.

In November 1946 assembly work was again commenced at Le Havre, so long under bombardment. Much interest was aroused and souls saved by the visit of Pastor's J. Cardwell and G. Purnell who also visited Sanvic, Harfleur and Lillebonne.

Ps. Carl Naeser died during the war while his friend Ps. S. Bjorner passed away in 1951 (his wife being taken home in 1955).

Although membership in 1956 is not large, a progressive work is being superintended by Ps. A. Dupont with assistance from Evangelist Francois Jequier (Switzerland).

Canada

Pioneers Andrew Turnbull, Frank Hodges and the brothers D.P. and Jones Williams took the opportunity, on October 22nd 1922, of visiting Canada. This account too should follow, chronologically, the visit to the United States of the same brethren, yet the faith of God makes the step from France to Canada but small.

time; I have placed my hand on the gates. I am asking before I break them open unto me. But I have authority, without breaking them, I have strength to break them but I have a key and I will not break the gates; I have a key to every gate at my girdle. The key of the hell and the key of the death of that nation (France) are there at my girdle; consequently I desire you to make a valuation of the worth of her redeemed ones.

Some of you have the keynote, "In the shadow of His wings there is peace" – peace for your neighbours. You shall take that message to your neighbours according to my will. I have, truly, honoured my servant (Pastor Naeser) because he has cleaved unto Me and has not let Me go. Is it right that I should speak of a man in this way today, as I did of one of old? (re: Jacob at Peniel) This one has been beating at my door as one in need of bread; he has sought and importuned as one who wishes to feed the need of the hungry. I will not turn away from him; I will honour his desire, saith the Lord."

It was not long before the Lord (again using the same channel), at a midweek meeting at the Babell, Penygroes, said he wished to have a private word with a young man who was sitting at the back of the hall among the small congregation. At the close of the meeting, in the presence of Pastor Caleb Morgan and Prophet Jones Williams, the Lord said he was offering first to this young man (Brother Tom Roberts of Skewen) the honour of representing the A.C. on the French field. The offer was accepted and Pastor Roberts laboured successfully, his knowledge of the French language being gained with rapidity and thoroughness. Others joined him, Pastor W. Gummer (now in Quebec) being among them while later the superintendency was taken over by Pastor W.H. Lewis. Various servants from

Before parting, Brother Naeser gave a souvenir gift of 1,000 Kroner to the church in Wales towards having an open-air baptistery at Penygroes, subsequently constructed by a local contractor. It has proved a great blessing to the hundreds who have availed themselves of the baptismal-burial during the August, Penygroes, Convention.

Such was the first entry into France. We call the following from the 'Souvenir' issued in commemoration of the opening of the Apostolic Temple, Penygroes.

"It would be well to give an extract of the word concerning France: '*Inasmuch as I have said that you should ask for a new mission field, ask of that nation of whom I have declared that her gates are gates of iron, that you may enter therein....I would have you prepare to go to the iron gates which are against me. But if needs be, I shall send an angel to destroy the gates, to fulfil the purpose that has been declared.*" (This word, It should be remembered, was given through Pastor Jones Williams on Wednesday 5th August 1925. Pastor C.G. Naeser being present as representing the A.C. in Denmark and France). The Lord went on in the Welsh language, a translation being now given:

"*For I cannot be deaf to the cry of the righteous, and those who call upon me. This field I have mentioned, buy it, not with the money of the 'field of blood' (Aceldama), but buy it with the blood which that money bought, that I may have an opportunity of exalting myself.*" "*....If you are ready to go in or to come with me to the gates, I desire a sign – everyone of you, upstand on your feet; but with that I desire the young people, who have consecrated themselves (of which there were 70-80) to remember what I am doing. I am doing it at this* *home he would be disappointed at heart for he has intended to carry out his purposes in order to attain the ends namely that the friends in France should have an opportunity to hear and to believe in my spoken word. Since he has mentioned and chosen one, without emphasising the other, to some extent, I would have my wisdom to be considered. For it is better for my directing, guiding word to be obtained by my apostle (D.P. Williams) for the objects which thou wilt find necessary and to meet those needs which he (Pastor Naeser) cannot meet."*

The two brothers, with Pastor Naeser, arrived at Paris late on Saturday night, about three weeks later, and found a few of the scattered, yet thirsty, saints who came together. In the night service one soul decided for the Lord and a backslider returned home to his Father amid great joy. Other meetings followed.

At the time there was no one to take charge of a settled gathering, but faith looked forward to a better condition of things. Many came forward for a private word of exhortation and wisdom in their difficulties.

Invited to a Wesleyan Chapel, they found the minister addressing the congregation, but on the entrance of the brethren, he gave them the pulpit and the Word of truth was preached for which they expressed gratitude.

Pastor Naeser acted, as interpreter throughout the stay of the two brothers and, during all the difficulties, never gave way although standing for and saying things which previously he was not assured of.

While waiting on the Lord on the last Tuesday of their sojourn, the Lord filled Pastor Naeser with the Holy Ghost and he spoke in tongues. The Lord confirming him in interpretation through the prophet Jones Williams.

CHAPTER 12

THE BUILDING UP OF THE WORK

The opening of doors to other countries was, and is, usually preceded by prophetic utterances through one or more prophets of the Church. This was the case with France.

France
While the brethren already named were in Denmark, the Lord indicated, through W.Jones Williams, that He wished the desire of Pastor Carl G. Naeser to be met in relation to a visit to Paris:-
"This is not the first time for the servants whom I send to separate from one another in order to accomplish the demands, which demands are more clamant than the feelings and desires of the human; and because of the measures to be taken, in the scales where eternal things are weighed, human desires and ambitions are not reckoned.

What I wish you, My servants, to rejoice about is that your leave-taking from one another (Brother's W.T. Evans and T. Davies left soon after for England) is not because of any differences of belief or partisanship, as happened in days gone by; for your separation as a delegation is in peace according to the perfect purpose.

Since my servant Naeser does not press for all to go, and some of you will need to remain in Denmark for yet another period, and you had some revelation concerning the time to be spent before you started upon this journey. If you all returned

ASPIRATION

What, my soul, was thy errand here?
Was it mirth or ease?
Or heaping up dust from year to year?
Nay, none of these

Speak, soul, aright in His holy sight
Whose eye looks still
And steadily on thee through the night
To do His will

                          Whittier.

EXHORTATION

Yet shrink not thou, who'er thou art
For God's great purpose set apart
Before whose far discerning eyes
The future as the present lies!
Beyond a narrow bounded age
Stretches thy prophet-heritage

Through heaven's dim spaces angel-trod
Through arches round the throne of God
Thy audience, worlds! – all time to be
The witness to the truth in thee

                          Whittier.

vision – an understanding to know the signs of the times and the seasons.

Mark My word, you will find the activities of given gifts again. of given ordinations, that will play their part in both the spheres of which I have spoken. But unless the government will be possessed with the Divine attribute of God, in understanding, you will be baffled, for the command will be contradictory to the human. When the word given towards the aggressive and progressive aspects of the activities, of that part and parcel of the Redeemed, earthward, is to move on, there is a switching over in the realms supernal and heavenly for to do the work ordained in that aspect."

Pastor Jones Williams, which stresses the co-operation of the saints and Church leaders. It is included because of its solemn implications. It was uttered on 4th November 1942 at Shrewsbury.

'Intercession of the Saints and Divine Guidance in Church Government'

"Government is the word that is on your lips and is heard of every day. It is becoming a common word but its meaning, power and possibility are foreign – foreign! When I say this then you must realise your weakness and nakedness. For government (I would have you to remember) means dominion; a swaying of the sceptre in strength; destroying, overcoming and even annihilating of the forces that are against you.

Remember that I am desirous that you should know of the government in its essence so that the effects may be seen; not a 'table talk' or a meditation of ambitious thinking, but rather an effectual destroying of the powers that are against. Government! I am still desirous, and still waiting, for the opportunity for the government to be placed in the places ordained so that it will not be a 'label' but rather a triumphant manifestation of the eternal resources, in all its aspects and activities, in the 'conquering and to conquer'.

There is that which I am wanting you to understand, as I have over and over again spoken, that there is an earthward aspect – a conflict and warfare – and there are those who have been called, chosen and trained even to war in that realm. But I want you to remember that there is a heavenly body that wars not on earth but in heaven. There are gifts and ordinations that are playing their part in the directing, stimulating and strengthening of the activities of the members in each sphere, and it is there that government must discern. For government not only means dominion and strength but

English and Scottish brethren. Among them were Pastors W.A.C. Rowe, J. Omri Jones, the late Andrew Turnbull, Hugh Dawson, V. Wellings, W.H. Lewis (the latter becoming superintendent of the Field. After severe experiences as Civilian Internee in the German Interment Camps during the second Great War he renewed and extended his former labours there and on the Continent).

The Church in Copenhagen became the Mother Church for the assemblies in Denmark that grew up rapidly, for the promise of the Lord that His chariots would stop at the doors of many throughout the land, rapidly fulfilled. That progress still continues.

From 1936 onward Pastor W.H. Lewis represented the General Council there, in collaboration with the Danish brethren, to further establish the vision. It is a melancholy reflection that in 1924 the Lord, through Pastor Jones Williams, predicted to the Pastor and Elders of the newly established assembly at Evangeliehuset, the coming second Great War in these words:

"Before long Europe will be bathed in blood, and your country (Denmark) will not escape."

How literally fulfilled that prediction was, our readers know, by personal experience or otherwise. How great is the responsibility of Church leaders who, bearing the prophetic word, need to consider what aspects its warnings affect others and, if at all possible, avert a predicted calamity, or warn those it may involve, so that measures may be taken to safeguard lives.

Through the prophets of the Apostolic Church how much has been made known which calls for the intensive intercession of the saints of God! This thought leads to the following prophetic utterance, through the brethren amid great rejoicing. A former Baptist minister, named Wulfe, became an opposer and when the news reached the Babell saints prayer was made that 'the wolf might be made a lamb'.

On 27th January 1924, following up the above events, a delegation of servants from the homeland visited Denmark. They were Pastor's D.P. Williams, W. Jones Williams, and Evangelist W.T. Evans. Pastor T. Davies, the scribe accompanied them.

The ministry of these brethren for a fortnight served to illuminate the saints, strengthening their faith, and making plain to all and sundry the purpose and scope of the Apostolic Vision. Among the converts to the vision was Brother Wulfe who conceded that a change, and a victory, had been wrought in his views and light was received as a result of prayer on his behalf. He was subsequently restored to the eldership.

Traditional views naturally opposed themselves to the heavenly vision but the visiting brethren satisfactorily answered all questions. On Wednesday evening, 6th February, the vast hall at Evangeliehuset, Trianglen, Copenhagen was again crowded out and, after unanimous testimony by the chief among the brethren of the blessings already received, with numerous testimonies from the saints, platform and congregation rose as one man to the testing challenge of whether they believed, and would become one, with the Apostolic Church in the British Isles.

There and then the bond between Denmark and the whole Church was sealed. A membership of seven hundred joining hands that night in one accord. Since that memorable fortnight many visits, fraught with untold blessing, have been paid by numerous Welsh,

Denmark

The revival, which started in 1904 in Wales, had, in 1905, reached Copenhagen where two ministers of the Palace Chapel had conducted revival meetings in the biggest hall in the city with blessed results. In 1907, however, the further truth of the baptism in the Holy Ghost reached the country and, in 1909, the Lord raised up Pastor and Mrs Sigurd Bjorner who gathered a congregation of several hundred people in Copenhagen. These formed themselves into a free Pentecostal assembly but, after two years, a great lack became evident but God had the remedy for His people in their need and extremity.

In 1922 one of the sisters, of the Copehagen assembly, visited the Penygroes Convention which made such a strong impression upon her that she persuaded Pastor Bjorner to attend the Convention the following year. A postcard from Pastor Carl Naeser (a friend of the Bjorners) duly arrived at General Headquarters asking for the name of a convenient hotel at Penygroes as he and his friends wished to attend the August Convention of 1923 (there is no hotel in the village yet!).

Duly arriving at Penygroes, the Spirit fell upon Pastor Bjorner almost straightway at the first meetings; and he spoke with new tongues. Then came the word of the Lord through Pastor Jones Williams calling him as an apostle to minister the gospel in the Pauline order of the Church among his flock.

Although anticipating opposition (which came in due course on his return to Copenhagen) he accepted the call. Arriving home, he found that the self-same Spirit had made the call known, and comprehended, by work has expanded. An annual convention was held in August of each year at East Lansdowne at which many came from the different assemblies in the country.

During the year 1931 Pastor H.V. Chanter was sent to America and continued working there with Pastor Larkins until 1935 when the latter moved to take the oversight of the Church in Canada. Pastor Chanter became superintendent of the work in the States. Other apostles and prophets have since then visited the U.S.A. (such as Pastor's T.Rees and W.A.C. Rowe) and, in 1934,

Pastor D.P. Williams and W.J. Williams again, in 1939 Pastor's D.P. Williams and J.Omri Jones and in 1945 Pastor's D.P. Williams, J.D. Eynon and Jacob Purnell (and later, Pastor W.J. Mcleod).

It is impossible to deal with all the changes that have taken place and the comings and goings of servants to the U.S.A. when under autonomy. Much was hoped for during more recent years, but the inevitable clash of personalities, warned by the Lord, has brought changes. The hall at Beverly Avenue was sold in order to concentrate on the work in Philadelphia; and a recent visit by Pastor T.Vaughan Lewis, to U.S.A. and Canada, shows that the blessing of God, in both countries, remains.

The Apostolic servants are acceptable speakers over the various radio networks and the going forth of Pastor Tom Saunders to U.S.A. will, undoubtedly, under the blessing of God, open up possibilities in West, Middle and East America. It will strengthen the hands of the A.C. leaders in the Western Hemisphere. Pastor T.V. Lewis reported a flourishing work in Jamaica under the care of Pastor W.T. Davies.

"Evangelebladet" in September 1952. Missionary offerings at home, for the year ending 31 March 1955 were £12,950.1.10 (twelve thousand, nine hundred and fifty pounds, one shilling and ten pence – ed). Truly a remarkable achievement. To God be the glory!

United States of America

By prophetic word through Pastor Jones Williams, many indications had been given of the divine desire to reach the United States. In the year 1922 a delegation of four (three Apostles – D.P. Williams, Andrew Turnbull and Frank Hodges with Prophet Jones Williams) were sent by the Missionary Council to visit a group of saints then meeting in the old brick Hall on Baltimore Pike, opposite Fernwood Cemetry, in East Lansdowne, U.S.A.. At first it appeared as though the whole purpose, for which the delegation had been sent, would be destroyed for the enemy had unleashed his evil forces in false propaganda.

In a mighty and wonderful way, however, the Lord undertook for the visitors. God blessed the brethren and the outcome of the visit was the establishing of the first Apostolic Church in America. This company continued services in a private house on Hirst Avenue (or possibly First Avenue – ed) for several months until a hall was secured in Baltimore Avenue, as stated, where regular services were continued until August 1930. A new church building was then erected on Beverly Avenue.

In 1927 Pastor Joseph Larkins of Scotland was sent to take charge of the work in the U.S.A. and the East Lansdowne Church became the General Headquarters.

Shortly after the church became chartered under the laws of the State of Pennsylvania and since then the

Lord. For all the manmade things are coming down, yea, coming down; and I am preparing to build up and no man shall bring down that which I build, for I am the Master Builder."

An Idea of the growth of the Missionary fields may be grasped by the following figures. At a meeting, which heard the above quoted word, the late President, Pastor D.P. Williams, said there was £91 in the Welsh Missionary Fund. Pastor Hollis had a gift of £50 from a friend while the need was £200 to send the three missionaries to Argentina. There was, at that time, three men representing the A.C. in the North of Ireland. Support was being given by the Hereford Area to a lady missionary (Miss Clark) in India. The Church celebrated twenty-five years of missionary effort in the month of September 1947 at the Bradford Missionary Centre. There were Apostolic missionaries also in China (Denmark being represented by Miss Pederson there), and a succession of missionaries have made progress in India, Nigeria, Calabar, Gold Coast, South Africa, U.S.A., Canada (both now autonomous countries) Ireland, France, Denmark, Norway and Germany. To the latter country, in its distress after the last Great War (1939-45) a proposal made by the President, Pastor Hugh Dawson, was supported and seconded by Pastor Lindsay and T. Stephens (both had lost sons in that war). It was carried, unanimously, and generously helped financially, by the whole Church at home and in Denmark, to send food parcels to Germany with clothing. Voluntary collections from Great Britain and N. Ireland assemblies totalled £800 per quarter.

Denmark celebrated thirty years of blessing in a special edition of the Apostolske Kirke magazine *of the Headquarters, for that work, I would have to be in this place where you are now standing, saith the Lord, for a great purpose have I in this. Are you willing for My will?*

This I would declare, the Headquarters of My Church would be in this place. I would have you to hold a monthly meeting in all the assemblies in all the nations, even in the three nations, yea, the first Monday in each month, a Missionary meeting and Missionary collection. That which My people will bring in through the collection should be sent forth unto this place saith the Lord. Are you willing?...."

"And, in connection with the Missionary Movement, I would have you to call it the Apostolic Church Missionary Movement; and again, 'The Apostolic Church Missionary Herald' – I mean the magazine that shall be scattered abroad through the land, and the printing of that paper, even that 'Herald', shall take place in this place, saith the Lord."

The Missionary Council, or Committee, was then set up. The arrangement of General Headquarters was at Penygroes with Financial Centre at Glasgow. The Missionary Centre at Bradford was later confirmed in 1934 and the event mirrored in the 'Unity Number' of the Apostolic Herald, October 1934.

How heartening for the future to read again the words of the Lord with regard to the A.C. Missionary Movement and to see its part fulfilment!

"Remember that you are listening and hearkening to great words at this season and that I am the Potter and you are the clay. Mark ye My word, that even those that are of dark skin shall rejoice for your gathering this night and many in this land, and the other side of the seas, shall rejoice in the knowledge that you shall spread abroad that you are one in this, for you are prepared of Me to save the situation, saith the

CHAPTER 11

PIONEERING IN WIDER FIELDS

Establishment of one Missionary Centre.

Since this chapter is devoted to the part played by Pastor Jones Williams in the building up of the work (although only an infinitesimal portion of the prophetic utterances can be quoted), it will be well to set down the Word of the Lord, through him, which established the united Missionary Movement. This uprooted and abolished the national tendencies that were then at work.

Speaking on Good Friday, April 22, 1922 at Albert Street Elders Room, Bradford, the Lord said:-

"*But I would have you to know this, that I am revealing at this season My will concerning the Missionary, for in unity I would have you to work in this matter. For I will not have the three nations to raise a Missionary cause of their own. Nay, verily, one Missionary Movement would I have you to know My will regards, for I have those of My choice in the midst of the three nations, but you cannot send them if you are going to act separately. Nay, verily, but if you are willing for My plan, yea for My will, I will cause them, who I have chosen in the assemblies of the nations to know that a Body I have prepared for that purpose; yea, My will shall I reveal unto you.*

This I would have you to know that all work, in connection with those the other side of the sea, ye are to reckon as a Missionary work. I would have you to be in unity. The centre

"Christ also pleased not Himself"
(Romans 15:3)

He so far thy good did plot
That His own self He forgot
Did He die, or did He not?

George Herbert

O Lord that I could waste myself for others
With no ends of my own
That I could pour myself into my brothers
And live for them alone

Such was the life Thou livedst; self-abjuring
Thine own pains never easing
Our burdens bearing, our just doom enduring
A life without self pleasing

F.W. Faber

not see eye to eye with the Missionary Centre regarding house rent, finance and the field of labour. He cabled that he could never agree to the arrangement suggested by the Missionary Council. He resigned in April 1924 and was followed in the superintendency of the field by Pastor David Morris (the latter, meantime, being married to Miss Davies of Skewen). Mrs Morris returned with her husband assisted by two missionaries; James Turnbull (son of the late Pastor Andrew Turnbull) and B. George Evans. Mrs. James Turnbull and Mrs. George Evans later rendered valuable help on

the field and much prosperity followed until it was expedient to withdraw therefrom.

Argentina has more recently, again, been referred to in prophecy through the mouth of Pastor J. Omri Jones and it remains to be seen whether the work will be taken up again by the Missionary Council. The Apostolic Church, U.S.A and Canada, has already a work in Jamaica and may some day reach Argentina and Bolivia again.

the Scottish assemblies, because you are the Missionary H.Q. now."

Preparatory for this, the Lord, through Pastor Jones Williams, indicated through prophecy (at the Plymouth Hall, Swansea, September 1921) that Pastor Hollis and his wife were to 'visit the assemblies in circuit as much as possible, that the saints might know him and be moved to support him'. (Incidentally, the Lord predicted that the following year Pastor D.P. Williams should visit America and, even this, was but a repititon of a similar indication in 1914).

As a result, the three missionaries (Pastor and Mrs Hollis and David Morris) sailed on the S.S Ortega and arrived at Tucuman, the chief city of Argentina, on 24th August 1922 (Accounts of the progress of the work will be found in the A.C. Missionary Herald from October 1922 onwards).

To show our readers how completely Pastor Jones Williams was in the possession of His Lord the following is recalled. While Pastor's D.P. and Jones Williams, H. Cousen, Evangelist W.T. Evans and the scribe Pastor T, Davies were in Copenhagen, Denmark, February 1924, at the breakfast table Jones described a dream he had had. "*You, Dan, with Pastor Cousen and myself were in a room together – the room having two doors. Pastor Hollis came through one of the doors and placed on the table a cable on which were the words 'Never!' then went out through the same door. The other door opened and a young couple (man and woman) came and knelt before you. Pastor Cousen and you, Dan, laid hands upon them and they went out through the same door as Pastor Hollis had gone.*"

As time went by, unfortunately, events happened that proved the dream to be of God, for, Pastor Hollis could

Argentina

United meetings of representatives from Wales, Scotland and England were held at Bradford in April 1922 (This culminated in the A.C. Missionary Movement being centred in Bradford).

Pastor D.P. Williams referred to the inception of the missionary work in Argentina in the following words:-

"Three or four years ago Pastor Joseph Hollis came over to Wales, before he joined the Pentecostal Missionary Union. He had had his baptism in Wales. Pastor Hollis is from England and his wife from Scotland.

Years ago he went from Bradford to Liverpool and from Liverpool to Penygroes Convention. He was shy, being a newcomer; but nevertheless on fire and there was something about us that made him afraid. He made himself at home with us, however, and we felt there was an affinity between us. The Lord had opened the door but I suppose he could not receive it very well and he went from us. "Let him go the length of the lead", the Lord said in prophecy through my brother Jones and, like a little dog, he could not go further than the length of the cord that held him. The Lord gave him a 'two years' lead and, at the end of the two years, Pastor Hollis came back to Wales.

We talked with him about commencing missionary work (never thinking of a scale such as this) and, in last year's Convention, August 1921, the Lord said that there would be a conference again on the Mount where Pastor Hollis would not be present. We had not a farthing to send him forth.

We collected £90 in Wales ready to send him, his wife and Mr David Morris (son of Mr. Wm. Morris of Trebanos). There is a collection tonight in Wales and Scotland in order that the missionary fund should send him forth. Now this belongs to you, Bradford people, as much as it belongs to the Welsh and becoming responsible for the administration of the Belfast Area in the persons of Pastor's J. Cardwell and J.F. Phillips. Pastor V. Wellings, and others, later joined these from the mainland including Pastor's William H. Humphreys, R.Stanton, W.L. Rowlands and J. Pridie.

The increasing number of elders, with other officers, in assemblies such as Ava Street, Frankfurt Street, Gt. Victoria Street, Old Park Road (Belfast), Lisburn, Lurgan, Waringstown, Battlehill, Banbridge, Portadown, Dromore, Muckamore, Ballymena and Portglenone have given loyal support attesting the blessing of God in the counties of Armagh and Down. Hopes look forward to Eire and the opening of doors there.

How truly fulfilled is that prophetic utterance, at 'Berachah', Dafen in October 1920, through the mouth of God's prophet W.Jones Williams to His servant Pastor Wm. Phillips:-

"Free thyself from all anxiety; leave it this side of the water; go forth in the light. I do not say there will not be difficulties and crosses with similar obstacles. If I did, it would not be Me for I always speak the truth and repeat that all should count the cost before setting forth. I declare that, whatever will come, I am mightier than all. I have not allowed any servant of Mine to do as they like and to be headstrong, though not a hair on their heads will be endangered, and yet, they were all martyred; but that responsibility and reckoning is in My keeping. Therefore, grip Me (that sendeth thee), in faith, for in sending I promise to be with thee. Thou shalt welcome with joy others of thy brethren, so all is safe guarded, and I will set-to My seal that I am with thee and this will suffice."

Then Brother's Tom Jones and Isaac Roberts appeared having travelled from Dowlais.

As the steamer crossed the bar, behold, we were twelve and remembered the word of the Lord, the previous February, when Brother Fisher was told, "*Be thou encouraged for I the Lord see another twelve on the water coming.*"

What did we see – the Sinn Feiners? No! The failure of the fifty-three? No, no! We would have been failures ourselves had not the word come through the prophet J.O. Jones. "*We saw the Lord God Omnipotent, Omnipresent and Omniscient*", writes one of the eye-witnesses recounting the story of this initial pioneering in Ireland, "*handling all blunders and mistakes yet bringing about His perfection*". A conference in Belfast, even in the days of trouble. When Brother Fisher, and the saints in Belfast, heard this testimony they had confirmation from heaven to believe the spoken word for others had tried to persuade them that there were no such thing as prophets in the Church today.

This victory opened two wells of prophecy in the first meeting and the living waters are still flowing in the prophetic word through other prophetic channels since. Twenty five souls came to the August Convention at Penygroes, Carmarthenshire God having given the increase.

Pastor's Evan D. Jones, Idris J. Vaughan, and others, who formed an evangelistic party and were the means of opening many doors, joined Pastor William Phillips, in later years.

The formation of the Apostolic Church Constitution led to two 'called out' men (those who had received the call to full time service through the A.C. Council – ed) published these things, letters came to Pastor Phillips saying that they (the writers of the letters) did not feel like going to the Convention in Belfast.

As the second week came the riots were of so desperate a character that three of the chosen ministers sent word to say that they did not feel like going. "*It happened*" someone will exclaim. No!, it was not "happening". When Pastor Phillips read the last letter in the presence of Pastor Thomas Jones of Llwynhendy, the prophet J. Omri Jones being also present, Thomas Jones remarked, "*That's the end of the Belfast Convention.*" Then the word of the Lord proceeded out of the mouth of prophet Omri Jones, "*Go thou, for I am God of land and sea. I would add that the bullet is not yet made to slay you; therefore, go thou and I will cause thee to return to the Mount (i.e. Penygroes, the Convention being in August) with the first-fruit of that land with thee.*"

So, next day Pastor Wm. Phillips left Swansea High Street (railway station – ed) for Liverpool. A few moments ere the train left David and Lemuel Morris of Pontardawe arrived saying, "*We are coming with you William.*" There was great joy as they crossed Landore Viaduct.

Arriving near the boat they heard a loud 'Hallelujah!' from the top deck. Looking up they saw Evangelist W.T. Evans of Pontypridd. So they sang together and, attracted by the singing, up came Pastor D. Kongo Jones and his wife, Miriam Jones, of Pontypridd. This added zest to the singing which brought another Apostolic saint to our company in the person of Brother John O. Jones of Crosshands (he is now in the Gloryland with some others of the already named e.g. Miriam Jones and W.T. Evans).

Will you not leave one of these men here? What about this man?" – laying his hand on the head of Pastor Wm. Phillips. Pastor Dan replied, *"What if we ask the Lord about it?"* – all agreed and Pastor Dan prayed: *"Lord, hast Thou a word on the matter?"* The divine answer came through Pastor W. Jones Williams: *"It is My will that you all return together; and I would add a word to My servant Benjamin, not to fear, but to be encouraged for I see another twelve on the water coming here. Be faithful and I will prove My word and you shall rejoice."* They returned February 22nd.

Brother Fisher, seeing the 12th July (Orangemen's holiday) coming, appealed to Pastor Dan for a convention and two good speakers from Wales. He asked that the convention be held in July. His letter was read before the Lord at the Skewen Overseer's Meeting and the Lord was asked who should be sent. The word came through Pastor Jones Williams: *"Write and tell him not to hold the convention in July but in the second week of June."* Brother Fisher, on being acquainted of this, replied that he could not agree because there were no conventions and holidays in Belfast in June, and July 12th was their national holiday. He added, rather candidly, that Welshmen did not know Irish customs. Once more, the Lord said, *"Wait and see!"* Brother Fisher acquiesced and a circular was sent around to the assemblies of England, Scotland and Wales inviting them to the Belfast June Convention.

Pastor Wm. Phillips received appeals from 50 persons to arrange lodgings for them in Belfast. Alas, however, on June 1st, the Sinn Feiner's fired upon the Orangemen at Seaforth Street, Belfast, and the riots commenced. Murder, and the shedding of blood, took place on a large scale all over the city. As the press

For I would have you to realise, My servants, that I am preparing to make a name for Myself in the way that I will accomplish my purpose in you, for great, indeed, is that which I have begun. Woes to that one that shall hinder Me for I will grind into dust those that shall set their hand against Me.

I would have you, My servants, to be willing in all things to suffer; if you suffer with Me you shall reign. You are not to seek for comfort but you are to be willing to sacrifice your comforts and be willing to separate yourselves from your families, if that will be My way. Yes, even to go and work and stay yourselves and also to move with your families as I will lead you."

Evangelist Evan D. Jones had been called to be a 'Home Missioner' during the meetings held to open Salem (local A.C. Church - ed), Skewen in December 1919. Indications were given, of the Lord that his training would lead to service overseas.

Pastor Wm. Phillips had, after a period of serving the Lord at Aberayron, ministered to the Assembly at Tygwyn, Llanelli. At the Dafen meetings (October 1919) held at 'Berachah' it was further indicated that Evangelist Evan D. Jones should accompany Pastor Phillips to the Emerald Isle (Northern Ireland).

On arrival in Belfast a fourteen-day mission was held at a Hall (113 Victoria Street) but for the first week without visible results. On the last Sunday 35 souls were saved, among them a family of seven. Eventually, eighty-seven accepted the right hand of fellowship.

Conversing with Pastor D.P. Williams and the brethren, brother Benjamin Fisher said, "*I feel rather discouraged seeing you all are going back to Wales leaving these souls on my hands, for I am working every day and they need teaching and visiting, especially at such a time as this.*

when the office was transferred to Penygroes with Pastor D. Caleb Morgan as Treasurer and Scribe Davies as clerk.

Northern Ireland

During 1919 the Lord began to speak concerning Ireland and the possibility of commencing a work there. On the invitation of an Irish brother (Benjamin Fisher), approved of the Lord through a subsequent enquiry concerning the wisdom of such a visit, Pastor D.P. Williams, W.J. Williams, J. Omri Jones, William Phillips, Evangelist Evan D. Jones, Wm I. James (Pontardawe) and Elder Alfred Lewis went over to Belfast in January 1920. They travelled with a warning from the Lord that the enemy had entrenched himself, but that the Lord would throw shells of tremendous calibre into the trenches.

There was a word at the Glasgow Convention on 1st January 1920 which had prepared the brethren for what was coming. In the presence of the late Pastor Andrew Turnbull, Pastor Brownlie, Weir, J. Macpherson and others, the Lord had declared through Jones Williams:-

"*For I even call that one in the midst, from the little nation (Pastor William Phillips from Wales) to send him forth unto that place (Ireland) that I may work indeed. For though they have been rebelling against one another, and rebelling against Me at this season, I have amongst those, and amongst that nation, My choice. I will cause My servant to go and you shall know that I am with him. Thou shalt not fear for I will give thee strength; I will give thee light and I will give thee power that, by the name by which you are sent forth, many shall bend, many shall bow indeed, saith the Lord.*

of short stature'), the saints rejoiced very often, at the Penygroes 'Babell' (their meeting place after leaving the 'Evangelical Hall'), with praises and dancing in the Spirit.

Foreign Missions

The needs of the heathen in foreign countries had exercised the minds of the servants and saints of God, in the Welsh section of the Apostolic Church, before the other sections in the Homeland had linked up their sectional efforts to form the A.C Missionary Movement with a Missionary Centre at Bradford in 1922.

During the brief affinity with the Apostolic Faith Church with Headquarters at Bournemouth, Hampshire, the Welsh assemblies had contributed from about 1911 onwards to missionary activities. Pastor's Wm. Roderick and James Brooke had been sent forth to South Africa. Withdrawing from that connection, for justifiable reasons, some forty servants (overseers of assemblies) met at Birchgrove, Swansea Valley on 31st January 1919 under the chairmanship of Pastor D.P. Williams. They decided that a missionary offering should be taken at each assembly and remitted to the then appointed treasurer, Overseer John Williams of Rehoboth, Crosshands with Overseer David Jones (Dentist) of Penygroes as Secretary (both brethren now in the Gloryland). Every six months accounts were to be rendered to the General Secretary (Welsh section), Pastor Thomas Jones, Lwynhendy. The office was in the middle room of 'Clifton House', Lwynhendy, near Llanelli, where (in 1920) Scribe Thomas Davies was added to the staff as shorthand writer and typist. Accounts and circulars were issued weekly until 1923

CHAPTER 10

A PROPHET
'TO THROW DOWN, TO BUILD
AND TO PLANT'

Our readers will, after a perusal of this chapter, notice how apt and true, as regards the subject of this memoir, are the references quoted from the Book of Jeremiah chapter eight. Though it may savour of impertinence to the reader, of the exploits performed by the late Pastor Jones Williams, there was nothing boastingly human or out of place in the incident we now recall concerning him. It can truly be said in the words of scripture, as in the case of Gideon - 'and God clothed Himself with Gideon' – that He also put on, as with a garment, His prophet, from the cradle of mystery.

At one of the August Penygroes Conventions, held in the Memorial Hall, Pastor Jones Williams took for his text, "*There was a man sent from God whose name was John*" (John 1:6). Proceeding to magnify his office, the speaker said, "*And there was a man sent from God whose name was William Jones Williams.*" It was not long before he justified his assertion, with the manifest approval of the audience, answering taunts of the Adversary and of men with chapter and verse.

As certain countries and nations were mentioned by the Lord in prophetic utterance through the 'gwr bychan' (as the Lord called him, i.e. 'small man' or 'man enlightenment and direction which were needed. Each member of the Body of Christ, as represented in the Movement known as 'The Apostolic Church' would know the Lord in a fuller sense from the least to the greatest. The Lord has faithfully kept His promise as His members can testify.

As we have to keep this volume within an expedient compass, a few only of the prophecies, on doctrinal matters, can be included.

Also, some which touched on the 'building up and pulling down' of nations. Others (culled from private enquiries by individual members) contain divine principles that are of great value.

It is regretted that the great wealth of prophetic inspiration, enshrined in the council reports, lying in the archives of the General Headquarters, Missionary Centre and Financial Centre can be drawn upon only to this limited extent and are confined, for the purpose of this memoir, to words spoken of the Lord though Pastor Jones Williams.

(In order to keep the continuity of the biography, examples of the prophecies are contained in the Appendix at the conclusion of this book – Ed)

CHAPTER 9

PROPHET

The reader's appetite will have been whetted to taste the spoken word of God that fed so many thousands of readers and listeners throughout the assemblies of the Apostolic Church, not only in these Islands but also in the five Continents.

The records of the prophetic ministry (not only through Pastor Jones Williams but other International Prophets such as J.Omri Jones, T. Napier Turnbull, W.A.C. Rowe, J.D. Eynon, Evan T. Edwards, G. Purnell and many others) have successfully been circulated to the A.C. Assemblies and printed in the various magazines and publications of the church.

Before unity was achieved in 1934, it was the custom within the Welsh section of the church, to circularise the Welsh prophecies with an English translation, for the inheritance of Christ's members permits bilinguality.

During 1911-1934 it was usual to 'enquire of the Lord' regarding various matters that pressed heavily on individual saints and never did the Lord refuse His guidance, being a God 'to be enquired of'. As the work increased, however, the Lord advised that the burden of private enquiry should be eased from the shoulders of the prophets and, the members of His Body, should seek Him in the secret. Thus, by prayer and waiting upon God, they would find that personal contact,

But the road stretched east and the road stretched west
There was no one to tell him which way was best
So my brother went wrong and went down, down, down
Till he lost the race and the victor's crown
And fell at last in an ugly snare
Because none of us stood at the crossroads there

Another brother on another day
At the self same cross roads stood
He paused a moment to choose the way
That would lead to the greatest good
And the road stretched east and the road stretched west
But I was there to show him the best
So my brother turned right and went on and on
Till he won the race and the victor's crown
He came at last to the mansions fair
Because I stood at the crossroads there

Since then I have raised my daily prayer
That I may be faithful standing there
To warn the runners as on they come
And to save my brother that runs along
When the road turns east when the road turns west
And I point him to the goal and rest
This gives me joy and my brother as well
To stand at the crossroads in order to tell
In order to warn and point the way
The runners of life to the goal and the Day.

Anon.

reported to have been given, by the then vicar of Llanon to certain of his parishioners at the time of thoughtless rage and riot against the servant of God:-
"*If this is not of God it will soon wither away.*"

The answer is – it has not withered away, it flourishes more and more in the Five Continents and will, before the Lord comes, have belted the globe, provided the Apostolic saints are faithful to the Lord."

But how true were the words of the Lord through Pastor Jones Williams! The persecutions of Lystra and Philippi have their place in scriptural history and convey their lessons. It is only the Gospel that can regenerate the human heart, for the loving kindness of the Lord God (a love commended by Himself, for that when we were sinners Christ died for us) is despised and His heralds misunderstood and rejected, until Jesus is received, and His words, in their entirety, believed.

Note.
It may be added that at Aberayron, near Llanon, Pastor Wm. Phillips providentially saved his friend Jones Williams from drowning, while sea bathing. Also in later years Pastor Jones Williams life was in peril from opponents to the truth in Aiguau, France and Australia.

THE WORD IN SEASON

He stood at the crossroads all alone
With the sunrise in his face
He had no fear for the path unknown
He was set for a manly race

Bowen, a Carmarthenshire man. Mr Bowen was covered in mud, his trousers torn and knee bleeding."

The proceedings may be read in the Welsh Gazette of January 7th 1915.

No blame was attached to the Apostolic Pastors but they were brought into the case that justice might be done. They made it clear to the police engaged in the case, and to the witnesses (villagers), that they bore no grudge whatever for the treatment meted out to them.

At least three of the Jenkins' household availed themselves of that grace in salvation by our Lord Jesus Christ that was offered at the meetings. D. Lambert Jenkins (one of the persecutors - now an Apostolic Church Pastor) had a vision of the Lord at Picton House and received the right hand of fellowship from the same Stephen Bowen some thirteen years later!

When standing before Shiloh Chapel, Llanon, at noon on Thursday 30th June 1927, Lambert heard a voice from heaven saying, *"It is new life you need." "Yes!"* was his reply, *"but who can give me this new life?"* The answer came: *"Jesus!"*

That day a cutting from a newspaper had come to the house stating that Pastor Stephen Jeffreys was holding Revival meetings at the Corn Exchange, Maidstone, Kent. Lambert went there, and believed, receiving life eternal from the Lord, through the faithful ministry of Stephen Jeffreys.

Nurse, Anita Jenkins, the sister of Lambert, has also embraced the Faith, she once in ignorance opposed, and is a happy witness. She is now the wife of Pastor Owen Roberts, minister at Tygwyn, Llanelli.

Mrs Jenkins, their mother, was called home a few years ago. How prudent and true was the advice, old lady of 84 and Tom Jones with his wife and I, got into the car (relates Pastor Wm. Phillips). A shower of stones greeted us as we moved away, and we got away.

As the driver, Pastor Stephen Bowen, came back and garaged his car at the Central Hotel, someone jumped on his back, managed to steal the key, and roughly handled him for some distance down the road. Pastor Dan helped brother Bowen into Picton House.

The evidence of Capt. Wm. Davies, 'Clarovine' Llanon, at the Petty Session Court was:-

"I am a retired mariner and have been captain of a ship for twenty years. I am acting as a recruiting agent at Llanon. On December 18th I was returning from Aberayron (which place I had visited that day) and arrived at Llanon at 10pm. I was met by my wife who asked me to accompany her to Picton House, which I did. There were about 200 – 250 people on the road from the van, which I had alighted, to the Picton House door. About 50 people followed us.

As soon as we turned from the by-road into Picton House we were pelted with stones and clods. My wife got into Picton House and I stood at the door to cover her while she entered. I went to the porch of the house next door and stood there for about twelve minutes. During a lull in the stone throwing I managed to get into Picton House where I remained for about fifteen minutes.

I took a candle into the front room and examined the room. I found all the window panes broken, except a few, whilst on the floor of the room were stones, some of which weighed two pounds and some two and a half pounds. There were also clods in the room.

When the crowd saw me in the room they continued pelting stones and I had to retire to a back room where I saw Mr

Jason hath received, and these all do contrary to the decrees of Caesar, saying that there is another king, Jesus." etc.

The Lord, through the channel Jones Williams, indicated that the pastors would experience within a short time a disturbance similar to that in the Early Church. Pastor Dan went on with the meeting but, very soon, stones began to be thrown at the house. After the meeting he called at the Police Station and made a complaint to the constable.

In the evidence before the Magistrates, at the subsequent Aberayron Petty Sessions on January 6th 1915, the constable was asked the following question by the defending barrister:-

Barrister – *"Do you know a gentleman connected with it? (The Apostolic Faith Church) who goes by the name of Pastor Williams?"*

Constable - *"Yes, he called to see me the night before the disturbance. He told me that some people had been creating a disturbance that night (Dec. 17th). I Called at Picton House early in the evening of Dec. 18th and told Mrs Rowlands (one of the ladies of the house) that I had to go to Pennant that night."*

The constable actually said that he was there to do us a kindness, that is, to save us from a storm. It had come to his knowledge that a crowd of young men were bent on chasing us out of the village altogether. So Pastor Dan thanked him very much and besought his protection for that night. The policeman explained that there was an eisteddfod (session – ed) in the Pennant and he was compelled to be present. *"Oh well!"* said Pastor Dan, *"you are responsible now, being that you know we shall hold our meeting at 7pm."*

The meeting, duly held, went on until 9.30pm. An

of you and you, as Elders, plead the promise on her behalf." Soon, the Holy Spirit fell upon Mrs Jenkins, she spoke in tongues, and went on her way rejoicing.

When she returned to Llanon the ark was removed to a relative's house (Picton House) and soon the company of believers was increased by the presence of Miss Annie Rowlands (afterwards the first wife of Pastor J. Omri Jones), Miss Jane Parry and her sister; John Rees – carpenter and a few more.

Candidates were baptised by immersion in water, after some local frustration which, we shall see, was soon increased in volume. The application for the loan of a room in the local Library to hold meetings was refused.

In the course of time it was made known that we intended establishing an assembly at Llanon, Cardiganshire. Pastor's D.P. Williams, J.J. Williams, W. Jones Williams and Stephen Bowen motored to Llanon for this purpose, opening a series of meetings at Picton House, with a Bible Reading, on the evening of Friday 17th December 1914. Little did they expect what was soon to happen.

The Lord, through the prophet Jones Williams, commanded Pastor J.J. Williams to read from Acts 17; reading the verses which declared:-

"But the Jews, which believed not, moved with envy, took unto them certain lewd fellows of the baser sort and gathered a company and set all the city in an uproar and assaulted the house of Jason, and sought to bring them out to the people. And when they found them not, they drew Jason and certain brethren unto the rulers of the city, crying, 'These that have turned the world upside down are come hither also, whom

to my gun while near me was a veteran, in a red tunic and medals, with scars of many battles.

The divine interpretation, when I enquired of the Lord in the presence of Pastor Dan and later through W. Jones Williams, was this: "*Doest thou remember the state of thy mind at the time of the dream?*" I answered, 'Yes Lord, I saw no indication of prosperity in the town and felt despondent, and that the favour of God had left me.' "*This is my word*" continued the Lord through the channel, "*The darkness which thou sawest was the darkness as of the ninth hour, 'My God, My God! Why has thou forsaken Me?' and the thorns and briars indicated the crown of the curse. The cannon or gun symbolised the Cross, and the veteran – He who came up from Edom and from Bozra with garments died red to help thee in thy need, telling thee to stand to the gun. Go to the village which thou sawest over the water and thou shalt see My hand moving with thee. I do not entrust this cannon to any man; I use it Myself in My purpose.*" The word encouraged me in the midst of my difficulties.

So, making my way to the village of Llanon, I met a good Lydia, who, inviting me to her home 'Millet Park', asked questions regarding the progress of the work. Lydia, in the person of Mrs Jenkins (mother of Pastor Lambert Jenkins – Carlisle A.C.) was desirous of all that the Lord Jesus had for her and, soon after, made her way to Penyfroes (en route to meeting her sea-faring husband at West Hartlepool). Attending a meeting at the Babell, she heard the Lord speak through His channel in the Welsh language which she understood and a privilege she had greatly desired.

The Lord spoke to the Babell Elders, "*I wish to do a work this night. My handmaid from the village by the sea is here to receive the promise (Acts 2). Let her stand in the midst preachers as the One that preached to that woman at the well! O this sermonic pride! When will you rid yourselves of it, my servants? Hearken to My word for I have something to reveal to you; do not look for results from this series of meetings now but in time to come you will see the results. When I shall judge men in righteousness and tell some to depart from Me, for as you are now my witnesses, so you shall be so then; that is the time you shall see the results of these meetings.*

I command thee, my servant William, to go and invite those whom I have laid on thy heart, plead with them to come to the feast."

I tried to persuade one man, a sidesman in the Anglican Church, his wife being a member of the board of Guardians, and he promised to come, but did not keep his promise. At the last meeting a master mariner attended and Pastor Dan spoke of the love of God and the aweful consquences of rejecting that love. The captain became uneasy, rose, went to the door and shouted at the preacher bidding him "*Go to Hell!*" and slammed the door. We closed with singing and benediction.

The man, who bluffed me that he would come to the meeting, was later found dead in bed by his wife. The blaspheming master mariner was torpedoed in his ship near Lundy and all hands lost except the cook (Thomas Enoch Jones son of the Aberarth shoemaker, Evan Jones). God is real, even if we are not.

During that time, in intercession, I had a vision of myself standing on the bank of Drenewydd surrounded by bramble and fern and seeing a long gun with its muzzle pointing over the sea to Llansantffraed. The darkness was lit up when the firing took place, the light widening as it reached Llanon. A voice bid me to stand *your specials in the Chapel."* I rejoiced and thanked him heartily.

It was too late to advertise the specials so I got 'Tom, the crier' of the place to take his hand-bell around and announce the meetings.

Prompt to time, Pastors D.P. Williams, J.J. Williams (his uncle from Trecastell), Thomas Jones – Llwynhendy and W. Jones Williams arrived. On Saturday night, apart from the visitors named, two constituted the congregation, I acted as usher, the two being the village crier and his good wife. Truly a night of small happenings for that part of Wales! The president gave a message on the woman of Samaria but the well was rather deep, we had just a taste to quench our thirst and then away home to bed.

Sunday we had a wee revival for another spinster had joined and J.J. gave a nice message short and sweet. Sunday night two more joined us, Mr John Roberts (Draper) and his wife. Pastor Thomas Jones from Llwynhendy, being a retired draper, did his best to fit Mr Roberts into an Apostolic outfit but it was rather a tight fit for we saw J.R. no more!

Monday night reduced the five to three again; ditto on Tuesday and Wednesday. On Thursday the revivalists felt like giving up. Before doing so, the two apostles (Pastors Dan and Thomas Jones) decided to have a word from the Lord. It came with tremendous force through the channel, Jones Williams, asking us if we believed His word sincerely, adding: "*I have proved to you every inch of the way that these meetings have been arranged of Me. I have led you into this chapel according to My word and, when I sent you the choice of My heart, you were reluctant to preach to them. You believe that you are as good* merciful rain and William came to know that he also was of the elect.) Evan Williams had left the 'consuming fire' (Heb.12) and had joined the 'Burning Bush' (a sect from Wisconsin U.S.A.) but the bush burnt out and Evan died in America.

God had called me out from King's Dock Tin Mills, Port Tennant, Glamorgan and sent me to re-open the Mission. We were just five in number at Aberayron and I lived in the 'Clifton', Aberarth which house is by the sea.

At that time I was greatly depressed not seeing anyone interested in our testimony; for Evan Williams had declared from the housetops that there was 'no gospel' from Caergybi to Cardigan town and that the 'tongues and prophets' were from hell.

I was sent to build a church there, like Nehemiah, but the ass could not pass through the rubbish. We opened the little Mission Hall in order to start afresh and the Lord, through the prophet W. Jones Williams, told me to pray for the space of three weeks for He had a large room prepared for the passover. So I watched and prayed for that period and, having only three days to announce the meetings, the room came not into sight until the Friday before the meetings.

I went to the Gaer, below Drenewydd Farm to weep and pour out my heart to God. Suddenly, I discovered that the Weslyan Minister and his mother, with two members, were passing and the preacher asked, "*How is the good work going on Phillips?*" I wiped my face and replied, "*Very well indeed, we are going to hold special meetings.*" "*Where?*" he asked. "*Oh, in the Mission Hall*", I replied. "*Tut, tut! our Chapel building is empty here, hold* duty it was to approve the building, was favourably impressed with it and its simple wooden emblem.

The hall was called "Pabell y Cyfarfod" or, for short, 'Y Babell' (Tabernacle or Tent of Meeting). Here gatherings were held under the unction of the Most High until 1933 when the congregation moved to the newly erected Apostolic Temple. The Lord's hand being evidently with the few, local prejudice was, among the enlightened, removed.

Elsewhere, the propaganda work of the leaders met with unexpected opposition, We were indebted to Pastor William Phillips, A.C. pioneer of the work in Belfast and Ulster, for enlarging upon certain aspects of the work in Wales in those early days.

Cardiganshire folk are known as being hard headed, though warm hearted when their hearts are won, The villages bordering the bay of Cardigan have supplied some of the ablest captains and mariners in the world; Aberystwyth once being an important harbour having its own shipbuilding yards. Llanon and Aberayron also providing doughty captains and pilots, the names of their sea going craft being transferred to the palatial residences which fringe the west sea coast of the principality.

Pastor Wm. Phillips writes:

"I was called to take the place of Evan Williams at Aberayron in 1912. (Here it may be explained that Pastor Phillips was, at the time of the revival in 1904, working in Martinsferry, Ohio, U.S.A.. Reading in the Swansea 'Cambrian Daily Leader' of the mighty visitation in Wales, he came home to his native Plasmarl and followed the revival meetings. The heavens were as brass but he persisted and, soon, down came the

Roberts that when their transitory fame, if fame may be the right word, is extinguished, they are condemned to live the balance of their days as a perpetual anti-climax.' How little the author knows! Evan Roberts resisted the most glamorous offers to return into the Methodist ministry. He never sought honour or position; he was content to serve God in the shadows as he had be called to serve Him in the intensive limelight of 1904/5.

Mystics like him are rare. He ended his days as he had planned – an intercessor. A truly great man of God is being laid to rest at Loughor tomorrow, and the whole of Wales mourns her greatest prophet since the eighteenth century."

We have before referred to the unction which fell upon W. Jones Williams at Llanllian, under the hands of Evan Roberts.

Misunderstanding and prejudice brought schism even within the little band that, after holding cottage meetings and gathering in local rooms at Penygroes, ultimately (in 1910) built the present Evangelistic Hall there. Some thought the events taking place were from the pit of Hell, others that 'speaking in tongues' was of the devil. Because of an ultimatum to Pastor Dan, it was decided, to avoid further controversy and a factious spirit, to withdraw. As many as believed the 'Apostolic Vision' withdrew to their own hall which was duly erected nearby. A wooden structure roofed with galvanised zinc upon a brick foundation and ornamented (by command of the Lord) with a cross. Put up in sections, the last addition, the wooden cross, found favour with the Ecclesiastical Authorities of the Parish. The then Vicar of Llandebie Parish Church, whose

Revival was of God. They helped a great deal to spread the flame that scorched the evil out of men's lives.

It reached the mission fields. I recall the testimony of the Reverend and Mrs. Rees Howells (afterwards leaders of the Bible College at Swansea) describing the beneficent influence of the revival in Portuguese East Africa where they laboured as missionaries, and similar reports came from countries all over the world.

Did it last in Wales? And what came of Evan Roberts? It did! There were sweeping social changes during the peak of the movement. Drink and gambling dens were closed down; the wife beater and the child starver became a model husband and father; the churches, for a change, were filled and the taverns emptied. In the course of time, the tide ebbed and left some flotsam on the beach, but, for the next generation, the bullies and drunkards, with a host of indifferent men and women, inspired by the revival, were the strength of the churches and enobling influences in their communities.

Evan Roberts retired to Leicester, to the hospitable home of Mr and Mrs Penn Lewis, where he was nursed back to health and helped Mrs Penn Lewis edit the devotional periodical, The Overcomer. Afterwards, he lived at Gorseinon and Cardiff paying long visits to London, where he stayed with Mr Sam Jenkins, the sweet singer of the revival – the Sankey of Wales.

To speak of Evan Roberts in his retirement as a physical wreck is false. He fulfilled the dream of the devout by undertaking a ministry of intercession, He avoided publicity and, if he were spotted at a meeting, steps were taken to keep his presence a secret.

Let me quote again from 'The Great Revivalists' (Thinker's Library):- 'It is the tragedy of men such as Evan

1904/5 will be laid to rest tomorrow afternoon (Wednesday 31st January) at the Moriah Church burial ground, Loughor. He died in a Cardiff nursing home on Monday 29th January 1951 aged 72.

It was at Moriah, 47 years ago, that the fire, lit at Newcastle Emlyn, began to glow and spread through Wales and the five continents. Evan was then 25. One year later he retired, exhausted by nervous strain. Now, after a long life of intercession in retirement, his body is committed to the hallowed ground of the church where he embarked on his mighty venture of faith.

Today, when religious meetings seldom find a place in the daily newspapers, it is astonishing to recall that the morning and evening papers in South Wales gave pages of space to the Revival. Hardly anything else mattered. Men said it was a time foretold by Zechariah the prophet, "In that day there shall be upon the bells of the horses, 'Holiness unto the Lord.'

London newspapers sent their special correspondents to inquire. Several would not accept the explanation given by the churches that the Revival was an outpouring of the Holy Spirit, the fulfilment of a Scriptural promise to a church on its knees. They called it 'mass hypnotism.' Or, as George Godwin maintains in a volume on revivals just added to the Thinker's Library, it arose from 'mental and physical causes among adolescents and unbalanced people, especially at times of intense, emotional fervour.' A natural enough view for a free thinker! But a whole nation of unbalanced people is a big mouthful to swallow!

Men like W.T. Stead (who met his death in drowning when the ill-fated 'Titanic' was sunk in collision with an iceburg), and cautious leaders of the various churches in England, went to see for themselves and they found the *to govern while Pastor Hutchinson stood for the principle that he, as an apostle, had the final word."* Other principles such as the need, in financial matters, of General Deacons were also involved.

There was nothing 'Judasaic' in their withdrawal and events subsequently proved that the Welsh brethren had been guided rightly within divine government.

The work in Wales (more particularly dealt with in a souvenir issued at the opening of the Apostolic Temple, Penygroes on Sunday 6th August 1933. Pastors Andrew Turnbull Snr., Thomas Jones, A. Gardiner, J.J. Williams, Hugh Dawson, Frank Hodges, the Architect Thomas Riley Esq. F.F.A.S., the Contractor Mr.

J.H. Grindall, Pastor Thomas Rees and Pastor D.P. Williams – President of the A.C. Council and Missionary Councils took a prominent part) went on apace, but not without encountering much opposition, prejudice and persecution.

It causes some wonderment that people, who should have known something of the history of the early Church, as set forth in the Acts of the Apostles and the Epistles, should have shown some bitterness against the work of the Holy Spirit since the first blaze of glorious enthusiasm evoked in the years 1904-5-6.

Mr Anthony Davies ("Llygad Llwchwr"), was converted under the ministry of Pastor Stephen Jeffreys and later immersed in baptismal waters at the famous Dirclawdd Farm, Llanon, Carmarthenshire. Recalling some of the reactions of that period, in the "News Chronicle" 30th January 1951, he wrote on the death of Evan Roberts:-

"Mr Evan Roberts, leader of the great Welsh Revival of

CHAPTER 8

PIONEERING AND PERSECUTION

The early prophetic ministry through many prophets had emphasised that the Lord intended doing a quick work in Wales. Through the same agency of His Spirit, that had commenced in the Welsh and Homeland assemblies, to ultimately belt the globe with the Apostolic Vision of divine government in His Church.

In November 1911, the Lord spoke through Pastor Blackman (Tunbridge Wells) as follows:- "*Go thou* (speaking to the late Pastor W. O. Hutchinson of the Apostolic Faith Church, Bournemouth) *to My people of the little Nation; they are a chosen people unto the Lord, though darkness be about their feet and trouble on every hand, yet, will I not forsake them. For I am their God and I will surely gather Me a people from the uttermost parts of the earth and they shall be one even as We are one, saith the Almighty.*"

Pastor Dan, and the Presbyteries of the Welsh assemblies, deemed it necessary, on principles of co-operation and co-ordination in Church Government, to withdraw from the Bournemouth Apostolic Faith Church. We quote from a letter written by Pastor Dan to Lewi Petrhus, Stockholm, from Copenhagen on February 12th 1924 as the latter had made some observations in his own magazine which called for enlightenment:- "*The Welsh assemblies stood for a presbytery*

"*In your patience possess ye your souls.*"
Luke 21:19

Endurance is the crowning quality
And patience all the passion of great hearts
These are their stay and when the leaden world
Sets its hard face against this fateful thought
And brute strength like a scornful conqueror
Clangs his huge mace down in the other scale
The inspired soul but flings his patience in
And slowly that outweighs the ponderous globe
One faith against a whole earth's unbelief
One soul against the flesh of all mankind

Lowell.

He has told me to walk up to you with the dollar." The Lord said to me, *"I have led you to sing in order to bring a soul to the front and I have made him to bring the dollar to the front."*

Our God is real, our God is true, no matter where He sends us and not matter what the difficulties may be. The half has not been told, but I am declaring to you that I have found God faithful for twenty-three years as I have walked every step on the word of God by naked faith and I feel like going on!

sitting alone in the kitchen, I heard you singing, 'O why won't you come in simple trusting faith.' I then went to the front room to get rid of the voice but the voice followed me there. I went up to my bedroom, and was preparing to go to bed, but I could hear the voice again. I have come in simple trusting faith to find Rest." He was looking down at me after standing up, and then turned to the congregation and said, "*It has taken God to bring a little man like this to bring me to the Saviour.*"

When he confessed, the cloud on the meeting went and the glory of God came down. After that, in every meeting, souls were saved and there is an Apostolic Church there today. After the stranger had finished I went back to the pulpit and the sermon came without effort to my memory.

Continuing to preach, and just about concluding my sermon, a man in the congregation stood up, with a Bible in his hands, and said, "*Pardon me, Mr. Williams, may I say a word?*" I prayed to God with instant prayer that he would give me wisdom to handle the situation that might arise from the unexpected question. "*Brother! If God wants you to speak I will not hinder you.*" He said, "*I am not wanting to speak but to tell you I have been a Congregationalist. I have been in every meeting and confess I could have been blessed more but for the bitterness that I had in my heart towards you when you came here, but everything is swept away now. The Lord has been telling me to give you a dollar, since I have been here tonight – a dollar – and I am ashamed to give you a dollar. I have been wanting to give you five dollars.*" Just think of it! – a dollar to a man 'on the rocks.' "*At any rate*" he said, "*I have been ashamed of the thought of coming to the front with a dollar so I have been asking the Lord to put a dollar in your hand and* not caring for me. You must save a soul and give me something today."

I went to the afternoon meeting to a full hall; another hard meeting. Again I went at night and as I was preaching my mind went blank and I lost the threads of my sermon. Yet there was harmony in my breast, there was music, and something was telling me all the time, 'Sing, sing, sing! But I had not the confidence, which was needed in myself, as a singer. Yet, after a second or two, I determined to sing:-

> *O why won't you come in simple trusting faith*
> *Jesus will give you rest*
> *O happy rest, sweet happy rest*
> *Jesus will give you rest*
> *O why won't you come in simple trusting faith*
> *Jesus will give you rest*
>
> (Redemption Songs 119)

I sang it about twelve times and I could see the congregation bewildered, probably thinking, 'He is out of sermons; he cannot carry on any longer.' But I felt constrained to sing. As I was singing the door opened and, a tall man, six feet in stature, came

in and walked to the front. He fell on his knees and I asked the congregation to take up the chorus while I went down from the pulpit.

I went to the stranger and placed my hands on his shoulder, saying, "*What do you want?*" "*Sir!*", he replied, "*I have lived the other side of the road for sixteen years, before this Hall was built; and although they have been holding meetings here since, I have never been saved. Tonight, as I was*

Two sisters had travelled eight hundred miles to the meetings and testified, "*We are going home to tell the assembly, to which we belong, about you*" and added that they would like me to visit them. I replied that if the Lord would have me to visit them then I would do so. A letter came in a week's time saying that, unanimously, they had decided to give me a two-week campaign in their church – which was eight hundred miles away.

I visited them and arrived penniless without the wherewithal to buy a stamp to send a letter home. I commenced the meetings.

I noticed that the majority of those present had their Bibles and found that, practically all, were Pentecostal saints from the districts around. They were carefully comparing my statements with the Scriptures to see if I was preaching the truth. I looked to God to help me.

The devil had managed to have misguided saints of God to be his channels to print, and broadcast, all kinds of things about me that were lies. I had to face all this.

From Saturday night onwards the place was like brass. Tuesday night I went to my lodgings broken-hearted; there was no move and no sign of acceptance. I decided to fast but my landlady remonstrated, "*You cannot stand it, Pastor Williams; you are labouring in this heat and it would not be good for you. I am fully in sympathy with you and know what it is to be in this environment but you cannot live without breakfast.*" However, I persuaded her otherwise and spent the morning wrestling with God, like Gideon, and said: "*Lord, you must save one soul today, that will be one gained for you. Also, give me something in my pocket, I am not going to beg nor tell anyone that I have nothing. It is not right for me to give a sign that you are*

Wherever you go, you find that we are 'a sect much spoken against'. No Movement has suffered more than the Apostolic Church has suffered and you find on every hand that Herod and Pilate are becoming friends when the question of the Apostolic Church, and what it stands for, comes up for discussion. But, Praise God! The fire of God is burning and His will is being carried out.

When this glorious work began people said, 'twas begun by man'; but it was not man who did it, it was God who inspired the plan. Many shook their heads and said, 'They will soon disappear' but, by the grace of God, we are still going on and here we are in Australia.

(The speaker having made reference to various fulfilment's of the spoken word, referred to elsewhere in this volume, concluded his address with the following)

In the year 1926 I was sent alone to America. My brother and I had been there with Pastor's Andrew Turnbull and Frank Hodges in 1922. In one city I was asked by the elders to preach for three weeks at evening services taking as the subject of each address, 'The Tenets of the Apostolic Church'. I had not done this before but had preached on a few of the Tenets. They wanted to advertise that I would so preach. I acceded to their desire and preached each night.

At the end of the meetings there was a wonderful time of rejoicing. Souls were saved during the meetings. I tested the meetings asking if there were any ready to step into the apostolic life. To my surprise eighteen walked to the front and one of them today is an apostle of the Lord.

the world and found ourselves penniless, but He has never been a disappointment. On all our travels we have always proved God's promises, 'I will never leave you'.

We never asked to come to Australia. It was because of a strongly worded cable, which Pastor Cathcart sent, that we are here. We had been to America, and when the call came from Australia, my brother and I said, 'Well, we trust that the Lord will send someone else this time since we have been away all these months.' We were longing to hear the decision to that effect but the news came from the General Council (while we were in America) that we were to come here.

When I arrived home, I found my wife rather down in health on account of labouring hard to try and help matters in her own sphere as deaconess in the church (I would ask everyone to pray for the wives of the servants of God). My own wife has stood by me in all the crises and difficulties I have encountered.

I thought, 'I have ample reason to ask the Lord to send someone else instead of me' but the cable from Pastor Cathcart said he would not be responsible if the faith, of the saints in Australia, was shattered, after God had revealed that we (my brother and I) were to be here. I felt that, whatever the cost, the will of God should be done by us. I thank the choir, and everybody in the congregation, for the wonderful welcome they have given us.

I would like to mention, to the glory of the Lord, that we have had the privilege of leading representatives of twenty-three nationalities to know the Lord on our travels. Was that prophetic word at the beginning true? Praise His name, it was true!

own arrangements. Not once have we gone from home without going on the 'simple' word of God. Surely we know what we are about at this time. Not once have we made one single pre-arrangement.

Another point I want you to realise is that money (i.e. personal profit) has never been mentioned at the beginning of our journeys, nor at the end; in all our travels nothing has been said, nothing has been asked – we have desired no personal gain. We sinply trusted God that speaks.

We have been to America, Denmark, France and Italy on the direct command of God. We have not asked for any door to be opened. You know the old idea, 'You preach well, and you will have the chance to come again!' The old idea is: 'You choose the best country, where there is money, and the largest congregation for you to reap the benefit.' This attitude is not known in the Apostolic Church. We are in the same place as when the church started as regards finance but we are much wealthier in grace, in faith and in confidence in God. We are richer in our love to God and His word.

Think of it. The door has opened in every country. Not one of the men (servants of God) present here, who has known the work from the beginning, can say that we have asked for an open door to our friends, or acquaintances, in any country. God Himself has opened the door every time. Praise His name forever!

So far, we have been six times to Italy, four times to Denmark, nine times to France, a dozen times to Ireland; to Scotland number's of times; all over England, every corner of Wales, Canada three times. Also, West Africa, Germany, Belgium, Spain, Holland and Switzerland. We have travelled to the largest cities in *thee to deliver thee, saith the Lord."* This is the divine comfort in the calling. *"Lo…I am with you."*

Is it true that the ministry of comfort builds up? I am able to say that I have had a part in the work of building up, in every nation. I am not saying this boastingly, but I am confirming the word of God that came through the boy lodger at Garnfoel who was saved. The divine word at the beginning concerning myself was: "A chosen channel to travel to the nations." I have had a part in the work as a prophet.

To a certain extent we can say that the Apostolic Church is a product of the Lord's condescension in making His will known through prophetic ministry through human channels, with other ministries of course. The word of God came through my lips that He desired to send Pastor William Cathcart by faith to this land of Australia; also Pastor Joseph McCabe and Pastor A. Gardiner. These men, on the occasions that God called them in that sense, do not know the agony that I went through as I realised that I (i.e.

from the human point of view) was sending them to Australia without anyone waiting to receive them there.

I will leave the result of these callings to speak for itself; you have some idea of the progress in Australia. It might possibly appear that I am boasting – but I am doing so in the Lord; let the effect speak for itself.

The Go! Of God.

I will now touch briefly on our travels. First of all, I want you to remember that we (my brother Dan and myself) have, up to this hour, travelled for twenty-three years and we have not once done so by making our dealing with the destinies of individuals. When I go to the assemblies I have been crushed under the weight of responsibility. I go in agony and pain again because of the misunderstandings that are taking place even in the realm of the intellectual. I am asking you, as one who has been used as a prophet for twenty-three years to this day, to pray for the prophetic channels whom God has called to the prophetic ministry.

II The Divine Commission

"*To destroy and to pull down.*" There is not time to dwell upon what that means. To pull down and destroy old ideas and old teachings. Take, for instance, the first command, practically, that came to the saints at Penygroes when I was called as a channel. The majority of the members were Congregationalists and had been taught, and believed, the rite of sprinkling infant children in baptism. When we were gathered together in the Hall the word of God came, and showed, that everyone, who said he or she was saved, must be baptised in water by immersion.

It was a struggle for me to be a mouthpiece of God to destroy old beliefs, old customs and ideas. Saints of God, if there are any among you who have been 'christened', I cannot find that rite in the Word of God. You must be buried with Christ by baptism unto death (Romans 6:4). In the Apostolic Church we dedicate our children to the Lord.

III The Divine Comfort

The divine comfort comes to build and to plant. "*Behold I have put My words in thy mouth.*" "*I am with* for a time; God saw to it that His healing touch preserved me.

The old adage says 'sticks and stones may break your bones but being called names will never hurt you'. I was able, by the grace of God, to withstand the misunderstandings from the outside world. We must be prepared for such misunderstanding and mistrust.

The opposition came nearer – the children of God also persecuted me. I know what it is to have the children of God stop me on the road and try to keep me for three to four hours endeavouring to draw out of me confessions that were not true. They tried to persuade me to confess to them that everything was 'made up' in the prophetic utterances in the Church. I have gone through all those things.

Then, again, even while God was speaking through my lips as His appointed channel, children of God have come to me and shouted in my face, 'You are a liar!'

Then there has been a third realm of suffering – the betrayers; children of God, who have been in the church for a time, but they became so hard and narrow that they turned back and followed no more. What they have said we will not repeat, but we will leave them in the hands of God.

Then there is another realm of suffering – that which comes into the life of every channel, when he realises the responsibility that is upon him, with regard to the calling of individuals into the work and purpose of God. No one, except a channel who has gone through similar experiences, can enter into the intense sufferings of the prophet because it is only those, in that realm, who can appreciate what it means.

I have enough understanding to realise that I am

much longer working every day and attending the meetings at night." I was down in the bowels of the earth for ten hours not seeing daylight for all that time. These representatives said that under the circumstances I could not stand it and said, *"We are asking you if you are prepared to leave the mine?"* This was the way I launched out into the work of the Lord.

One of the brethren said he would give me sixpence a week, another said he would give ninepence a week, and so on. I said I would leave my manual work if it was the will of God. So, I launched out into the Apostolic life, without any guarantee of salary, receiving sometimes thirty shillings and sometimes fifteen shillings a week as the money came in; but Jesus never failed me.

A prophet's life is not a playground but a battlefield. Whoever has been called to be a prophet you have something in front of you that you have never realised. If I had known beforehand what I have had to face, the persecution through literature, tracts written in opposition, the 'slights' (causes of offence) and the suffering that I have met, and endured. If I had known they were on my way, during the last twenty-three years, I would never have started the journey. But, Praise God! His grace has been sufficient and He has never failed me. I am able to say, to the glory of God, 'I am what I am by His grace!'

I have suffered much from outside opposition and misunderstanding of God's ways and purpose. As I have walked the streets some have shouted after me, *"That's the god of the Apostolic Church."* Then they have spoken in imitation of the 'tongues' and sneeringly asked, *"What is the interpretation?"* But that suffering was but

I have read to you the verses in the prophecies of Jeremiah that he was chosen of God before he was born. I make bold to say that I was definitely called of God before I was born. The very same God who called and chose Jeremiah also declared that the had chosen me. It is the prerogative and power of God to chose whom He will before they are born. I am declaring to you that this is the strength of my life, to believe, in face of everything, that I have been definitely called of God.

I have been asked several times if I have been ordained. Well, my reply is that I have been ordained three times. 'Have I been to college?' is another question that I am asked. Well, I have done my best with the aid of Bible Schools. I have not been to college, but I have the knowledge that I have been called and chosen of God Himself.

I have been ordained three times as I previously said. I was ordained before the foundation of the world – before I was born. I was ordained again, before I was saved, in a revival meeting during the Welsh revival (here Pastor Jones Williams repeated the facts previously outlined by his brother see page 18 – ed).

This was before I was saved, before the Apostolic Church began and before I realised what was being done. Then, for a third time, I was ordained again in the Apostolic Church.

After I began to serve God I remained in the mine for about fifteen months. I was working all day and had very few evenings to myself at home. The representatives of different assemblies, that had been gathered together, asked me one day if I was prepared to leave the colliery. They explained. *"We are blessed through your ministry and we realise that you cannot carry on* the Holy Spirit descended and each one of the fourteen converts were baptised with the Spirit. That was the beginning of the Apostolic Church. The very same night, some of the saints were in the Hall having a prayer meeting and God visited them and baptised them. A few saints had called at the home of a deacon of the church and, again, the Holy Ghost came down in the midst. Thus on the same night, in three different places, people were baptised with the Holy Ghost. The Apostolic Church commenced that night.

When the power of God was working on these new converts, (so I learnt afterwards) Ivor Thomas, my lodger friend, began to speak in English (mixed with tongues) as though the Lord wished to use him in that language to prophesy (the first language being Welsh – ed).

At this time at 'Brynteg' Gorsgoch Road, where my brother Dan lived, there were evening meetings. Through my friend Ivor Thomas, the Lord told Dan, "*Go thou, My servant (naming the house to which he was to go) there are two persons in that home, sitting, and the smaller in stature is an ordained and chosen channel to travel with thee through the nations.*" My brother said to his wife that he was going to obey this word. If he found it true, then no man would hinder him from believing, and following the voice of God; but if he found it was not true, he would say nothing about it and no one should hear anything about the spoken word.

Dan and his wife started out from their house and found, at the house named according to the word, the two persons. I was one of them and I was the smaller in stature. Now no one could have known that I was in this particular home but God Himself.

mother is not worse.' She had told me Sunday morning that she was not well. A second and third time the voice said the same sentence. It was not an 'inward' voice but it was a real, practical experience of hearing a voice outside me. I stopped when the voice spoke a third time, "*Your home is not the same tonight as it was this morning.*" I was puzzled. What could the matter be? The voice gave the answer; "*The boxer (pugilist) boy is saved!*" This happened before I entered the home. Then I gathered myself together and said, "*He needed salvation! I am not going to be sorry, after all, he was a real down and out!*"

Going into the cottage I saw that the family were all downstairs waiting for me. Straightway the boxer boy came to me in the passage (hallway – ed) and said, "*Jones, I did everything you told me but I failed to run out of the meeting.*" Another 'Hallelujah' man in the home! I was now left like an orphan.

I went to work the next morning and I met my village friend, told him the story and he said, "*I sympathise with you.*" His mother was saved but others of his family were not. He added, "*It is bad enough for me, but I don't know how you are going to manage.*"

He said he had a little money and was prepared to take a journey to America to get out of the way.

To cut a long story short, during the first of the Christian experience, of this lodger friend of mine, there were fourteen converts in my brother Dan's assembly. Bible readings, for the benefit of the new converts, were given at his home so that they might learn Scriptural truths.

Before starting the Bible class at his home Dan prayed and asked God to give light. The result was that

"*What pleasure do you get in puffing at straw?*" I gave him the remainder of the cigarettes.

Later on he used some swear words; I tried to copy him but as soon as I did my blood seemed to turn cold. I realised it would be impossible for me to live a life like this. How miserable I was after being for hours in this young man's company!

We went home and I began to preach to the lad, who was something of a pugilist as well. I told him straight, "*You are a real sinner; there is no sense or meaning in the life you are living.*" I recalled to him the things he was doing and added, "*Tomorrow is Sunday, I am going eight miles from home with three others; four is company, but if we take you, you will spoil the company. I am going to give you orders; stay in bed in the morning and mother will bring you breakfast. Then go out into the field and enjoy God's creation. Go to the meeting in the evening, to the hall where my brother Dan is, and sit by the door. If my brother comes to you and asks you a question don't answer him. If you will answer one question he will ask you a second question and, if you answer the second, it won't be long before he has you on your knees. If you feel 'the creeps' coming on you during the meeting, run out!*"

Mother tried to persuade me the following morning not to go from home with my friends. I said to her, "*Don't tell me not to go, because I have promised, and I want to hear these preachers we are going to meet. You can take my word that everything will be alright.*" So I went.

Coming home that night (it was nearly one o'clock on Monday morning), as I was walking along towards my home, I was suddenly stopped on the road and heard a voice distinctly telling me, "*Your home is not the same as it was this morning.*" I said to myself, 'I hope clasped, her eyes closed and dancing. As soon as she opened her eyes, and saw that I had come, throwing her arms around my neck she said, *"Jesus has saved me and healed me"* – and I lost my friend!

I went to bed planning and wondering what I should do. Now that I was friendless, no one sided with me in the home. I decided in bed that night that I would ask my mother to take in a lodger, whom I could have as a friend.

Before going to the mine I told mother that, as my sister had been saved, I must have a lodger young man for company. My mother looked at me and asked, *"Where are you going to put him?" "He can sleep with me"* I replied; *"I must have someone here as company. You are all shouting 'Hallelujah'- I must have someone."* (I was the sole support of the family at the time. Mother gave me my desires on that account. Every member of our family had been taught to give every penny of their wages, when working, for the support of the home and for my mother, who had sacrificed so much for us.) *"All right, my boy"* said mother, *"bring a lodger, but bring a nice lad like yourself."*

That day I went to the colliery and met the friend I had in mind. I asked him if he would like to change his lodgings. He said he would and I settled terms with him.

The following Friday night I went to his lodgings and helped him to remove to Garnfoel. On our arrival, mother went to another room and shed tears. Next day we went together to the nearest town, four miles away, where we bought some cigarettes. I tried to imitate the lodger in smoking. Afetr smoking one cigarette I said, point a finger at me, yet I was a rebel against God's mercy and love. For years I continued in that rebellious state Until, at last, I grew bold enough to say, "You carry on with your 'Hallelujah Chorus!' I am enjoying life in the realm that I am living." There was one sister in our home, unsaved. She sided with me and I helped her. The 'Hallelujah' gang were in one part of the house, and we were in the other.

One, never-to-be-forgotten Sunday, my sister became very ill. The doctor was called and said she would have to go to hospital the following morning if she did not improve. I was vexed and troubled and became very miserable because my sister was so low in health. That Sunday a missionary ministered at the Hall where my brother Dan was Pastor. I said to a friend, "Shall we go to hear this missionary tonight? I understand he is a 'good man'. That was my life then – I liked to run after different preachers. My friend and I went to the meeting. Conviction rested upon me; so much so that I jumped over fours seats past the people, in order to get away from the environment that was conquering me. I found myself outside the hall on the roadway.

As I watched the crowd coming out, I noticed my brother and the missionary having a talk. I said to my friend, "*I believe Dan is going to take the missionary home to pray for my sister who is ill. Well, I am not going home tonight!*" I stayed out until twelve midnight. Then I thought; 'Well, surely Dan and his friend have parted by now.'

When I came near the cottage I heard an actual repetition of Luke 15, for I heard the noise of music and dancing – at 12.30 (in the night). When I went in the first thing I saw was my sister with her hands

I. The Divine Call

In 1904 God set little Wales ablaze with the divine light of His divine love. I well remember those days though I was very young. I remember very well that the public houses were empty, that there were prayer meetings in the railway station waiting rooms, on the platforms, and in the trains. Children sang in the streets as they came home from the day schools. Wherever you went you heard music and the praises of God on every tongue, with joyous dancing.

God visited our home and saved father and mother with the majority of the family. I was one that was not saved, with another sister. For six and a half years, from the time the others were saved, I lived at Garnfoel, unregenerated. It was not an easy thing for an unsaved person to live in a home where all were saved and shouting 'Hallelujah'.

I worked with my brother Dan in the mine. He brought me out of that pit; but it was out of a deeper pit – the pit of sin – that the Lord delivered me. I worked with my brother for six and a half years and, if anyone tried to save a person, he did; for he used all means and ways (I called them tricks) to convert me, but each time he tried I became harder and harder. I was getting more rebellious against God's love towards me. Remember that, judged by my outward conduct I was not what is termed a 'down and out'. I never tasted any kind of strong drink and never liked the idea of swearing or doing anything that would bring me, as a young man, down to a plane of degradation.

I became a member of the Congregational Church at Penygroes and was a regular communicant. I went to the Sunday School and did my best; no one could

CHAPTER 7

FROM PIT TO PULPIT
(Autobiographical)

The following extracts are taken from an address delivered by Pastor W. Jones Williams (at various places), originally on Sunday evening 28th October 1934 during his visit to Australia.

The verse that I want to read is this:

"*He brought me up also out of an horrible pit, out of the miry clay, and set my feet upon a Rock, and established my goings.*"

(Psalms 40:2)

I should like you to turn also to the first chapter of Jeremiah.

v.5 "*Before I formed thee in the belly I knew thee; and before thou camest forth out of the womb I sanctified thee, and I ordained thee a prophet unto the nations.*"

v10 "*See, I have this day set thee over the nations and over the kingdoms to root out, to pull down, and to destroy, and to throw down, to build and to plant.*"

v19 "*And they shall fight against thee; but they shall not prevail against thee, for I am with thee, saith the Lord, to deliver thee.*"

In this chapter there are three headings, namely:
I. The Divine Call.
II. The Divine Commission.
III. The Divine Comfort.

SAVED TO SERVE

To tread our rough streets, He left those that were golden
Unrecognised, walking 'mid eyes that were holden
That perishing lambs to His heart might be folden
He wandered and suffered and died
O love so unselfish! Thy zeal has inspired me
I'm glad as a labourer that God ever hired me
Ashamed at Thy feet that the cross ever tired me
I choose the lone path Thou hast trod

It might be a pathway less lone and laborious
To lead just myself out of danger victorious
But let me win souls for the mansions all glorious
Win thousands for God and for Home
For this let me wake while companions are sleeping
For this while they laugh at the altar be weeping
For this while they rest in the harvest be reaping
That loaded with sheaves I may come

I die to the good things for Jesus is calling
I die to myself to save others from falling
I will not go free when the yoke that is galling
Is keeping the millions from rest
But – wonders of grace – how my soul is receiving
To keep was to lose I get all by my giving
I lost my own life but I ne'er had such living
The joy of the Lord is the best

                         Constance Ruspine.

asleep" at his youngest daughter's house, 'Glanyrafon' (Bank of the river).

The chapters that follow have been collated from the literary remains deposited with Pastor T. Davies by the late Pastor Jones Williams, diaries and chronicles of his 'journey's oft'. It is to be deplored that Pastor Dan was 'cut off' before completing the biographical plan that he had conceived.

an Overseer at the Babell, Penygroes, his mantle fell upon Overseer (and General Deacon) John Williams, the latter faithfully gave water to many to the end of his days.

Dear Reader – you have before you the six chapters of "The Cradle of Mystery" as they came from the pen of the late Pastor D. P. Williams. He wrote them, the most part, when in Canada, and which were re-written by his widow, Mrs. Talitha Williams at 'Glanyrafon', Gate Road, Gorslas during his life and after her husband's decease (amplified also when necessary).

On the occasion of the return of Pastor T. V. Lewis (the second president of the Apostolic Church) from Oslo, Norway on the 10th January 1947, Pastor D. P. Williams was present at the welcome of his co-adjutor at the Temple, Penygroes. When his turn came to speak Pastor Lewis said, sadly, but predictively, that there would be no need to give him (Pastor Dan) such a welcome as that again.

At that gathering, Pastor Dan confided to Pastor Thomas Davies, his literary assistant since July 1919, that he would not be able to complete his memoirs of his deceased brother; much as he would like to. The premonition of the impending home call was already knocking on his heart's door. A month later, on Thursday morning, 13th February 1947, at age 64, "*after he had served his generation by the will of God, he fell* (mentioned later) now stands there. At the same time he was shown what a great work would be done at Penygroes and the neighbouring districts. A company of saints, at a later period, assembled in a house at Crosshands.

Our late beloved friend, Pastor D. Caleb Morgan (who was presenter at Penygroes August Conventions for very many years, Treasurer of the Welsh section, before a more complete unity became possible with the other countries of England, Scotland and Northern Ireland and, finally, General Secretary), whose death on February 3rd 1942, aged 65, was much lamented, had the oversight of the little band. Caleb believed God and many will remember his often repeated wish to die in the faith, with his head as that of Caleb of old, resting within the borders of his Canaan inheritance. There is a fragrance arising at the very mention of his name.

We were directed, by the word of the Lord, to buy a piece of ground to build upon it a place of worship large enough 'to seat as many people as He gave of years the antediluvians to live' – that is one hundred and twenty (Gen. 6:3). The building was to be called 'Rehoboth' for it was to be a 'well of water' for which the people would not strive (Gen. 26:22).

The well has been springing up now for over thirty years. When Pastor Caleb Morgan was removed to be

---

*Asaph, as Pastor Caleb was called, had in his successor, John Williams, one possessed of a musical ear. Despite a painful recurrence of asthma during the last years of his Overseership, John faithfully ministered to the needs of the saints and, by his own example, showed what an 'Apostolic' servant should be in constancy and fellowship.

and, before the building was completed, it was paid for as declared by the Lord.

Again, travelling conveniences were very limited; the nearest railway station to Penygroes was four miles away. Definite prayer was made for the Lord for the way to open for us to have a motor car. The Lord gave us this promise:- "*A swift chariot I will send you soon, so that you may be able to travel according to the demands of My will, and I would have you to prepare a place*" (i.e. a garage).

It was done as the Lord directed us and, no sooner did we step out on His word, than He fulfilled His promise by sending us a new Ford car. This swift chariot proved indeed a gift, for in it we travelled far and near, by night and by day, in every kind of weather; and, for most of the journeys, filled to capacity with God's servants to meet the increasing and varied calls.

Passing through a village, one day in the car, we were prompted to hold and open-air meeting, making the chariot a pulpit. At the end of the service the Lord declared: "*I will gather in this place a people unto Myself and you shall come again and gather them together.*"

Today we have a building in that place with a company of faithful saints.

While the divine directions were becoming, weekly, more comprehensive, there were also previous indications, given to other's outside our immediate circle, of the Lord's purpose at Penygroes and neighbourhood. A dear saint of God, used in prophetic ministry for many years, in the person of Elder Thomas Richards of Felinfoel, near Llanelli, on his drapery sales round, was told of the Lord, while visiting the 'Company's houses' at Crosshands, that He would cause a place of worship to be built nearby (indicating the site). 'Rehoboth'

Similarly, by many signs and wonders, the Lord proved veracity of His word in order to establish us in the faith and in the ultimate fulfilment of the purpose He had for us. We proved His sovereign love and grace in His dealings with us, as with Israel when He said: "*That thou mightest know that the Lord HE IS GOD; there is none else beside Him.*" We proved His supreme power, glory and authority over all agencies and spheres, as we dared to obey Him.

As the work continued to increase, hardly ever were we without visitors. People came from distant places to enquire of the way, having fellowship with us in the vision that was dawning upon us.

Our correspondence also greatly increased, so that the Lord desired us to have convenient rooms for the work, and office and enquiry room. We were counselled not to despise the days of little things, for great was the work laid in store for us for the future.

I was, at that time, directed to ask a contractor, to place upon my own private ground, adjacent to 'Brynteg', Gorsgoch Road, Penygroes, where I then resided, a convenient timber built office and, by the time the building would be ready, the money would be available. As a token of this, the Lord said through His channel, my brother Jones, "*Tomorrow, at this time, thou shalt receive ten pounds as a sign unto you that this is My will.*"

With great expectation we waited for the promised time; but, to our dismay, nothing came by the morning's mail. By midday a telegraphic order came for ten pounds from Bournemouth. Although the sum was small, it was great as a confirmation of the spoken word

CHAPTER 6

PIONEERING WORK

In every sphere of life, a measure of pioneering work and of adventure must be undertaken before any measure of success can be expected or achieved. With every divine calling, there is an impartation of faith, and an element of advancement in the nature of faith. But faith is inevitably confronted with difficulties and, by overcoming them, the soul grows in the knowledge of God and faith increases with the triumphs ahead. The history of all men and women of faith is full of the supernatural, that is, of God.

When the voice of God is heard, and deals directly with the moral condition and mental capacity, enlargement of the soul takes place inwardly while there is also advancement outwardly. Through many supernatural signs and wonders, wrought of God through human channels, faith within themselves, and others who behold them, is strengthened and sustained. Such manifestations are tokens of the supernatural both in their nature and design. Wonders are the objective side of miracles – the extraordinary and marvellous, the evidence of Deity; and, wherever manifested, they produce wonderment and astonishment.

As on the Day of Pentecost (Acts 2), when the multitude that gathered heard the disciples speaking in tongues and magnifying God and His wonderful works, they were all amazed (vv11,12).

ONWARD!

The battle wages fierce, my servant true
In this contested land
And I, in truth, have very much to do
And need thy hand.

The path of purpose lies through mountains rough
As well as valleys sweet
But 'til My voice shall say 'It is enough'
In need thy feet

Shrink not to see the warfare on ahead
And tasks therein enshrined
Calmly thy vision hold, though sore bestead
I need thy mind

My message has to ring from shore to shore
Till earth and heaven rejoice
Slack not for deadness, nor for fast closed doors
I need thy voice

But most of all I ask of thee, keep for Me
An inner shrine of rest
Whence undisturbed I may give forth through thee
Even My best

Love! Love that casts out fear, thy portion be
Even unto the end
And life and power, that proveth Me to be
More than thy friend

Anonymous.

in life to the delinquents. Thus we commenced to have 'all things in common'.

Various assemblies in the near-by towns and villages were established, set in order, and elders and deacons appointed. At that time Pastor Thomas Jones (Llwynhendy) was called to the pastorate. He proved himself a most devout and faithful pastor and, later, apostle in the Apostolic Church. He was highly esteemed by all, and has left behind him memories of a holy man of God.

As a prophet, Jones played a great part (at the side of Pastor Thomas Jones) in that district.

Special meetings were held in the council school at Llwynhendy at which the word of the Lord came though my brother Jones that I was to anoint and lay hands upon Pastor Joseph Omri Jones, and to impart to him the gift of prophecy. Immediately we laid hands on him. A prophetic ministry flowed through him and, in due time, he became one of the most valuable prophets in the Body of Christ. His services in that capacity cannot be over-estimated.

By this time the work had so increased that the presbyteries of the already established assemblies decided to call my brother Jones out to the work as a paid servant.

Demands from all directions came upon us, giving us hardly time to rest; and all this time, Jones by his persevering ministry, made his calling and election sure. The purposes of the Lord, and the reason why the Lord called the cottage of our upbringing "The Cradle of Mystery", was becoming clearer to us, causing us to rejoice in His condescension and grace.

while debts were unpaid. Those utterances brought us to a pass.

Then, we were commanded by prophetic ministry, but not knowing the purpose at the time, to "bring our tithes to the storehouse" and to keep them until He would further speak to us. The word of the Lord was after this manner:

"*It is My will that you My people should walk circumspectly and prove unto all men that I, the Lord, have surely appeared unto you. In order to prove this, forget not what is written in My Word. That you should carry one anothers burdens, and thus fulfil the law of Christ. Bring the tithes to the storehouse, and then you shall prove that the windows of heaven will be opened unto you. See to it that full account shall be kept until I will give you further instructions.*"

Obedience was given to the word of the Lord, even as it is recorded of Agabus, who signified by the Spirit that there should be great dearth throughout the world, and, in obedience, the disciples, every man according to his ability, determined to send relief to the brethren who dwelt in Judea. They promptly obeyed the spoken word, before the dearth came, and made the collection (Acts 11:27-30).

So we brought our tithes regularly, until the sum of eighty pounds was in the storehouse. Then the Lord gathered us together to hear His further word when He gave us instructions to pay the debts of those who, owing to hard and trying circumstances (others through negligence), had failed to meet their obligations to the local tradesmen. It was a time of rejoicing when the Lord divided His portion to everyone, according to the need, and gave a new start bring things to order. The ship was without a helm or captain; yet the mariners were ready, if only they knew how, to bring things under control.

The came a voice from the middle of the congregation:- "*Stand on thy feet, My servant, for I have appeared unto thee to shepherd My flock; therefore, feed my sheep*".

Then I stood and said, "*What wilt thou have me to say, Lord?*" and He said unto me: "*Open my Word in the last chapter of the fourth book in the second Book*". By this time a great calm rested upon the congregation.

This voice and mode of utterance brought a silent sensation and wondering what manner of words, these that were heard, were. To the few who were beginning to become acquainted with the prophetic voice, without any difficulty, knew that the Lord meant the last chapter of John's Gospel in the New Testament. Thus the Book was opened and the sheep were fed.

The meetings continued and were brought to perfect harmony and peace day after day. Such an occasion as this, proved to be the means of bringing a new revelation of God's divine order and purpose in the early days. It also brought us in touch with many other places, which had already been visited with His Pentecostal outpouring.

Another incident worthwhile recording is the following. Many who had been marvellously converted were, through sin and trying circumstances, unable to meet their obligations to the tradesmen of Penygroes village. Strong exhortations were received, through prophecy, from the Lord, concerning this condition of things that we were to owe no man anything and that it was not His will that we should hold street meetings fluid state, as it were, without being patterned on Church (Pauline) order).

This gradually did take place as the Holy Spirit, from time to time, brought us to a vital understanding of His purpose. Pastor Hill deemed it wise to withdraw; so he returned home. It was the desire of those in responsibility for the meetings to send for me, to be with Pastor Dan Jones.

I was very reluctant to comply with this request as my ministry, hitherto, had been in the Welsh language and considered myself a novice in experience to meet such important demands and expectations. So I, with the elders, turned to the Lord and enquired of Him and His will was made known before the elders in the following utterances:

"*Hearken ye unto My word, for have I not spoken unto you that from this place I will work. I have, therefore, caused this call to come to you, for this door has been opened by Me for you, My servant, to enter in. If you will refrain from answering this request, you will hinder My purpose for you. Therefore, go on My word and I will be with you. Let my young servant also go with you.*" (The young servant was my brother Jones).

On the Monday many proceeded from Penygroes to Swansea. So, with fear and trembling, I went, conscious that the occasion was beyond my ability to meet the demands but, at the same time, the power and the glory seemed to overshadow my being.

When we arrived, the tumult and confusion, amongst the crowd that had gathered, was such that the place was like a seething pot. I had nothing to do but to lie prostrate under the pulpit, for the hand of the Lord humbled me. There were many who cried to God to ienced that we had entered into the order of worship and ministry set forth in 1Corinthians 14:26:-

"How is it then brethren? When you come together, everyone of you hath a psalm, hath a doctrine, hath a tongue, hath a revelation, hath an interpretation. Let all things be done unto edifying."

In fact, this Corinthian chapter became the experience of the assembly. Well could we declare that, *"We never saw it after this fashion before!"* If all were recorded that happened in those days, it would take volumes; we can make mention of some particulars only. We read on Proverbs 18:16 that *"a man's gift maketh room for him"* we were soon to learn that this was so.

We also came to realise the difference between natural gifts, the force of 'soul' in personalities and the gifts of divine origin – spiritual gifts. The tone and production of divine gifts were of a different nature, quality and influence.

We had now arrived at a time when the fact, that the word of the Lord was being declared in our midst, was noised abroad and our faith God-ward was spread in many districts so that there was no need to make announcements. Believers, seekers and sinners gathered to us from the surrounding villages and districts. God began to work amongst them also and we made visits to their gatherings in turn.

Later, a special convention was held in Bellevue Chapel, Swansea, when people from far and near came together. Pastor Hill and Pastor Dan Jones were the speakers. It appears that some misunderstanding arose concerning the order of the meetings (our readers should understand that at this time things were in a *found faith in him, the silent believer* (Evan Thomas, Taberah).

Another one have I brought from afar, the one who shouts 'Glory' like a trumpet (Evan Jenkins Cwmcoch); *and the one whom I use occasionally to give forth my word* (W.J. Evans, Penpont).

The shall be the elders of My choice in preparation for the future for I have many things to reveal unto you; but let this suffice for the present."

Needless to mention, this was very amazing and hard to bear by some who were present, as well as by myself, as it was the first time for me to ordain servants into office. Nevertheless, in faith, hands were laid upon them as Elders, and they were reckoned as such in our midst. As for my own ordination, it took place previous to this under different circumstances. It could naturally be expected that this fact would bring a division, but to the contrary, God's choice was received with satisfaction.

At this time, the new work was passing through great crises. The demonstration of the Spirit and the sense of the supernatural presence of God occasionally were beyond description. Under God's hand some lay prone in great prostration, others in ecstatic transportation, carried away on the wings of the Spirit. Others sung spiritual songs (in tongues) and ecstasy of rapture and praise.

The Spirit filled saints were carried, as it were, by a gale from Glory. The heavenly bliss was such as though we had entered the heavenlies. Some, in the midst, were mightily inspired to preach the Word with boldness. The ordinary became extraordinary. We truly exper-

Lord to set His church in order. As we sat with awe, listening to the word of the Lord, we came to the conclusion, concerning some who were present (who disapproved of the 'new order', namely, obedience to the spoken word of God as uttered by His prophets), that they might not be mentioned, while others would be called of God.

To our surprise the choice of the Lord was quite contrary to our expectations, when He made known unto us His will in the following declaration:-

"For all power and authority is given unto Me. Unto some I say, 'Go!', and they go; unto others I say' 'Come!' and they come. Some who are in the midst of you at this hour never expected to be here, but, being constrained by My 'Come' they have come for the purpose that I have in view for the future on this Mount of My choice. I will cause my word to run swiftly to the ends of the earth from this place, and I must lay down a foundation that will remain firm in the Faith, when My movements will appear to be strange.

My servant *Roderick, as it has already been revealed unto you, shall go to a far-off land, as my messenger, and the one who is of great strength (David Jones, Bryntirion) *shall stand at the side of My shepherd* (D.P. Williams) *to be his right hand support. The one whom I have brought into your midst by surprise, and has proved my healing hand upon him, "For a purpose thou hast been drawn into this place to be a pillar* (Daniel Williams – uncle of Pastor D.P. Williams), *it is well that thou has brought with thee thy friend, for I have*

---

*William Roderick became a missionary with the Apostolic Faith Church in Johannesburg for a period and still serves the Apostolic Church in the Rhondda.

CHAPTER 5

CALLINGS AND DIVINE ORDER

Well can we record here, in the words of Isaiah the prophet: *"For My thoughts are not your thoughts, neither are your ways My ways saith the Lord"* (Isa. 50:8). Even as it is written, when Samuel called the sons of Jesse, even as his sons passed by one by one, before the prophet, the father really thought the chosen channel of God for the kingship of Israel would be the eldest, Eliab. The prophet said, "*Surely the Lord's anointed is before him*", but the Lord said unto Samuel, "*Look not on his countenance, or on the height of his stature; because I have refused him: for the Lord seeth not as man seeth; for man looketh on the outward appearance, but the Lord looketh on the heart*" (1Samuel 16:6-7).

So it was the case at the commencement of the Apostolic Church; some who might be expected, on account of ability and publicity, to be separated in to the office of eldership, were 'refused', while those who, hitherto, were not foremost since the Revival, were drawn nearer at this time. It was evident that the 'eye of the Lord' was searching for men of faith in His Word, whom He could rely upon, to commence the great work that was to be accomplished.

As we assembled together, in the 'Babell' (lit. 'tent' this was the first meeting place, formerly an army building ed.), the great unction of God rested upon the assembly, it was evident that the time had come for the

This is His will, He takes and He refuses
Finds Him ambassadors when men deny
Wise ones nor might for His saints He chooses
No! such as John or Gideon or I

He, as He wills shall solder and shall sunder
Slay in a day and quicken in an hour
Tune Him a chorus from the sons of thunder
Forge and transform my passion into power

Ay! For this Paul, a scorn and a reviling
Weak as you know him and the wretch you see
Even in these eyes shall ye behold His smiling
Strength in infirmities and Christ in me

'St. Paul' by F.W.H. Meyers

Thus, the cottage continued to be the Cradle of Mystery.

THE MOLDING

Once for the least of the children of Manasses
God had a mission and a deed to do
Wherefore the welcome that all speech surpasses
Called him and hailed him greater than he knew

Asked him no more, but took him as He found him
Found him with valour, slung him with a sword
Bade him go on, until the tribes around him
Mingled his name with the naming of the Lord

Also of John a calling and a crying
Rang in Bethabara till strength was spent
Cared not for cousel, stayed not for replying
John had one message for the world, 'Repent'

John, than which man, a grander or a greater
Not till this day has been of woman born
John like some iron peak by the Creator
Fired with the red glow of the rushing morn

This, when the sun shall rise and overcome it
Stands in his shining desolate and bare
Yet not the less the inexorable summit
Flamed him his signal to the happier air

was the profound and correct language used, as though Jones were an educated young man well grounded in the Welsh Classics when, in fact, he had no such previous knowledge. Many of those prophecies are to be found in the records of the Church today.

Again, the Holy Spirit would, often times, move upon him to speak of those things that were far beyond his capacity and learning, such as astronomy, music, physiology, the philosophy of life and moral ethics. When Jones would try to expound, of himself, and such matters, everybody was made aware of his inability and his limited knowledge of the subjects named. All who had the least conception of such truths, and knew who he was, and also his age, were constrained to acknowledge that none other than God the Holy Ghost spoke through him.

Nevertheless, as it is recorded in the written Word (and there are many instances), some believed, others doubted, while others believed not at all. It was only what could be expected at such a new procedure and order of things, that contentions would arise, and divers opinions manifested that would eventually lead to division. Others waxed stronger in the Faith and thus were confirmed, and established, as they believed the prophets.

The continual strain of those days bore heavily upon him, for he continued to work hard in the mine as well. By this time others, from the neighbouring districts, paid visits to the home and to the assembly and, with longing hearts, gathered to the Mount of Penygroes to worship with us. They became recipients of God's grace and faith as they availed themselves of the privileges of hearing the word of the Lord.

purposes of God were unveiled continually and progressively as he matured in the prophetic ministry.

"The Word of God grew and multiplied", and its substance was profound. Many others were occasionally used as the Spirit moved heavily upon them, and in many instances they were used for edification, exhortation and comfort. Thus, through the mouths of many witnesses the Word was verified, but we learned that there were further revelations, with wider and deeper mysteries made known unto us by the Spirit through him (Jones) as channel.

So significant were the manifestations of the Spirit through Jones, as a channel of blessing, that we were persuaded that there was a specific and elective purpose for him. Time and again we were kept before the Lord until late hours of the night while we listened, with astonishment, to the great and marvellous things which we were privileged to hear.

Many considerations, which occurred to my own mind, gave us all substantial proofs of the Divinity of the utterances. My brother was young , and had never been privileged to study the works of any theological authors, neither had he read any treatises on subjects of moment, or the fundamental doctrines of the Scriptures.

In fact, his general knowledge of the Bible was very limited at that time; but even men of advanced knowledge, strong in their acquaintance with the Scriptures, sat listening, with amazement, as the Spirit of God unfolded the depths of Truth, expounding the written Word. Subjects, that he had not the least conception of, were made plain to our understanding.

Another proof of the divinity of the prophetic words

house of Simon, the tanner, who lived at the seaside, and called for Peter to minister unto him (Acts 10:1-8).

Meetings were held continually in many houses. New converts were added to these little companies, and greater assurance was found in the Divine visitation, with new light on the purposes of God. There were many who were used as channels to give out prophetical utterances of various kinds, some foretelling and giving guidance, others edifying and exhorting, with no little assurance of their inspired nature.

All this was a means of creating faith, although occasionally we hesitated, as we found ourselves in a realm, hitherto, unknown to us. Undoubtedly, they were days in which we could say we were being trained in the school of the Holy Spirit.

Assiduously we continued to search the Scriptures so that our experience should be based on God's written Word, knowing that the scriptures were the true evidence of safety. Nevertheless we were continually confirmed by the fulfilment of the prophetic word, as it is written, *"Howbeit, when the Spirit of Truth is come, He will guide you into all truth, for He shall not speak of Himself, but whatsoever He shall hear, that shall He speak; and He shall show you things to come". "He shall glorify Me, and shall show it unto you"* (John 16:13, 14).

We were now beginning to learn somewhat of the ministry of the Holy Spirit, unifying us in the One Faith, for with great assurance we were established as we received the word in power and in the Holy Ghost. We were conscious of the progressive nature and revelation that was given, as time went on, through the mouth of my brother Jones Williams. Our ministry in the written Word was greatly confirmed, and the *unto you this night, for not without a purpose have you gathered in this place. It is My will that you should proceed to 'Disgwylfa', thy brother's house; there thou shalt find two young men whom I have purposed to bring into the fold. When thou shalt meet with them, say unto them, 'My Spirit shall not always strive with man.' Declare unto them that thou hast been sent of Me, with this message, for a great purpose I have for one of them to be with thee on thy travels in the coming days, for he is mine elect."*

Who was I to doubt or to hesitate to obey such a definite command? Immediately I made my way to the appointed place (opposite the Penygroes Council School, Waterloo Road, Penygroes) where my brother, Ivor, lived and found even as the Lord had declared unto me. There was therefore no ground to disbelieve God's word, for He had caused the two young men (my brother Jones, and his friend David Henry Williams, locally known as David Herbert Williams) to be there before me. My brother and his friend looked at me with astonishment, as I declared that I had been sent to them by the word of the Lord. I delivered the message with a strong word of warning and exhortation; then offered up a prayer; after which I asked them to follow me to the Evangelistic Church Mission Hall.

A short time after my arrival, both followed me, and sat in the congregation. After the message was given, an appeal was made, and both decided to yield themselves to the claims of the Lord and signified as such.

The service ended with great joy. We realised the fulfilment of the word of the Lord, many being present to bear attestation to it, for it was the same principle as in the case of Cornelius, who sent his soldiers to the all, the members of the home had the evidence of the baptism of the Holy Spirit 'with signs following' (Acts 2:4).

In the little Evangelistic Hall (built with the gifts and collections of many saints) at Penygroes, when the fire-filled saints gathered together (as so many brands from the burning), God's bush burned brightly.

My brother, Jones, appeared to be, at that time, rather antagonistic, because this advanced experience demanded complete surrender, which, he was evidently not prepared to make. He tried to escape the crisis and made various attempts – going out of meetings prematurely on some occasions – but it was hard for him to kick against the pricks. The time had now come for God's will to be revealed concerning him.

As we gathered in our home, at Brynteg, Gorsgoch Road, Penygroes, for prayer and meditation in the Word, in order that the new converts should be well established to stand the opposition that was being manifested in the place in no small degree, it became essential that they should be confirmed by the Word of God in their new experience. So I took, as our meditation, 1 Corinthians 12. Soon we were to find that the unction and sanction of God were upon this gathering, for the Holy Spirit spoke through one of the young men present most emphatically. Yet, the Lord was putting our faith to the test as to the accuracy of the prophetic utterance we were now to listen to, as it would have been impossible to prove the divinity of the words without obedience.

In February 1911, at Brynteg, Gorsgoch Road, Penygroes, with Ivor Thomas as prophet. The Lord told us, *"Hearken, My servant, unto the word that I am speaking* brother, Jones, kept full interest in my ministerial career, when, in time, it was revealed that he was to join me in the ministry.

The tide of spiritual fervency was declining at this time in Wales; yet, through the country, there were many new 'mission' movements coming to sight, which kept the fire burning. Soon, the news spread abroad that the Holy Spirit was again poured out in England, Scotland and Wales. Even from the United States some came to give their remarkable testimonies and add fuel to the fire.

The great emphasis that was laid (on the first visitation of God) was the 'new birth' and 'assurance of salvation', with a measure of God's fulness.

Although, on many occasions, we heard 'speaking in tongues', 'interpretation' and 'prophecy', nevertheless, emphasis was not so much laid upon the 'gifts' (Ephesians 4 & 1 Corinthians 12).

The second visitation of God appeared like an invasion of further revelation of Truth, and a manifestation of God's purpose, in various places. The ground was quite prepared for this at Penygroes, so that many were endowed anew by the baptism of the Holy Spirit, as on the Day of Pentecost. Many homes in the neighbourhood witnessed this.

At the same time meetings were held during which the manifestations and administration of God's Spirit, through the gifts, were further realised, understood, and their benefits rejoiced in. All this developed into a new order of services when the saints commenced to gather with the same object in view.

At this juncture, Garnfoel cottage continued to be the scene of extraordinary experiences, when, nearly

CHAPTER 4

THE PENTECOSTAL BLESSING AND ITS PURPOSE

The gracious hand of our God continued to be upon the family at Garnfoel from the days of the revival of 1904. During those years the cottage was none other than the sanctuary of the Lord. Continual prayer, praise and witnessing were heard, and many were the visitors who came to join us, while others found their Saviour and Lord, returning to their homes with great rejoicing. Time and space will not permit us to record some marvellous visitations. God's Word was continually on the table, and mother could often be heard reading it aloud, while our blind father endeavoured to interpret the meaning.

Undoubtedly, this mode of life proved to be an excellent method of keeping the young family in the consciousness of God's presence, and preserving them in His ways. Also, it prepared us all for a further revelation of God's will and purpose as it gradually dawned upon us.

During those years it pleased the Lord to privilege the writer to be called to the ministry by the minister Rev. William Bowen and congregation of Penygroes Welsh Congregational Chapel. For nearly six years I engaged in the Congregational pulpits of Wales with the object of being an ordained minister. Nevertheless, God had purposed another plan. Meanwhile, my

*I sought for faith, the kind that moves a mountain
Then staggered when my plea for alms seemed spurned
I said that, "God, His love for me hath holden"
How strange, though all, His will was not discerned
And after weeks and years of constant trying
I seemed to stand fast where I stood before
At last I noted there was not advancement
"Why is it, Lord?" my heart seemed to implore*

*He spoke, when I had ceased my bitter struggling
And quiet was I, passive in His hands
And to my great surprise (almost rebellion)
He said, "You have not heeded My commands;
You wanted peace and joy and love and patience
But daily you have shrunk from sacrifice
You loved the hollow 'romance' of Mount Calvary
But for the crown you will not pay the price*

*I see it now! I do not like the chastening
But now instead of seeking human aid
I let each stroke He sends be just a weapon
To bring the thing for which I long have prayed
And when I shrink in terror from the trials
I only cling still tighter to my Lord
And then emerging from the loathsome testing
I find I am more like Him – My reward*

(Anon)

the Lord restrained us from interfering with His Hand when bringing Jones through the valley of decision.

Some discernment was given to us who observed his spiritual conflicts that there was some object in view with God in His elective grace. So it proved, for he was placed in God's mold to be His prophet and, it became manifest, that the cottage was nothing less than the Cradle of Mystery.

THE MYSTERY OF GOD'S MINISTRY

I prayed to be made holy like the Saviour
To be patient, gentle, mild and meek as He
The straightway came some bitter disappointment
I pushed the instrument away from me
I kept on praying still to be like Jesus
And trials of every sort I seemed to face
But every time one came I fled in terror
And sought me out some human refuge place

I cried for love, that dying love of calvary
At once it seemed my foes were everywhere
I could not stand to meet with opposition
Injustice I had never learned to bear
And once again I fled for consolation
To some I knew were loyal through and through
And then kept wondering at my heartfelt hunger
As day by day my prayer I would renew

always kept him at high tension in all his activities. He became a very skillful worker in the colliery, indeed, it was surprising how much work one of such small stature could accomplish at such an early age. His untiring, determined and defiant efforts manifested strength of character and his indomitable will seemed able to surmount formidable obstacles. Occasionally we feared that those commendable qualities would prove to be a hindrance (good as they were) to his spiritual attainment, for soul-strength has so often proved to be detrimental to true spiritual life, without a crushing defeat to the natural man. When those qualities pass through a crucifixion and death, becoming subservient to the power and will of God, they prove to be of the highest value and qualification.

This, however, proved to be so in his case as he grew older, when the impressions and work of grace, done in his heart, had time to sink down to his nature - analogous to the corn of wheat which remains alone and unprofitable except it fall into the ground and die.

Thus, by a visitation of God's mighty Pentecostal blessing, resurrection came with renewed evidence and promise of some great future purpose in his life. Nevertheless, with this second appearing of God's purpose unto him, he passed through a deep sense of contrition and brokenness of spirit. Indeed, so humbling was the process as he passed through the agony of the death-union and spiritual burial into Christ, that he appeared, to some, to be on the verge of death.

Many requested us, on more than one occasion, to persuade him not to be so intense in the struggles, but revival meetings; and in every way he eagerly pursued the trail of God's blessing. On one occasion, in the Methodist Chapel at Llanillian, in the vicinity of Penygroes, Evan Roberts the Welsh Revivalist and Dr. D. M. Phillips M.A. Ph.D of Tylerstown (one of the historians of the Welsh Revival) held meetings. The place was overcrowded, making it impossible for many to find a seat. My brother, characteristically, found his way up to the stairs of the pulpit and was eventually welcomed to sit between those two great men. While the large congregation was ablaze with praise and prayer, Evan Roberts turned to Jones and asked him, *"Do you love Jesus?"*, he answered, *"Of course I love Jesus!"*. Then he asked, *"Would you like to be a minister?"* Jones answered, *"Yes! I would love to be a minister sir!"* Mr. Roberts called the attention of Dr. Phillips and said, *"This young boy would like to be a minister for God"*, and both laid their hands on his head and asked God to make him a preacher of the Gospel.

Often, afterwards, Jones said that God ordained him then to the ministry, before he was saved, and before the Apostolic Church was established. He continued to show signs of future possibilities, as he grew older, though the tidal wave of revival was receding, seemingly.

Difficulties increased, and following the Lord at the same pace was by no means easy. The allurements of the world, with its various attractions, caused him to become cold and he became a backslider. Natural ambitions grew upon him as a young man but he still showed interest in the Lord's work.

His industrious nature, high inclination for prosperity in all that he engaged, and his aim of noble living so in the human realm when Christ, the Sun of Righteousness, rose with His rays on the land of Palestine of old. What a summer that was when publicans and sinners caught the fire of Christ's glory, and common fishermen were called to be apostles! But oh! What a withering, on the other hand, when the Pharisees and Scribes criticized, opposed and endeavored to bring a blast upon the good work in the presence of the Christ.

When the 'Revival Summer' of 1904-5 poured upon us its radiant beams, and the fervency of God's heavenly fire was felt, the moral surface of the nation was transfigured. The sinners of every description came teeming from the far off country of prodigality to their Father's home with singing, rejoicing and feasting. Then it was that many homes became as a burning bush, our cottage included, for it burst into divine flame, and every branch within it caught the fire.

My brother Jones, although young, was bright in his testimony, and his voice was heard often in earnest prayer amongst the crowd. One cannot remember him on one occasion, seated in the front seats of the gallery of Penygroes Chapel, uttering such words as these: "O Lord! grant that the taps of every cellar may become rusty, and every tap-room idle and empty, so that there shall be no more drunkards in the land." Time and again his original manner of utterance and fervency appeared. He played a constant part in the devotions at the family altar, which gave us an inkling of what was taking place within him and afforded ample signs of the future possibilities that awaited him in the Lord's service.

He also traveled to the surrounding villages visiting

at such an early age, until the Divine call came for me to leave the bowels of the earth; and he also, in due time, followed the same course.

When at the age of fourteen, the burdens of home life became lighter and prospects brighter, there was heard 'a sound in the tops of the mulberry trees'. It signified to us that a great and mighty rushing wind was on the way, when God's interventions were going to be experienced in thousands of homes in Wales. Soon, the Welsh Revival came in mighty power.

We had read and heard, around the fireside, of the visitation of God in 1859 and previously to our forefathers. Oft-times we had wondered whether we would like to see some such extraordinary visitation; but at last it came upon us with such overwhelming conviction and realization that it was nothing less than God's day of awakening from the torpor of sleep. Without hesitation we flung wide the door of our hearts and our homes.

So strong and deep was the conviction and repentance, that this outpouring of the Spirit of God created, that there followed a mighty upheaval in the life of everyone who dwelt in the cottage. There was not time to hesitate or analyze whether this was of God or of man. It was too Divinely supernatural, too penetrating and gracious in its influence, too severe in its nature of condemnation against sin, and the life of mere profession.

We have noticed from time to time that the sun, with its burning heat, causes all nature to flourish and every bush to burst in to glory and beauty; the coming of spring and of summer causes nature to thrive and burgeon, and all creation is pregnant and prolific. It was the quarry (to the right of the approach to our home), digging and chiseling stones to sell for building purposes. When it was too hot during the day for hard work, he would rest in order to be able to dig during evening hours, for, to him, day and night were the same.

Later he decided to open a little business of his own in the village where he continued, on a small scale, until the end of his earthly pilgrimage. All his efforts and skill were a wonder to all who knew him.

My mother's care and devotion to her family surpassed commendation. In a measure, all the children contributed to the welfare and comfort of the home. Space would fail to make mention of each, individually, since our concentration must be upon the object of this biography.

As regards home comforts, it is meet that we pay tribute to our late brother Jones, for he played an excellent part in the life of the household, in his demeanor and obedience, as well as in carrying a good share of the responsibility. His devotion and obedience to his parents were beyond praise up to the day he left the home to embark on his married life. An incident will illustrate this: the last pay, which he earned before leaving home, he divided between his mother and his wife.

When only twelve years old, my brother Jones's feet were directed to the colliery. Small of stature, weak in appearance, he yet had an abundance of energy, a 'live wire', sharp and always on the alert in his work, so that we often wondered at his vigilance; he held his own early in his miner's career. It was my prerogative and privilege to have had him work with me underground the house in silence, but its ministry was not to be spared when called for!

On Lord's Day morning, everyone (as far as possible) had to go to a place of worship. There was a strong religious sentiment about everything on that day, in fact, attention was paid to all the church services; the Sunday School, the 'society', and especially the cottage prayer meeting (from house to house). There was something sacred in the paths across the fields trod at evening in the light of the lantern.

Memory delights to linger in meditation over the sacred hours, when prayers were offered to the Throne of Grace in fervency, and solemn hymns were sung. One cannot but believe that deep impressions were made upon our hearts, although, at the time, we may not have been conscious of them. We were set to learn to recite Psalms, and portions of Scripture, sacred poetry and songs for the Sunday School 'Children's Quarterly Meetings'.

Though we knew not, experientially, the power and assurance of salvation, yet we were religiously inclined (the effect of tradition) and we felt the sense and influence of God's Holy Spirit working upon our hearts in a great measure. It could be said of us, as of that one of old, *"Thou art not far from the Kingdom of God"* (Mark 12:34) – so near and yet so far! – for, not being born again we had not entered the Kingdom.

The Church and minister were locally the highest institution in our esteem and regard. All this was undoubtedly a preparation for better days.

My father's efforts and skill (although blind) verged on the miraculous; gardening, cobbling (repairing shoes ed.), basket making, sewing and, above all, his skill in

CHAPTER 3

THE COURSE OF EVENTS

By the courage and confidence of my father, the sacrifice and diligence of my mother, and the contribution allotted to each one of the children in the home, and, above all, the loving-kindness of God, the barque of the family survived the storms of life.

Certain duties were allotted to every one of us as children. The necessities of life had to be carried a distance of a mile from the village; water, from a well down in the field below the cottage; while the cleanliness of the surroundings at home was given to the hands capable of scrubbing etc. A large garden had to be cultivated, it was the heritage of the family, over which my father kept strict oversight, for even after blindness befell him, he took the same interest therein, and could weed the rows with the best. The older children had to nurse the babies.

During the school holidays we as children were fully occupied in gathering coal (by permission) from the colliery tips (hills of waste coal at the coal mine ed.), endeavoring to stock as much as possible against the coming of winter. All duties had to be finished on Saturday night, so that nothing was left to be done on the Lord's Day.

When obedience was called for, the word 'No' was not heard. The Birch rod on the mantelpiece policed

God moves in a mysterious way
His wonders to perform
He plants His footsteps in the sea
And rides upon the storm

Deep in umfathomable mines
Of never failing skill
He treasures up His bright designs
And works His sovereign will

Ye fearful saints fresh courage take
The clouds ye so much dread
Are big with mercy and shall break
In blessings on your head

Judge not the Lord by feeble sense
But trust Him for His grace
Behind a frowning providence
He hides His smiling face

His purposes will ripen fast
Unfolding every hour
The bud may have a bitter taste
But sweet will be the flower

Blind unbelief is sure to err
And scan His work in vain
God is His own interpreter
And He will make it plain

William Cowper

he uttered many things when he could not trace God in his trials. He wished he had never been born, longed for death, and to lie in the grave with departed kings and counsellors, princes and prisoners, at rest. That would have been to him a relief. He had instructed many, and had strengthened the feeble knees; but Eliphaz said to him; *"But now it (calamity) has come upon thee, and thou art troubled"* (Job 4:3).

It was hard for him in such a crucial hour to realise that God was preparing him for a higher purpose, and to be an example of His grace unto all who would pass through the crisis and crucible of life. It is thus recorded of all, in God's Word, whom He had purposed to be the recipients of the purposes of His grace.

Even so, we have all reason to believe that the bitter disappointment, and hard struggles of life, through the seeming misfortune of a blind parent, were the means in the end of preparing and leading our family to a state of receptivity of His salvation in the days of God's visitation. For, when it pleased God, through His mercy to remember us, the cottage of Garnfoel became the *"Cradle of Mystery"*.

of joy and victory for the whole family. It was as though the God of Noah, who told him, "Come thou and thy family into the ark", had ushered the family at Garnfoel into the ark of safety and eternal Salvation and shelter.

Many there are who have not acknowledged God's providential care and sovereign rule in the kingdom of men, in the days of adversity and calamity, but rather have complained against His ways making Him responsible for their misfortune, and have therefore missed His spiritual favour.

It is better to believe that He deals righteously in all His ways, and cannot err, even when things appear to be the contrary. Such an attitude of submissive expectancy towards God enables the soul to be sustained and, in the end, causes hard measures to minister unto good. Through trying circumstances, God may be preparing us to be in line with His hidden purposes in a realm higher than temporal circumstances, namely the realm of His Divine election of grace. Very little did Jacob realise that God was working on his behalf in his sorrow and loss. When Joseph had disappeared, when Simeon was in prison, and when the remaining brethren sought to take away Benjamin also, their aged father sadly mourned, saying; *"All these things are against me"* (Genesis 42:36). *"Ye shall bring down my grey hairs with sorrow to the grave"* (Genesis 44:29). But if he could then have pierced through the darkness, he would have seen the king's chariots coming for him to take him, and his household, to the land of plenty. Job also, the comforter of all men in the days of prosperity, had to pass through the deepest feelings of despair. In his misery and bitterness of soul months old when our father saw him last; and was the seventh child born to the family (a number usually associated with perfection). The others subsequently born he was not privileged to see. It was not easy under such circumstances, to bring up such a large family. From time to time, the neighbourhood expressed their sympathy in various ways, until the time came for the oldest boys at ten and a half to twelve years of age to commence work at the colliery (coal mine ed.) in order to earn (what proved to be a meagre wage) towards the upkeep of the home. God blessed the barrel of meal and the cruse of oil so that we were well fed and clad. God's miraculous provision is still in operation.

Although by this time our parents have left the humble cottage for the mansions on high, they left upon our hearts indelible impressions of noble principles of honesty, righteousness and upright living. Out of that family three generations have sprung, and have scattered far and near, carrying with them the saving knowledge of a gracious Redeemer, and a testimony to God's goodness and grace.

In the days of God's visitation and the outpouring of His Holy Spirit during the Revival of 1904, it pleased the Lord to pay a visit to that cottage. With His power of repentance and grace, the Lord caused the family to be saved bringing the glorious light of God's Kingdom and glory to the hearth, which hitherto had been so bereft of that comfort and consolation, knowing only the misery of misfortune.

God's visitation lifted the cloud, drove the gloom away, and brought to Garnfoel the wealth of untold riches in Christ Jesus. They were days that led to years declivity of rock. Within this cottage my father and mother, William and Esther Williams, commenced their married life together sixty-six years ago. I have tried to set out their mutual characteristics in an Elegy written in the Welsh language in my booklet *"Odlau Hiraeth a Bywyd" ("Poems of Longing or Pining for Life")*. The wheels of industry turned very slowly in those days, so that to commence married life was an adventure. However, soon there came a gradual spiritual awakening, and circumstances promised better days.

There were born to my parents twelve children, nine sons and three daughters. Three of the sons died at an early age, leaving nine alive until April 15th 1945, when it pleased the Lord to take unto Himself the subject of our present biography.

His body lies at the Apostolic Temple, Penygroes, where it was interred on Friday, April 20th 1945 in the presence of a lamenting concourse of relatives, saints and friends from the surrounding neighbourhood. The writer was at that time in Canada.

As the family increased, there seemed to be every possibility of increasing home comforts through the diligence of our parents, but as the sunbeams of prosperity cast their rays upon the happy household, a gloom of disappointment darkened the hearth. As the result of rheumatic fever, our father became blind. It was a bitter experience having to face the future in this distressful state, with a growing family, and without any support, except the Hand of Providence which has never failed in the crucial hours of life.

As the light gradually left my father's eyes, the eyes of my dear brother, the late William Jones Williams, opened to the light of this world. He was only ten

CHAPTER 2

THE CRISIS OF LIFE

The beautiful mining village of Penygroes, Carmarthenshire, stands on the brow of the Great Mountain facing the north-east, overlooking the rich valley of the Amman, from Derwydd to Pontardulais, and even down to the banks of Loughor (the home of Evan Roberts, the great Welsh Revivalist). Rising up towards the north is the Black Mountain (Mynydd Du), terrace after terrace ascending towards the Sugar Loaf; with Carregcennen Castle on a prominent spur, a memorial to Welsh history. In the far distance the highest peak of the Brecon Beacons is halo'd with clouds.

Towards the east is the long range of Bettws Mountains like the waves of the sea billowing from Brynamman to Swansea. Towards the south we view the Gwendraeth Valley, enclosing Burryport, Kidwelly and Carmarthen. These glorious views in all directions make the village of Penygroes most attractive, while the lake called Llyn Llech Owain, to the north-west with its legendary story, adds a romantic touch to the neighbourhood.

There are many mines of anthracite coal in the adjacent districts, which have flourished for the last fifty years.

A distance of about a mile from the village stands a cottage called Garnfoel, nestling in the shelter of a steadily worked out in these days, and He will see to its consummation.

Consequently, as God will be wholly responsible for its growth, we have only to follow, with seeing eye, listening ear and with unerring obedience. Only thus, finally, will everyone in His Temple be able to shout 'Glory!'. Christ shall see of the travail of His soul, and shall be satisfied.

CHAPTER 1

CONCEPT

God's beginnings are unending, moving towards an endless goal. *"Hast thou commanded the morning since thy days?"*, asked the Almighty of Job, *"and caused the dayspring to know his place; that it might take hold of the ends of the earth...?"* (Job 38:12).

All God's beginnings and doings, and immeasurable plans, have a cradle; small beginnings, when the child is born; when the seed is sown. God has ever wanted to choose a man, a family, a nation. His plans have been entrusted to men like Adam, Enoch, Noah, Moses, David; to fishermen, and to great persecutors. These men had their cradles. The plan of God was revealed in their calling, as they obediently carried out the unfolding will of God.

The most hallowed cradle of all was at Bethlehem, watched over by a young and lowly maiden. The Babe grew; the mystery was gradually unfolded; the things which are revealed belong to us.

God still has His cradles in the individual hearts of men and women, in communities, in nations. The Church is the cradle of the final mystery of God. *"He that hath ears to hear, let him hear!"*. We stand in awe as the mystery of the Church unfolds itself to us by the Spirit. God grant that our vision may not be blinded or dimmed by any earthly glare, and that we miss not any of His shafts of light. The vision given of God has been

Nyni fu'n gweini arno
Nyni fu'n gwylio'i gryd
Pan oedd peryglon yn amgau
O gylch ei wely clyd
Daeth llawer ysbryd heibio
A difrod yn ei gol
Ond nid oedd elyn allai droi
Bwriadau DUW yn ol!

Twas we who waited on him
Twas we his cradle kept
When he mid danger heedless still
Of danger calmly slept
And many a friend passed by us
That fain the child would seize
But powerless was every foe
To alter God's decrees

(From "The Children of Heaven" by Dyfed and Rev. J, Bodvan Anwyl with acknowledgements)

The final word, however, must come from Pastor Dan himself taken from one of the many hymns he composed:

> *Father, what can to Thee be given*
> *For all Thy mercies blest*
> *For riches of Thy glorious grace*
> *And for the bliss of rest*
> *Within Thy hand I place my own*
> *And thus my path pursue*
> *Content to walk with Thee alone*
> *Til Glory fills my view*

INTRODUCTION

It is a great honour to publish *"Cradle of Mystery"*, the biography of Pastor and Prophet W. Jones Williams by his brother Pastor D.P. Williams. The family of 'Pastor Dan' (as he was affectionately known) continued writing the book after his passing into the presence of the Lord on 13th February 1946. Subsequently, the manuscript was completed, and ready for print in 1956.

Rev. James Worsfold believed that the writings of D.P. Williams would be *"exhumed in future days"* and so, fifty years after the manuscript was completed, his words come to pass. For the first time we can share with Pastor Dan his personal thoughts and vision regarding those early Apostolic days and particularly his love and appreciation for his brother William Jones Williams. It has been a wonderful insight into the ministry of both of these servants of God, as I have read and digested page after page, and I trust that it will be a blessing to each reader also.

It has been my intention to change as little as possible from the original manuscript so that the Welsh flavour and period is maintained. The only changes are the occasional explanation of colloquialisms, Welsh language and some grammatical adjustments.

The heart of these brothers was to be truly apostolic in 'belting the globe' with the gospel and vision of Jesus Christ. It is therefore my desire to honour their memory by committing the main profit from the sales of this book to the missionary work of the Apostolic Church.

the twenty-first century this book will inspire us to a fresh understanding and appreciation of the eternal purpose of God revealed in Jesus Christ and expressed through the Church, which is His Body.

Warren Jones
National Leader
The Apostolic Church UK

London
2nd June 2006

PREFACE

That a worldwide movement should begin in a small Welsh mining village, with two coal miner brothers, is amazing. This is the intimate account of the way God moved at the beginning of the twentieth century in the Williams family of Penygroes, Carmarthenshire, South Wales.

Almost one hundred years on, the names D.P. Williams and Jones Williams are unknown to many, but it is important that a new generation become acquainted with the miraculous events that took place at the birth of the Apostolic Church, particularly the role revelatory prophecy played in those formative years.

We are privileged to be able to read a first hand report of those episodes from the pen of Pastor D.P. Williams himself. He speaks with great affection of the conversion and spiritual development of his brother Jones and, in the process, gives us fascinating glimpses of the unfolding of spiritual truth that, although now almost universally accepted, was at that time revolutionary. The brothers not only expounded the contemporary ministry of the apostle and prophet, but through their own ministries, demonstrated it in remarkable ways.

Although this is Pastor D.P. Williams' testament to his brother, it breathes the spirituality, godliness and Christ centred-ness of the author himself. My prayer is that in biography of Pastor D. P. Williams will follow this publication.

HUGH DAWSON
Bryncwar House
Penygroes

FOREWORD

I have very happy recollections of the ministry of Pastor W. Jones Williams when he was first called to Bradford. At that time I was in business, and had not had much time for study of my Bible etc., nor had I traveled to many conventions to hear the ministry of the Word. But when Pastor Jones Williams came to Bradford he commenced a Bible class during the time the younger scholars were in Sunday-school classes. Here he gave us Bible readings commencing with the book of Genesis. I can really say that these studies whetted my appetite for the Bible more than any other ministry I had heard up to that time.

I was also blessed to see his aptitude and enthusiasm for pastoral work. The Assembly at Great Horton flourished under his care.

Since that time we have seen many changes and progressive moves in the Lord's work. God has called Pastor Jones Williams, and his brother Apostle D. P. Williams, to their heavenly reward.

As President of the General Council of the Apostolic Church, I was privileged to broadcast on November 25th 1954 a fifteen minute summary of the progress made within, and through, the Church in which the two brothers were used of God to co-operate by acts and deeds owned by the Holy Spirit. It is hoped that a

CONTENTS

Chapter		Page
	Foreword	9
	Preface	11
	Introduction	13
1	Concept	17
2	Crisis of Life	19
3	The Course of Events	25
4	The Pentecostal Blessing and its Purpose	34
5	Callings and Divine Order	43
6	Pioneering Work	52
7	From Pit to Pulpit (Autobiographical)	59
8	Pioneering and Persecution	79
9	Prophet	95
10	'To throw down, to build and to plant'	97
11	Pioneering in Wider Fields	109
12	The Building up of the Work	120
13	The Consolidating Work of Apostle and Prophet	136
14	'He Spake the Word' (Ps. 105)	148
15	Reminiscences	164
16	Preacher	181
17	The Apostolic Church 1904-1955	212
18	The Home Call; Funeral Report	225
	Appendix	257

Finally, I dedicate this book to every man and woman who is willing to follow in the footsteps of such men as Pastors Dan and Jones Williams in taking the gospel to the ends of the earth.

Peter K. Yeoman – Editor

For all God's purposes in heaven and earth
He sets a time when they shall come to birth
And then He seeks a cradle clean and fair
And a strong love to be a watcher there

God ever seeks for cradles; see His love
His patient eye through time and space doth move
Willing to intimate His great design
Whispering low: 'This work is Mine and thine

That which is born of God shall ever be
Triumphant to its purpose and its goal
God's ordinations cycle to eternity
And His designs shall compass all in all

D. P. Williams

APPRECIATION AND DEDICATION

I wish to thank Pastor Alun Morris and the Williams family for allowing me the privilege of publishing the manuscript, *'Cradle of Mystery.'*

I want to thank my wife, Lynne, for thirty years of married life, with her unstinting support and encouragement in evangelism and church planting, as well as putting up with me during the preparation of this book.

Thank you Mum and Dad for an apostolic upbringing.

A word of encouragement to my son Andrew, and his wife Helen, 'the mission is apostolic.' Also to my daughter, Hannah, and her husband Lee, thank you for a wonderful grandson 'Joshua' (a future pastor?)

Thank you to Andrew Griffiths for the use of 'the room' and your expertise in the cover design.

Thanks to Barney Harper for proof reading.

Thanks Andy, Emma, Dave and Alison (the Leadership of Swansea Valley Bible Church) and all the members for your love, support and enthusiasm.

Thanks to Peter and Jenny Williams for your encouragement and fellowship in the gospel.

Lastly, my brother John, and his wife Margaret, who is a prophet in the Body of Christ, presently serving the Lord with the Apostolic Church in Latvia. "You shall speak My words to them" (Ezek.2:7)

There are a host of friends and mentors, who have been a great influence in my life and ministry, of whom there are too many to name. I thank the Lord for every one of you.

First published in 2006 by
Kingdom First Publishing
Unit 19, Ynyscedwyn Enterprise Park
Ystradgynlais, Swansea SA9 1DT

Cover design by Andrew Griffiths
(www.agmusic.co.uk)

Copyright 2006
The Apostolic Church General Council

All rights reserved. No part of this book may be reprinted or reproduced or utilised in any form or by any electronic, mechanical or other means, now known or hereafter invented, including photocopying and recording, or in any information storage or retrieval system, without permission in writing from the Publisher.

ISBN 0-9553551-0-9

Printed by Gomer Press, Llandysul, Ceredigion SA44 4JL

CRADLE OF MYSTERY

By
D.P Williams

A Biography of W. Jones Williams
(Pastor and Prophet)

By his brother
D. P. Williams
(First President of the Apostolic Church General Council)

With autobiographical and other additions

Edited by
Peter K. Yeoman